"In *Spirit-filled Protestantism*, Luther Oconer revises and revitalizes the history of the arrival of American holiness revivalism into the Philippine Islands via Methodist Episcopal missionaries. Following revival practices and doctrines as they made their way into the islands behind the American military and alongside the larger colonial project, Oconer re-narrates a tired and simplistic one-way story of western religious imperialism into a stirring drama of pan-Pacific 'Holy Spirit revival.' Tracing the movement and subsequent reconstructions of holiness thought, practice, and performance through revivals in India that spread to the Philippines, Oconer provides a full and convincing portrayal of Filipino intellectual, emotional, and institutional engagement with the religious offerings of the missionaries. This *culto Pentecostal*, which Oconer argues opened the space for Filipino participation in the global Pentecostal healing movement in the 1950s, became the kernel for the development of Filipino Methodist identities, practices, and schisms."

—**Morris L. Davis**, Associate Professor at Drew University

Spirit-Filled Protestantism

Spirit-Filled Protestantism

Holiness-Pentecostal Revivals and the Making of
Filipino Methodist Identity

Luther Jeremiah Oconer

FOREWORD BY
David Bundy

PICKWICK *Publications* · Eugene, Oregon

SPIRIT-FILLED PROTESTANTISM
Holiness-Pentecostal Revivals and the Making of Filipino Methodist Identity

Copyright © 2017 Luther Jeremiah Oconer. All rights reserved. Except for brief quotations in critical publications or reviews, no part of this book may be reproduced in any manner without prior written permission from the publisher. Write: Permissions, Wipf and Stock Publishers, 199 W. 8th Ave., Suite 3, Eugene, OR 97401.

Pickwick Publications
An Imprint of Wipf and Stock Publishers
199 W. 8th Ave., Suite 3
Eugene, OR 97401

www.wipfandstock.com

PAPERBACK ISBN: 978-1-4982-0360-9
HARDCOVER ISBN: 978-1-4982-0362-3
EBOOK ISBN: 978-1-4982-0361-6

Cataloguing-in-Publication data:

Names: Oconer, Luther Jeremiah. | Bundy, David D., Foreword

Title: Spirit-filled protestantism : holiness-pentecostal revivals and the making of Filipino Methodist identity / Luther Jeremiah Oconer ; foreword by David Bundy.

Description: Eugene, OR: Pickwick Publications, 2017 | Includes bibliographical references and index.

Identifiers: ISBN 978-1-4982-0360-9 (paperback) | ISBN 978-1-4982-0362-3 (hardcover) | ISBN 978-1-4982-0361-6 (ebook)

Subjects: LCSH: Methodist Episcopal Church—Philippines—History.

Classification: BX8316.P5 O25 2017 (print) | BX8316.P5 O25 (ebook)

Manufactured in the U.S.A.   10/10/17

For those who have kept the flames of renewal alive
among the people called Methodists in the Philippines

The most successful innovation in the Philippines has been the Methodist revival because it has so perfectly fitted the psychology of the people. They find the passion and drive of Methodism almost irresistible. A revival breaks out . . . a sense of joy witnesses to the presence of the Holy Spirit; the impassioned preacher sweeps across the heart strings of his hearers, with no attempt at logical order, but with every effort to convict of sin and to portray salvation in such beautiful terms that unsaved men and women and children will be wooed to the altar in quest of it.

—Frank C. Laubach, *The People of the Philippines*

Contents

List of Illustrations | viii

Foreword by David Bundy | xi

Preface | xv

Abbreviations | xix

Introduction | 1

1 American Holiness Roots and Methodist Missions | 11
2 Methodist Beginnings in the Philippines | 29
3 *Culto Pentecostal* Revivals Begin | 70
4 Seasons of Pentecost, 1911–1924 | 93
5 Refinement, Moral Crusades, and Schism, 1925–1933 | 139
6 The Methodist Healing Revival and Its Consequences, 1934–1965 | 163

Conclusion | 191

Bibliography | 197

Index | 211

List of Illustrations

Figure 1.1. William Taylor | 25

Figure 1.2. Bishop James Mills Thoburn | 26

Figure 1.3. Bishop Francis Wesley Warne | 27

Figure 1.4. Bishop William Fitzjames Oldham | 28

Figure 2.1. Nicolas Zamora | 60

Figure 2.2. Pioneer Methodist workers in Manila | 61

Figure 2.3. Cornelia C. Moots and Genevieve Cutler | 62

Figure 2.4. Felipe Marquez | 63

Figure 2.5. Key MEC sites in Manila, 1899–1910 | 64

Figure 2.6. Narcisa Dimagiba | 65

Figure 2.7. The congregation of Mexico MEC | 66

Figure 2.8. Philippine Islands Mission Conference, 1905 | 67

Figure 2.9. Women's Conference, 1907 | 68

Figure 2.10. Central District Bible Institute | 69

Figure 3.1. Pandacan MEC chapel | 88

Figure 3.2. Procession Preaching | 88

Figure 3.3. Pentecostal Procession | 89

Figure 3.4. Charles W. Koehler | 90

Figure 3.5. Pentecostal meeting, Tondo, Manila | 91

Figure 3.6. Philippine Islands Annual Conference, 1910 | 92

Figure 4.1. Bishop William Perry Eveland | 129

Figure 4.2. Philippine Islands Annual Conference, 1914 | 130

LIST OF ILLUSTRATIONS

Figure 4.3. Joshua F. Cottingham | 131

Figure 4.4. Arthur L. Beckendorf and family | 132

Figure 4.5. Filipino Methodist Pentecostal meetings | 133

Figure 4.6. Joseph and Mary Knapp Strong Clemens | 134

Figure 4.7. Dionisio D. Alejandro | 135

Figure 4.8. The first Filipino graduates of Asbury College | 136

Figure 4.9. Wilhelmina Erbst | 137

Figure 4.10. Central District women workers | 137

Figure 4.11. Epworth League Christmas Institute | 138

Figure 4.12. Knox Memorial MEC prohibition sign | 138

Figure 5.1. Filipino District superintendents, 1932 | 157

Figure 5.2. Jorge C. Bocobo | 158

Figure 5.3. Samuel and Mary Boyd Stagg | 159

Figure 5.4. Samuel W. Stagg with the Central Student Church evangelistic teams | 159

Figure 5.5. Cipriano Navarro | 160

Figure 5.6. Interior view of Central Student Church | 161

Figure 5.7. Philippine Islands Annual Conference, 1935 | 162

Figure 6.1. Curran L. Spottswood preaching | 183

Figure 6.2. Philippines Central Conference, 1948 | 184

Figure 6.3. Lester F. Sumrall | 185

Figure 6.4. Lester Sumrall and Clarita Villanueva | 186

Figure 6.5. Clifton Erickson's Revival | 186

Figure 6.6. Ruben V. Candelaria | 187

Figure 6.7. David Candelaria | 188

Figure 6.8. Taytay Methodist Community Church | 189

Foreword

A good case study can open vistas for research that can transform one's understanding of the subject. Such is the case study of Luther Oconer on Methodism in the Philippines. Many histories of churches are institutional studies, focusing on the development of structures. Others are sociological. Often the beginnings of a church are precisely defined in the historiography and few questions asked. The work of Oconer is so much more. It is a multivalent study that takes all of these aspects into account, including theology, international politics, and the structures of religious belief.

Beginning with a situation in which Oconer and others found themselves censored by leaders of their church, he examined the situation synchronically and diachronically. The results of his research are important for World Christianity, Methodism generally, and specifically for the development of Methodism in the Philippines and other regions of Asia. The volume provides a carefully documented situation in which the networks and influences of the global Radical Holiness traditions struggled with the birth from within it of a more radical religious tradition, Pentecostalism.

Luther Oconer is singularly qualified to undertake the study. He is an ordained elder in the Pampanga Philippines Annual Conference of The United Methodist Church. Oconer studied at Mapúa Institute of Technology (BS 1993) and Wesley Divinity School (MDiv 2001), which is part of Wesleyan University in Cabanatuan City, Philippines. He continued his studies at Drew University (MPhil 2006 and PhD 2009). He was personally involved in the situations that led to the case study and had access to the other principal actors for his research. He has already established himself as an authority on the history of Methodism in the Philippines. This work demonstrates that the breadth of his expertise goes far beyond the history of Methodism in the Philippines to Methodism in the rest of Asia, the United Kingdom, and the United States.

The central question with which Oconer deals is the origin of "Pentecostal" Methodism in the Philippines. It has often puzzled observers that religious traditions with roots in North America and Europe share liturgical styles and theological emphases with "Pentecostals" while not being generally recognized as Pentecostal. This happens despite the fact that the churches to which they are related in North America and Europe are anything but "Pentecostal" in liturgy and theology. Thus, many churches that are nominally Methodist, Presbyterian, Baptist, Lutheran, Anglican, and Catholic can be observed to share "Pentecostal" liturgies and theological foci. Luther Oconer has the distinction of demonstrating that for the Methodists in the Philippines, this is due to the Radical Holiness tradition, a tradition which has been little studied.

Radical Holiness was a self-designation and a self-identifying code for the radicalized Holiness movements that grew out of Methodism and other denominations in the post-Civil War period. The main hermeneutical shift was to move from the Gospels as normative for church life, as Wesley and the Methodists had assumed, to insisting that the book of the Acts of the Apostles, especially the first two chapters, presented a normative and ideal vision for spirituality, church life, and mission. Hence, the identifier "Pentecost" or "Pentecostal" churches that became popular from the early 1890s, famously led by Richard Reader Harris in the United Kingdom and Samuel A. Keen in the United States was supported by publisher and God's Bible School founder, Martin Wells Knapp. These Radical Holiness movements, and the leadership in them, reached across denominational, ethnic, gender, and class lines. They were quite open, initially, to theological experimentation. As versions of Methodist ideas about spirituality (sanctification or theosis) were introduced into diverse religious traditions, ideas alien to Methodism (faith healing, premillennialism, inerrancy, Darbyist dispensationalism) were adapted by groups with a Methodist heritage.

Simultaneous to this, fissures over the nature of the Methodist/Holiness Movement doctrine of "sanctification" or "baptism of the Holy Spirit" were developing. In England, after Wesley there had been a less "enthusiastic" approach to sanctification fostered by Jabez Bunting and Richard Watson, and there were similar developments in the United States. In both the United States and the United Kingdom this paralleled Methodist upward mobility, less involvement with the poor and less enthusiasm in worship. Renewed appeals for attention to sanctification in British Methodism (and other British churches) were little influenced by the perfectionistic theologies of sanctification developed at Oberlin and promoted by Charles Finney and Asa Mahan. In the United States, the more vigorous renewed calls for attention to sanctification were shaped by Oberlin perfectionism.

However, within the missionary community, changes in Methodist and Radical Holiness theology were beginning to happen. William Arthur, William Boardman, Bishop William Taylor, John Hunt, Thomas Champness, and later Bishop James Thoburn realized that cultural structures around the world were different from those of the United States and the United Kingdom, and that a different understanding of and presentation of Radical Holiness ideas on holiness were needed. The thinking and preaching of these missionary theologians resulted in a tradition that might be described as "global holiness." The ideas would, with some intellectual shifts, be institutionalized (indigenized) in European Holiness movements, for example, in the United Kingdom (Keswick) and in Germany in the *Gemeinschaftsbewegung*. European Holiness movements rarely combined the more exuberantly enthusiastic liturgical styles of their North American religious cousins with this tradition of "global holiness" that would become popularized by the Keswick Convention. Despite their evolving perspectives on holiness, all of these thinkers and mission leaders remained in good standing in the Radical Holiness movements.

However, in many areas of the world these two interrelated streams, the Radical Holiness movements and the "global holiness" intertwined to become part of the fabric of World Christianity. Thanks to this volume, it becomes clear how this happened in the Philippines! For that, we owe Luther Oconer a debt of gratitude. It is to be hoped that this research encourages others to reexamine the traditional scholarship on the Radical Holiness, Pentecostal, and Methodist movements.

David Bundy

Associate Director, Manchester Wesley Research Centre, Nazarene Theological College, and Research Professor for World Christian Studies, New York Theological Seminary

Preface

This book grew out of a desire to learn more about John Wesley that dates back to my time as a youth leader in my home church in the Philippines. This passion has set me off on a journey of discovery that eventually brought me to the Wesleyan and Methodist Studies program at Drew University fifteen years ago. As my understanding of Wesley's vision for the Christian life deepened, I began to focus my attention on his teachings on sanctification and the ways by which they influenced the rise of the Holiness movement in the United States. This movement provided a fertile seedbed for the emergence of modern Pentecostalism and helped shape missionary thought and practice in foreign fields at the turn of the twentieth century.

Hence, this book explores how holiness spirituality, with its varied forms and expressions, influenced Methodist missions in the Philippines. This inquiry led me to sieve through volumes of conference journals, official records, memoirs, and manuscripts piecing together the spiritual culture of early Philippine Methodism. The process has enabled me to uncover the significance of *culto Pentecostal* (Pentecostal meeting) revivalism in the development of Methodism in the Philippines, which became the subject of my doctoral project at Drew. *Culto Pentecostal* revivals were not mere footnotes to the history of Wesley's spiritual descendants in the Philippines but key to discerning how Filipino Methodist identity developed. This study therefore endeavors to offer a rich and nuanced retelling of the early history of Methodism in the Philippines by using *culto Pentecostal* revivalism as a lens. It is also my hope that it will deepen our understanding of Methodism in the Philippines and advance our knowledge of American Methodist mission history.

I am deeply indebted to my United Theological Seminary family—the faculty, staff and students—for their constant support during the course of this project. David Watson and Scott Kisker were the first ones to motivate me to get this study published. Andrew Park, Tom Dozeman, Peter Bellini, and Justus Hunter have served as conversation partners during the various stages of the project. Chad Clark assisted in the preparation of the manuscript and edited my drafts. I deeply appreciate his attention to detail and editorial expertise. Zeppellin Canlas also assisted my family in so many ways so that I could be away for research. I am also grateful to our board of trustees for the much-needed sabbatical that allowed me to finish this book.

Since the book has been initially conceived as a doctoral project, I also owe a debt of gratitude to my former mentors and colleagues at Drew. Donald Dayton provided early inspiration on the subject through his lectures and writings on the Holiness and Pentecostal movements. I pay special tribute to his *Theological Roots of Pentecostalism* for introducing me to the fourfold gospel as a framework for understanding these two movements. My dissertation committee also deserves special mention. Morris Davis, Jesse Todd, and L. Dale Patterson provided guidance and valuable insights that sustained and saw the completion of the project. Methodist Librarian Chris Anderson provided resources as he was working on his research and, recently, granted permission to feature some images from the Methodist Library Image Collection. Kevin Newburg and Patrick Eby served as sounding boards throughout the course of the project.

I also appreciate the connections and resources made available to me through the Wesley Seminars at Duke University (2006 and 2016) and Asbury Theological Seminary (2013). I am very grateful to notable Wesley scholars Randy Maddox, Richard Heitzenrater, and Kenneth Collins for the opportunity to participate and learn from these two seminars. Other specialists who provided valuable insights include Floyd Cunningham of the Asia Pacific Nazarene Theological Seminary in the Philippines, William Kostlevy of the Brethren Historical Library and Archives and David Bundy of the Manchester Wesley Research Centre. I extend my deep appreciation to David for writing the Foreword.

For the many important discoveries made during research, I thank all the librarians, archivists, and staff at all the repositories I have visited. These include the United Methodist Archives, the Drew Methodist Library, the Drew Library, the Duke Divinity School Library, the Duke Bridwell Library, the American Bible Society Archives, the Syracuse University George Arent Library, the Asbury University Archives, and the Asbury

PREFACE

Theological Seminary B. L. Fisher Library. Mark Shenise and Frances Lyons-Bristol, associate archivists at the United Methodist Church Archives, deserve special mention for the many ways they have assisted me with my research. Louis Sechehay and Kathy Juliano of Drew Library's Inter-Library Loan diligently fulfilled my dozens of requests for rare Philippine Methodists materials from other libraries. Suzanne Gehring, head of archives and special collections, and Hannah Armour, assistant archivist, at the Asbury University Kinlaw Library generously provided me some of the images used in this book.

I also commend a number of individuals for their assistance. The late David Candelaria graciously granted me an interview in his home in Taytay in May 2005. Esther Javier, the daughter of Ruben Candelaria and wife of the late Eleazar Javier, and Bishop Jesse Candelaria, the son of David, shared significant insights about their fathers. Julie Dizon provided documents pertaining to the history of the Philippine Assemblies of God, Inc., a group founded by Ruben in 1966. Jay Yamomo sent me unpublished research from the Institute for Studies in Asian Church and Culture (ISAAC) on Philippine Protestantism and Filipino religious culture. My uncle, Pol Galvez, a renowned artist and former cartoonist with the *Manila Bulletin*, selflessly devoted his time to draw illustrations for this book. Rita E. Owen, the granddaughter of Philippine missionaries William and Edna Teeter, was gracious to share photos from her family's collection.

I can also never thank Patria Agustin Smith and her husband Paul enough for their extravagant kindness to my family that dates back to our time at Drew. Their generosity has allowed me to feature a number of rare images from the United Methodist Church Archives' Mission Photograph Collection. My appreciation also extends to many friends in the Philippines including Bishops Solito Toquero, Daniel Arichea, Pedro Torio, Rodolfo Juan, and Ciriaco Francisco for their unwavering support during the various stages of my ministerial career and my calling to the academic ministry. My friends from the Pampanga Philippines Annual Conference and Aldersgate Renewal Ministries Philippines, whose names are just too many to enumerate, for praying for me and providing inspiration to finish the task.

My loved ones also deserve special commendation. My parents supported me during the most difficult years in graduate school. My father passed away in April 2014. I regret that he will never see this book. My mother spent six months in Dayton to help us with the kids in the midst of my wife's intense studies and as I worked on this book. I also thank Jose

PREFACE

Padang, my father-in-law, and my siblings, Lester, Lemuel, and Lesley, for the countless manifestations of encouragement they have sent my way. Last, but not the least, I am deeply grateful for my wife, Marion, and our children, Ilana and Wesley. Marion served as an associate during my research trips by helping me sort material and scan hundreds of pages. Our children, on the other hand, kept me grounded throughout the writing process by constantly reminding me about what matters most in life. The book is better because of them.

Abbreviations

ABS	American Bible Society
BFC	Badley Family Collection. United Methodist Church Archives—GCAH, Madison, New Jersey.
JTDJ	Diaries and Journals of Bishop James M. Thoburn, 1857–1918. Allegheny College Library, Meadville, Pennsylvania (microform).
AG	Assemblies of God
BFBS	British and Foreign Bible Society
CA	*Christian Advocate*
CMP	Cornelia C. Moots Papers. United Methodist Church Archives—GCAH, Madison, New Jersey.
CI	Christmas Institute
ELI	Epworth League Institute
GIAL	*Gospel in All Lands*
HDHM	*Historical Dictionary of the Holiness Movement.* Edited by William C. Kostlevy. 2nd ed. Lanham, MD: Scarecrow, 2009.
IW	*Indian Witness*
LW	*Lucknow Witness*
MBUMC	Mission Biographical Reference Files, 1880s–1961. United Methodist Church Archives—GCAH, Madison, New Jersey.
MCUMC	Missionary Correspondence, 1846–1912. United Methodist Church Archives—GCAH, Madison, New Jersey.

ABBREVIATIONS

MEC	Methodist Episcopal Church
MFUMC	Missionary Files, 1912–1949. United Methodist Church Archives—GCAH, Madison, New Jersey.
MFMUMC	Missionary Files, Misfiles, 1912–1922. United Methodist Church Archives—GCAH, Madison, New Jersey.
MSMEC	Missionary Society of the Methodist Episcopal Church
NHA	National Holiness Association
NIDPCM	*The New International Dictionary of Pentecostal and Charismatic Movements.* Edited by Stanley M. Burgess and Eduard M. van der Maas. Rev. and exp. ed. Grand Rapids: Zondervan, 2003.
NPAC	*Official Record of the Philippine North Annual Conference of the Methodist Episcopal Church*
PAC	*Official Record Philippine Annual Conference of the Methodist Episcopal Church*
PAG	Philippine Assemblies of God, Inc.
PCA	*Philippine Christian Advocate*
PCC	*Official Record of the Philippines Central Conference*
PE	*Pentecostal Evangel*
PH	*Pentecostal Herald*
PFCC	Philippine Federation of Christian Churches
PIDC	*Minutes of the Annual Session of the District Conference of the Philippine Islands of the Methodist Episcopal Church*
PIMC	*Official Journal of the Annual Session of the Philippine Island Mission Conference of the Methodist Episcopal Church*
PO	*Philippine Observer*
SVM	Student Volunteer Movement
SVMIC	*Addresses at the International Convention of the Student Volunteer Movement for Foreign Missions.*
TMCC	Taytay Methodist Community Church

ABBREVIATIONS

UMC	United Methodist Church
UP	University of the Philippines
UTS	Union Theological Seminary
WCPIAC	*Official Report of the Woman's Conference of the Philippine Islands Mission of the Methodist Episcopal Church*
WCTU	Woman's Christian Temperance Union
WFMS	Woman's Foreign Missionary Society
WFMSAR	*Annual Report of the Woman's Foreign Missionary Society of the Methodist Episcopal Church*
WMF	*Woman's Missionary Friend*
Works	*The Bicentennial Edition of the Works of John Wesley.* 17 vols. to date. Edited by Frank Baker et al. Nashville: Abingdon, 1984–.
WWM	*World-Wide Missions*
YMCA	Young Men's Christian Association

Introduction

The Filipino Methodist Pentecostal Impulse

It was Easter of 1998 in Angeles City, Philippines, when three young pastors of the United Methodist Church (hereafter UMC) were summoned by a committee of senior clergy from their district to respond to the charge brought against them. Apparently, their troubles had begun a few days earlier when the District Superintendent was appalled to find emotional outbursts and other unusual occurrences at a joint revival gathering they had organized in one of their churches. Featuring a number of reputed Pentecostal preachers from Manila, and attended mostly by young people, the event also agitated a band of local Methodists who were repulsed by what they felt were acts of desecration to their church. After a quick deliberation, the committee found the three guilty of the chargeable offense: "dissemination of doctrines contrary to the established standards of the doctrine of The United Methodist Church."[1] They recommended that the pastor who hosted the event be expelled from the ministry and the other two be withheld from entering seminary until rehabilitated. Nevertheless, at the annual conference weeks later, before their case was to be deliberated upon by the Conference board of ordained ministry, the bishop and his cabinet intervened. As a compromise, he separated the three by assigning them in three different districts. Since then, all three have been ordained elders in the UMC and have served in different capacities within the denomination. One of them is the author of this book.

Unbeknownst to me at that time, the event that summer was but a microcosm of a larger phenomenon within Methodism throughout most of the second half of its existence in the Philippines. There have been many

---

1. *The Book of Discipline* (1996), ¶ 2624.1. All citations are in their shortened form. Please refer to bibliography for full citations.

instances of Pentecostal-related controversies, which rattled the denomination in varying degrees throughout the years. The first and, perhaps, the most turbulent and publicized of all was the one that took place in 1954 involving two prominent Methodist ministers: Ruben V. Candelaria, district superintendent of the Manila District, and his cousin David M. Candelaria, pastor of Taytay Methodist Church. Ruben became the pioneering Filipino pastor of the newly established Bethel Temple, the first church built by the Assemblies of God (hereafter AG) in the City of Manila. David, on the other hand, led half of his congregants in Taytay to form an independent "full gospel" Methodist congregation. This church would eventually figure prominently in the growth of the Charismatic movement in the Philippines in the years that followed.

While small compared to the two major schisms that had rocked Philippine Methodism decades earlier,[2] the Candelaria defection, nevertheless, served not only as a significant milestone in the history of the denomination but also as a harbinger of things to come. For years to this day, Filipino Methodists continue to grapple with similar tensions and defections, though to a lesser degree, wrought by a persistent Pentecostal influence creeping within their churches.[3] The emergence of the Aldersgate United Methodist Renewal Fellowship harkens back to this Pentecostal impulse, for example. Launched in 1992 by a group of UMC ministers and laypersons, the movement attracts about a thousand Filipino United Methodists to its annual Aldersgate Conference in Baguio City. Questions raised regarding Aldersgate's teachings and relationship with the UMC shortly after its founding led Bishop Emerito P. Nacpil of the Manila Episcopal Area to issue a circular on 19 August 1993, to "not oppose the charismatic movement within our United Methodist constituency."[4] Though the movement has increasingly attained mainstream acceptance in recent years, it continues to spark new tensions that either leave churches divided over issues pertaining to liturgy and practice or result in the exodus of individuals or small pockets of Charismatic Methodists to join or form independent Charismatic groups. For example, in 2001, Hiram Pangilinan, a highly

2. These are the Zamora schism of 1909 (in chapter 2) and the Stagg schism of 1933 (in chapter 5).

3. This is somewhat substantiated in a recent analysis that further suggests that, in the ensuing years, especially in the 1990s and onwards, non-Catholic Pentecostalism "grew at the expense of Protestant mainline denominations." Kessler and Rüland, "Responses to Rapid Social Change," 80–81.

4. Quoted in Padang, *Primer for United Methodists*, 79–81.

popular United Methodist minister known for his healing and deliverance ministries, led about a hundred lay persons, mostly young people, to form what is now known as Church So Blessed, which is now a network of more than fifty churches spread throughout the country.[5]

Nevertheless, with the increasing acceptance of Charismatic spirituality among Filipino United Methodists during the first decade of the twenty-first century came the birth of the Ablaze Conference, an annual conference on the Holy Spirit to activate "spiritual gifts" and "equip people to live in the Spirit and move in signs and wonders." The Ablaze Conference also brought about the Revive Conference, a quadrennial gathering spearheaded by former Supreme Court Chief Justice Reynato Puno, a prominent layperson from Puno Memorial UMC, to "spark revival" among Filipino United Methodists. Scheduled a week prior to the episcopal elections on November 2012, it attracted approximately 10,000 Methodists at the Philippines Sports Arena in Pasig City. Since 2016, Revive had become a project of the Philippines Central Conference of the UMC.[6]

Thus, the Candelaria case provokes the primary questions framing the course of this book. Despite the presence of other Protestant denominations in Manila at that time, what made Philippine Methodism a fertile seedbed for the AG revival in the 1950s? How does one get from Methodism to Pentecostalism? What was Filipino Methodist revivalism like prior to this? What comparisons can be drawn between early Philippine Methodist revival practices and the later AG revival practices? How did the early Methodist missionaries and their Filipino counterparts develop and promote these practices? What were the sources and configuration of this early revivalism? Pursuing these questions illuminates a similar dynamic operating in the broader Christian culture—the interaction between doctrine and practice.

The narrative that follows provides an ideal probing ground for these questions because, not only does it provide the setting leading up to the defection, it also brings to the fore the Methodist revival ritual known as "Pentecostal service" or "Pentecostal meeting," which Filipino Methodists called *culto Pentecostal*. Borrowed from the Spanish lexicon, *culto* is equivalent to the English noun "worship" or "religious service." Vigorously promoted by a significant subset of Methodist missionaries and Filipino

---

5. For more about the history of Church So Blessed, see Pangilinan, *What if God Comes.*

6. Charles M. Puno, e-mail, 20 September 2016.

workers in the Philippines, Pentecostal services were first introduced in the United States in the 1890s in Methodist annual conferences by Holiness evangelists commissioned by their bishops. They were revival gatherings whose doctrinal content was the Methodist doctrine of entire sanctification, and whose intent was to awaken nominal Christians towards a deeper spiritual life. However, during this period, the classic Wesleyan term of "entire sanctification" was already being equated with the New Testament experience of "the baptism of the Holy Spirit" or explained through other pneumatological expressions from the New Testament. It was for this reason that the meetings were called "Pentecostal." Contrary to assumptions, this term even predated the birth of the modern Pentecostal movement that traces its roots from the Azusa Street Revival under the leadership of William Seymour in Los Angeles, California in 1906.[7]

Though commonplace and integral to the life of early Philippine Methodism, *culto Pentecostal* revivalism has, unfortunately, been overlooked by scholars for years. It is, therefore, the primary intention of this book to fill this particular gap in Philippine Methodist historiography, for it offers an opportunity to discern not only early Filipino Methodist spirituality and practice, but also how Philippine Methodist identity was shaped in the years covered by the study to eventually become what it is today.

What the Book Hopes to Accomplish

The research presented in this book was set in motion by existing literature affirming the preeminence of evangelistic work in early Philippine Methodism. While this was self-evident in a number of publications written by Methodist Episcopal Church (hereafter MEC) missionaries, even non-Methodist missionaries have acknowledged Philippine Methodism's overt emphasis on evangelism over other "civilizing" endeavors. For example, veteran Presbyterian missionary James B. Rodgers, in his *Forty Years in the Philippines* (1940), summed up his observation of Methodist efforts as "almost entirely on the evangelistic work of the Kingdom."[8] Though "evangelistic work" may refer to many things, it was Congregational missionary

---

7. To minimize confusion, I will hereafter use "modern Pentecostalism" or "modern Pentecostal movement" to refer to the movement mostly associated with the William Seymour-led Azusa Street Pentecostal Revival in Los Angeles (1906). For this usage, see, for example, McGee, "Latter Rain," 648.

8. Rodgers, *Forty Years in the Philippines*, 149.

and self-described mystic Frank C. Laubach who, in his *People of the Philippines* (1925), clarified such a thrust as a "Methodist revival," even suggesting that emotionally-charged Pentecost-themed revival meetings had dominated the work of the MEC mission and helped account for its phenomenal growth in the country. He argued that Methodist revival work was the "most successful innovation in the Philippines" since it "perfectly fitted the psychology of the people."[9]

While Philippine Methodist revivalism is an established fact among historians of Philippine Protestantism, the doctrinal contents of this revivalism have not yet been fully explored. In fact, only a few historians have scratched its surface, such as Bishop Dionisio D. Alejandro in *From Darkness to Light* (1974), which remains the most definitive chronicle of Philippine Methodism to date. It was Alejandro, the first Filipino elected to the Methodist episcopacy, who first traced the beginnings of Philippine Methodist *culto Pentecostal* rituals to the nineteenth-century North American Holiness movement (hereafter Holiness movement). According to him, these revival gatherings persisted in Philippine Methodism even until the Second World War.[10] Richard L. Deats also affirms the strong revivalistic culture in Philippine Methodism in his book, *The Story of Methodism in the Philippines* (1964). Although failing to underscore their connections with the Holiness movement as Alejandro did, Deats, nonetheless, acknowledges the importance of revivals, with their attendant emphasis on the "moral life," by suggesting that they helped create a strong social service and social reformist impulse among prominent Filipino Methodist laity in the public sphere.[11] In *Holiness Abroad: Nazarene Missions in Asia* (2003), Nazarene historian Floyd T. Cunningham, however, revives Alejandro's claim by attesting to the existence of a "faction strongly influenced by holiness teachings" among Philippine Methodists. Cunningham also points out that former Methodists formed the pioneering membership of the Church of the Nazarene, and Pilgrim Holiness Church in the country.[12] In another article, Cunningham not only reaffirms Philippine Methodist revival culture,

---

9. Laubach, *People of the Philippines*, 221.

10. Alejandro, *From Darkness to Light*, 33, 104–7. I am using "nineteenth-century North American Holiness movement" to simply acknowledge that there were other movements in other Christian traditions with similar concerns on holiness, broadly conceived, during the same period and in earlier periods of Christian history. This point is highlighted, for example, in Bebbington, *Holiness in Nineteenth-Century England*.

11. Deats, *Story of Methodism*, 52–58.

12. Cunningham, *Holiness Abroad*, 62.

but also underscores the role played by Methodists in the rise of the AG in Manila in the 1950s. Unlike Alejandro, however, Cunningham extends the lifespan of this holiness revivalism up to the post-war years.[13] In his memoir, Eleazar Javier, former general superintendent of the AG in the Philippines and ex-Methodist from Taytay, also acknowledges the Candelarias and the Methodist connection in the growth of the AG in the 1950s.[14] Prior to Javier's most recent work, none of the extant scholarly texts on the history of AG in the Philippines mentions the Candelarias or any Methodist connections in their accounts, despite the obvious importance accorded to them in primary AG texts.[15]

Hence, the book hopes to fill a gap not only within the history of the Methodist Church in the Philippines, but also in the history of the Holiness movement in the early decades of the twentieth century. This work, however, will not merely add to the emerging corpus of scholarship on the global impact of the movement. By highlighting the dynamics of Philippine Methodist holiness revivalism and its relationship to the rise of the AG in the country in the mid-twentieth century, this book challenges both conventional narratives of the history of Pentecostalism in the Philippines, and the standard social scientific analyses that have interpreted Filipino Protestant Christianity as too rational. An analysis by Filipino social anthropologist Melba P. Maggay is representative of this paradigm when she argues that Protestant missionaries brought with them a "cold and highly intellectualized" or "left-brained" religion that proved to be incompatible with the "highly mystical" or "right-brained" popular Filipino religious consciousness.[16] It is precisely this lack of recognition of "heart religion" or "subjective" Protestantism, which was surely never scarce in early Philippine Methodism and other related movements that this book hopes to address.[17]

The book also has implications for mission history. It hopes to be situated among what mission historian Dana Robert dubs as "new mission histories," which challenge the usual "colonialism paradigm" that

13. Cunningham, "Diversities," 33.

14. Javier, "Personal Memoir."

15. For standard texts on Philippine AG history, see, for example, Seleky, "Six Filipinos," 119–29; Trinidad, "Assemblies of God in the Philippines."

16. Maggay, "Early Protestant Missionary Efforts," in Ma and Ma, *Asian Church*, 33. A similar argument is given by Bautista, "Socio-Psychological Make-up," 11–12.

17. I borrow Leonard Gurley's use of the word "subjective" to refer to advocates of the Holiness movement. Quoted in Schneider, "Heart Religion," 127.

dominated not only mission historiography discourse in the second half of the twentieth century,[18] but has also influenced the analysis of early Philippine Protestantism in recent years.[19] Emerging from a growing realization that the "center of gravity" of Christianity has shifted to the "global south," and of the "changing face" of Christianity on account of its unexpected growth in former colonized countries,[20] this new direction offers a fresh and multifaceted reading of missionary sources. In particular, it moves beyond the usual caricature of missionaries as "moral agents" of imperialism by reading them instead as "concrete" actors with particular historical and theological locations.[21] Similarly, the story of Philippine Methodist Pentecostal revivalism shows that mission historiography does not exist in a vacuum—it cannot be understood apart from the spirituality that missionaries imported with them. This, then, constitutes what German missiologist Andrea Schultze similarly calls "new approaches to mission history," whereby Christian doctrine—with its various interpretations throughout history—can provide "a better understanding of missionary sources and their implicit perspective."[22] Accordingly, this endeavor provides the opportunity not only to trace the founts from which Philippine Methodist spirituality sprang forth, but also discern more broadly, like José Míguez Bonino in his reflection on Latin American Methodism, "which Wesley" was introduced to the Philippines.[23]

Synopsis

Chapter 1 outlines the development of the Holiness movement from the second quarter of the nineteenth century up to the early decades of the twentieth century. This is in no way intended to be a comprehensive presentation of the history of the movement, as it only aims to flesh out elements that

18. Robert, *Converting Colonialism*, 1–2.

19. A good example of this "colonialism paradigm" in Philippine Protestant historiography is Apilado, *Revolutionary Spirituality*.

20. Jenkins, *Next Christendom*, 2–6; Walls, *Missionary Movement*, chap. 6; Robert, "Shifting Southward," 53–56; Sanneh, "Introduction," 3–5.

21. Robert, *Converting Colonialism*, 4–5. The approach to mission understood as a "moral equivalent of imperialism" is found, for example, in Hutchison, *Errand to the World*, 91–124; Schlesinger, "The Missionary Enterprise," 336–73. A counter argument, however, is found in Porter, "Cultural Imperialism," 367–91.

22. Schultze, "Writing of Past Times," 327.

23. Bonino, "Wesley in Latin America," 172.

can help us discern the roots of Philippine Methodist Pentecostal revivalism. Hence, special attention is given to the theological transitions and the various expressions that emerged from the movement, most particularly the Pentecostalization of the Wesleyan doctrine of holiness as advocates began to equate it with the "baptism of the Holy Spirit" or explain it as "the Spirit-filled life," an ideal popularized by the Keswick movement. The shift to Pentecostal expressions later set the stage for the emergence of revival meetings known as "Pentecostal meetings" within MEC conferences mostly in the American Midwest. The chapter also examines the movement's intersection with the Southern Asia mission of the MEC in India, where Keswick expressions of holiness had become more dominant. This then provides the context to the Pentecostal revival work of Bishops James Thoburn, Francis Warne and William Oldham, pioneering bishops of the MEC mission in the Philippines, and some missionaries who came from India.

Chapter 2 examines the beginning of Methodism in the Philippines at the onset of American colonial rule in the country. The chapter's primary objective is to outline the many ways in which Pentecostal revivalism was utilized by American Methodist pioneers, including Bishops Thoburn and Warne, and Woman's Foreign Missionary Society (WFMS) missionary Cornelia Moots, in their ministry among American soldiers. Such ministry inadvertently spilled over to masses of eager Filipino hearers who gladly welcomed Methodist work in their communities. Pioneer Filipino preachers, who emerged from among these early converts, helped spread Methodism to neighboring districts and towns in and around Manila, and further north. Accordingly, the chapter outlines the dynamics involved in the MEC's northward expansion that allowed it to experience phenomenal growth, and eventually organize the Philippine Islands Annual Conference in 1908.

Chapter 3 emphasizes the events and factors leading up to the introduction of *culto Pentecostal* rituals in Philippine Methodism. It begins by outlining the MEC's Protestant crusade against Roman Catholicism, and its eventual shift to a crusade against sin. Such change took place under the initiative of Bishop William Oldham, but was catalyzed by the Zamora schism in 1909, which forced the MEC to evaluate its mission. While missionary Charles Koehler was the first to introduce *culto Pentecostal* revivals in the Philippines to help stem the tide of schism, it was the famous Holiness evangelist Henry Clay Morrison that helped galvanized their place in Philippine Methodist culture. Hence, the chapter also lays out Morrison's highly successful Pentecostal meetings during the Annual Conference in Manila in 1910.

Chapter 4 describes the contours of MEC Pentecostal revivals in the Philippines as they began to take a prominent place in the fabric of Philippine Methodism in the years following Morrison's visit and up to the first quarter century of the denomination's existence in the country. This includes underscoring the contributions of those who prominently functioned as evangelists and those who labored on the sidelines to promote them—the bishops, male and female missionaries, Filipino clergy and women workers. Also, the chapter's careful reading of the performative elements of *culto Pentecostal* allows us to discern its success and longevity in light of socio-economic changes under American colonial rule. Nevertheless, its success was not merely limited to the revival gatherings themselves, but also through the ways by which it shaped Philippine Methodist self-identity. Therefore, the chapter demonstrates how *culto Pentecostal* revivalism influenced Methodist youth formation, and compelled Methodists to maintain high moral standards. Such standards found their way through official resolutions, and through the moral crusades of prominent Methodists in the public sphere.

Chapter 5 focuses on the status of the Philippine MEC Pentecostal revival culture following the first twenty-five years of Methodism in the country up to the "Stagg Schism," the split led by missionary Samuel Stagg in 1933. It highlights the status of *culto Pentecostal* culture and the circumstances that allowed it to flourish during a period of Filipino Methodist refinement. WFMS missionaries and Filipino clergy kept the Pentecostal revival flame burning even though newly arrived male missionaries like Stagg were less committed to it. Furthermore, the chapter brings to fore Jorge Bocobo's moral legacy to illustrate the moralizing tendencies of Filipino Methodists during the period. This provides the milieu for understanding how holiness standards inspired by the *culto Pentecostal* revivals helped create the Stagg Schism.

Chapter 6 examines the status of Methodist revivalism after the Stagg Schism and the post-war years and the context that allowed for the coalescing of Philippine Methodist Pentecostal impulses with divine healing revivalism. It details the arrival of the worldwide healing revival movement in Manila in the mid-1950s and the relationship between AG missionary Lester Sumrall and Methodists Ruben and David Candelaria. Through the Candelarias, the Methodist Church became fertile ground for the dissemination of the healing revival in Manila and in the provinces. Consequently, Methodists who were deeply involved with the healing revival increasingly found themselves drawn to the Pentecostal movement, and eventually away from their denomination. Thus, the chapter concludes with a discussion on the events that precipitated the defection of Methodists to the AG, and how these defections helped dictate the shape of Methodist revivalism in the years that followed.

Finally, the conclusion weaves together all the major findings from the previous chapters and accounts for *culto Pentecostal* parallels or implications that persist to this day in the UMC in the Philippines.

1

American Holiness Roots and Methodist Missions

> It is thus that we wait for entire sanctification, for a full salvation from all our sins, from pride, self-will, anger, unbelief, or, as the Apostle expresses it, "Go unto perfection."
>
> —John Wesley, "The Scripture way of Salvation"

Methodism itself was a reaction to the nominal Christianity or Anglicanism of John Wesley's day and that Methodist societies were designed to make "real Christians" out of those who desired to "flee from the wrath to come."[1] Wesley's doctrine of salvation extended the Protestant Reformation's call for salvation by faith with a post-conversion experience of holiness or entire sanctification. Consequently, Methodists for decades emphasized this experience of holiness, and, therefore, have set high moral standards as benchmarks for true conversion. This quest for real Christianity was also accompanied by Methodist enthusiasm expressed through noisy and emotionally charged revivals that ritualized one's conversion or entrance into a deeper level of Christian experience. The appeal of heart revivalism was not lost among Methodists for years as it contributed to its vibrancy and growth not only in the British Isles, but also in the American frontier where it primarily found full expression in the camp meetings and other gatherings.

Revivalism had become so embedded to Methodist identity that by the time American Methodists launched into the mission field in the nineteenth century, it was natural for them to carry the same revival impulse to usher people into an experience of justification and sanctification.[2]

---

1. Collins, *A Real Christian*, 148–51; Wesley, *General Rules*, II.4, *Works*, 9:70.
2. Oconer, "Methodism in Asia," 160–63.

However, by the turn of the twentieth century, as Methodists reached the Philippines, their revival preaching had already been dominated by Pentecostal motifs that expressed the Holy Spirit's power to bring about holiness and renewal to the person. It was for this reason that their revival meetings were called *culto Pentecostal* (Pentecostal meetings). In order to understand the *culto Pentecostal* meetings, it is important that we first turn our attention to the Holiness movement.

The Holiness Movement

Though scholars offer different arguments to account for the emergence of the Holiness movement, most agree that its theological roots were in John Wesley's doctrine of Christian perfection or entire sanctification, which he taught as a distinct second religious experience or "second blessing" subsequent to regeneration.[3] Although Wesley, as scholars contend, explained such experience as having both instantaneous and gradual elements to it, the Holiness movement emphasized the former.[4] The doctrine initially found a great following through the Methodist movement in America as it expanded from the eastern seaboard to the frontier throughout the closing decades of the eighteenth century. Some scholars suggest that Methodist interest in the doctrine went through a brief period of decline until it was reinvigorated by the emergence of a much broader perfectionist thrust within American culture during the second quarter of the nineteenth century.[5]

Within American Methodism, the increasing level of interest in the revival of the doctrine of holiness became evident in Timothy Merritt's immensely popular book, *The Christian's Manual, a Treatise on Christian*

---

3. Among those who make this connection include: Dieter, "The Wesleyan Perspective," 11–36; Dayton, *Theological Roots of Pentecostalism*, 38–48; Jones, *Perfectionist Persuasion*, 1–2; Synan, *The Holiness-Pentecostal Tradition*, 1–8.

4. Wesley's weaving together of both the gradual and instantaneous elements in his understanding of entire sanctification is substantiated by a number of scholars. See, for example, Lindström, *Wesley and Sanctification*, 123–24; Tyson, *Charles Wesley and Sanctification*, 298–99; Maddox, *Responsible Grace*, 180–87; Collins, *Theology of John Wesley*, 293–96.

5. See for example, Peters, *Christian Perfection*, 67–132; Jones, *Perfectionist Persuasion*, 2; Dieter, "The Wesleyan Perspective," 36–37. Some scholars, however, argue that the teaching of Christian perfection never declined in the denomination. See, for example, Coppedge, "Entire Sanctification," 34–50; Kostlevy, *Holiness Manuscripts*, 1.

Perfection: with Directions for Obtaining That State (1824), which was a compilation of the writings of John Wesley and John Fletcher on the subject and was meant to be a guide for those who sought to experience the second blessing.[6] Such interest also found denominational support when the bishops of the MEC made an appeal before the General Conference of 1832 for a revival the doctrine.[7] Another prominent development was Sarah Worrall Lankford's "Tuesday Meeting for the Promotion of Holiness," launched in 1835 in New York City, which eventually catapulted her sister Phoebe Worrall Palmer to the forefront of holiness revivalism. Some scholars, in fact, attribute the beginning of the Holiness movement to the Tuesday Meetings.[8] Charles Jones even suggests that it was to Palmer, more than Wesley, that the Holiness movement owed much of its distinctive practices and teachings.[9] Palmer taught a "shorter way" to experiencing entire sanctification through her "altar theology" by insisting on the immediate or present availability of entire sanctification through the following elements: 1) "entire consecration," 2) faith in God's promises to sanctify those who would come before the "Altar of Christ," and 3) public testimony. Palmer's holiness teaching represented a significant shift from that of Wesley's by making holiness the beginning, rather than the culmination, of the Christian life.[10] Though challenged by some, Palmer's teachings found support among Methodist bishops and gained wide acceptance among lay people and clergy both within and outside Methodism.[11]

The perfectionist impetus in Methodism also found parallels in the Reformed tradition as the "Methodization" of Calvinism became more apparent among "revivalistic Calvinists"—like New School Presbyterians, most Congregationalists, regular Baptists, and others—who increasingly manifested a similar concern for Christian holiness.[12] By the time the Worrall sisters started the Tuesday Meetings, Charles Finney, who had been

---

6. See Merritt, *The Christian's Manual*, iii–v; Smith, *Revivalism and Social Reform*, 115–16.

7. See Smith, *Revivalism and Social Reform*, 116; Dieter, *Holiness Revival*, 22.

8. Scholars debate the origins of the movement. Some attribute it to Timothy Merrit while others trace it to the Lankford sisters's Tuesday Meetings. See Kostlevy, *Holiness Manuscripts*, 1.

9. See Jones, *Perfectionist Persuasion*, 5.

10. Dieter, "The Wesleyan Perspective," 40.

11. See Dieter, *Holiness Revival*, 22–38; Long, "Palmer, Phoebe Worrall," 226–27.

12. Dieter, *Holiness Revival*, 18; Smith, *Revivalism and Social Reform*, 32–33. See also, for example, Shiels, "The Methodist Invasion," 257–80.

influenced by the works of John Wesley and other Methodist writers, had begun promoting holiness with his "new measures" revivalism before Reformed audiences in the "burned-over" district of western New York.[13] Some of the other prominent non-Methodist leaders who were particularly influenced by Palmer were: Asa Mahan, Congregationalist, Oberlin College president, and Finney's colleague; William Boardman, Presbyterian, and author of *The Higher Christian Life* (1858); Thomas Upham, Congregationalist; and A. B. Earl, prominent Baptist evangelist.[14] We should note, however, that although they generally sprang from the well of Wesleyanism, Reformed articulations of holiness doctrine flowed back to greatly reshape the Wesleyan Holiness tradition.[15] This particular stream would also make way for the rise of the Keswick movement years later and influence the formation of the Christian and Missionary Alliance Church under Albert B. Simpson, who emphasized the "four-fold gospel" of Christ the "Saviour, Sanctifier, Healer and Coming King."[16]

The nascent American Methodist Holiness movement, on the other hand, initially finding its center in the respectable urban parlor setting of the Palmer meetings, eventually blossomed into a much broader grassroots movement, as embodied by the establishment of the National Camp Meeting Association for the Promotion of Holiness (later renamed National Holiness Association) in 1867. Organized by Methodist ministers John A. Wood, John Inskip, and William McDonald, who were greatly influenced by Palmer, the National Holiness Association (hereafter NHA) "facilitated a resurgent, anti-genteel populism," Kathryn Long argues. While "disciplined Methodists" led the NHA on the national level, it increasingly took an interdenominational and radical social coloring in the regional and local chapters of the NHA, which reacted heavily against Methodist *embourgeoisment* in a manner reminiscent to that of the Genesee Conference "Nazarites" who had left the denomination to form the Free Methodist Church years earlier.[17] By the turn of the twentieth century, Methodism had to brace itself against ruptures brought about by the tide of radicalism within the

---

13. Carwardine, *Transatlantic Revivalism*, 16–17; Smith, *Revivalism and Social Reform*, 103–13.

14. Dieter, *Holiness Revival*, 32–33.

15. See Dieter, "The Wesleyan Perspective," 38.

16. Ibid., 39; Dayton, *Theological Roots of Pentecostalism*, 22.

17. See Long, "Consecrated Respectability," 305; Dayton, "Good News to the Poor," in Meeks, *Portion of the Poor*, 83–86, 89.

local associations that eventually metamorphosed into separate holiness denominations. Holiness advocates from the regional or local associations either separated themselves or were "put-out" by pressures within the main branches of Methodism, and gathered themselves and their non-Methodist converts to form holiness churches. Charles Jones estimates that about 150 groups came out of this, which included some who would later amalgamate into churches like the Pentecostal Church of the Nazarene (later renamed Church of the Nazarene), the Pilgrim Holiness Church, the Church of God (Anderson, Indiana), and many others. Later, most of these denominations affiliated with the Christian Holiness Partnership (a successor to the NHA) and the more conservative Interchurch Holiness Convention.[18]

Pentecostal and Keswick Holiness

Another important subtext to the rise of the Holiness movement is that by the mid-nineteenth century, the formulation of holiness doctrine would undergo a major shift. The increasing articulation of entire sanctification as a second "crisis" experience eventually paved the way for the reappearance of "Pentecostal sanctification," or the identification of entire sanctification with the "baptism of the Holy Spirit."[19] Such a formulation, which Donald Dayton traces from the Methodist theologian John Fletcher, would eventually have a "broader impact" among Baptists, Presbyterians, Quakers, and other groups during the "Great Prayer Meeting Revival" of 1857–58.[20] As interest in the doctrine of the Holy Spirit grew, the Holiness movement throughout the rest of the century increasingly preferred Pentecostal imagery over the more controversial themes of Christian perfection. Representative of this shift was the popularity of books like William Arthur's *Tongue of Fire* (1856) and Phoebe Palmer's *The Promise of the Father* (1857), and the prominent use of the word "Pentecostal" and other similar language within Holiness circles, which was carried on well into the early decades of the twentieth century.[21]

---

18. See Jones, *Perfectionist Persuasion*, 121–42; Dayton, "Holiness Churches," 197.

19. Dayton, *Theological Roots of Pentecostalism*, 70–71.

20. For a detailed treatment of the 1857–58 revival, see, for example, Carwardine, *Transatlantic Revivalism*, 159–69; Smith, *Revivalism and Social Reform*, 63–79; McLoughlin, *Revivals, Awakenings, and Reform*, 141–45; Dayton, "Holiness Churches," 197.

21. Dayton, *Theological Roots of Pentecostalism*, 71–80.

The Great Prayer Meeting Revival of 1857–58 also set the stage for an increase in transatlantic revival activity by a number of prominent American Holiness evangelists.[22] This allowed a number of "Arminianized Calvinists" to gain access to the much broader evangelical circles across the Atlantic and the continent, like the Mildmay Ministries and the Evangelical Alliance, which in turn helped create the milieu from which the Keswick movement was born.[23] The work of Mahan, Boardman, Quakers Hannah Whitall Smith and her husband Robert Pearsall Smith, and others made the holiness message more palatable to English Reformed sensibilities through their "higher life" teachings at the Oxford and Brighton union meetings "for the promotion of scriptural holiness." This provided the impetus for the eventual rise of a summer convention "for the promotion of practical holiness" in 1875 in the resort town of Keswick in northwest England.[24] Led primarily by Anglican evangelicals, among them Canon Thomas Harford-Battersby, the resulting "Keswickian" movement increasingly reshaped the holiness doctrine propagated by its Wesleyan promoters. We should note, however, as Charles Price and Ian Randall argue, that in its early stages, both the purveyors of the Wesleyan instantaneous crisis experience, and that of the distinctive Reformed-inspired non-perfectionist Keswick articulation, as it is known today, shared the platform at Keswick, and were in tension for the first seventy years of the movement. It was only after the post-war years that the latter indisputably became representative of Keswick thought.[25]

The resultant Keswick concept of holiness is essentially a *via media* understanding that is neither Wesleyan nor Reformed, in their strictest sense. It shies away from the Wesleyan perfectionist notion of the "total eradication" of sin while staying in agreement, to some extent, with the Reformed notion of the inevitability of sin in this life. But what makes Keswick different from Reformed is that it also retains, to some degree, a modified Wesleyan optimism in terms of the possibility of overcoming the sinful nature. While submitting to the Reformed argument that sin cannot be totally eradicated, it believes that sinful predispositions can be "suppressed" or "counteracted" through the "Spirit-filled life" or through the constant "indwelling" or "fullness" of the Spirit. Thus, it comes as no

---

22. Carwardine, *Transatlantic Revivalism*, 169–200.
23. Bundy, "Keswick," 118–44.
24. Dayton, *Theological Roots of Pentecostalism*, 104–6.
25. Price and Randall, *Transforming Keswick*, 14–15.

surprise that Keswick's ambivalence about totally agreeing with mainstream Wesleyan/Holiness notion of holiness is reflected in its preference for more nuanced catchphrases such as "higher life," "deeper life," "victorious life," and "fullness of the Spirit" to describe a less finite ideal for the Christian life or a "more moderate form" of holiness piety.[26] As we will see later, the influence of this Keswick understanding holiness would later manifest itself in various ways among Methodist missionaries in India and in the Philippines.

The Keswick movement eventually came full-circle when it gained popular appeal in the United States through the revivals brought by famed American evangelist Dwight L. Moody, and produced a number of important figures on the American scene, such as Albert B. Simpson, Adoniram J. Gordon, Arthur T. Pierson, Reuben A. Torrey, and others.[27] Moody, for instance, as David Bundy argues, was initially "marketed" as a Holiness revivalist during his English tour (1873–75), but eventually turned against holiness perfectionism upon his return. Moody carried this Keswick influence through his Northfield Conference, which focused more on "ecumenical" or non-perfectionist expressions of holiness and millenarianism.[28] Northfield helped inspire commitment towards overseas missions, and was instrumental in the founding of the Student Volunteer Movement (hereafter SVM) by members of the Young Men's Christian Association (hereafter YMCA) in 1886.[29] As we will see later, the SVM was very instrumental in compelling a good number of young Methodist "volunteers" to heed the call to serve as missionaries in the Philippines. A number of them have also been educated at the Moody Bible Institute in Chicago, a school founded by the highly revered evangelist the same year the SVM was founded.

---

26. For a summary of Keswick distinctive teachings, see McQuilkin, "Keswick Perspective," 151–83. See also Russell, "Counteracting Classifications," 86–121; Dayton, "Pneumatological Issues," 115.

27. Dieter, *Holiness Revival*, 249–50; Dayton, *Theological Roots of Pentecostalism*, 104–6. For further discussion on the Keswick movement and its understanding of sanctification, see McQuilkin, "Keswick Perspective," 151–86; Kent, *Holding the Fort*, 340–55.

28. Bundy, "Keswick," 124, 131. For more on Moody's English tour, see Kent, *Holding the Fort*, 132–68.

29. For more of SVM's connection with Keswick, see Price and Randall, *Transforming Keswick*, 116–19; Parker, *The Kingdom of Character*, 36–41. See Clymer, *Protestant Missionaries*, 11–12; Phillips, "Changing Attitudes," 5–6.

Methodist Pentecostal Services and Missions

While many Methodists left to join separate holiness denominations, many Holiness Methodist "loyalists" persisted within mainstream American Methodism as they continued to command a large presence in the NHA in the early decades of the twentieth century.[30] Much of this holiness entrenchment in Methodism can be attributed to bishops who sought to counter both the decline of holiness preaching especially among *bourgeois* urban congregations and the rise of liberalism among young university and seminary men. Northern bishops, in particular, gave their stamp of approval to the numerous Pentecostal services conducted by Methodist Holiness evangelists in several annual conference sessions. These found remarkable success in Ohio, Indiana, Iowa, Nebraska, and Washington, as well as in the border conferences where MEC was a minority denomination.[31] Northern bishops and individuals even intentionally "bombarded" the border conference of Alabama with holiness revival tactics throughout the 1890s to attract Southern Methodist holiness partisans to MEC ranks, but met with little success.[32]

The burgeoning Pentecostal services represented a culmination in the shift towards the articulation of entire sanctification to "Baptism of the Holy Spirit" in American Methodism,[33] which, as we will show later, would also find vigorous application in the Philippines. Popular among Methodist Holiness evangelists was Samuel Ashton Keen, a presiding elder from Ohio, who was called by the bishops to conduct Pentecostal services among ministers and others in seventy-six MEC annual conferences beginning in 1891. Four years after Keen's death, he was succeeded by Joseph Smith, who emerged as the foremost Holiness evangelist within the denomination at the beginning of the twentieth century. Smith, who was elected president of the NHA in 1925, was also asked by the bishops to conduct Pentecostal meetings at the 1904 and 1908 General Conferences together with Henry Clay Morrison, renowned southern Methodist Holiness evangelist and future president of Asbury College.[34] Morrison would later play a pivotal

---

30. See Rose, *Vital Holiness*, 96; Jones, *Perfectionist Persuasion*, 188.

31. Smith, *Called unto Holiness*, 53; Smith, "Holiness Crusade," 626–27. See also Peters, *Christian Perfection*, 177–80.

32. Brasher, *The Sanctified South*, 50–52, 211; Brasher, "The North in the South," 41–44.

33. Dayton, *Theological Roots of Pentecostalism*, 91–92.

34. See Rose, *Vital Holiness*, 95–96; Smith, *Called unto Holiness*, 53. For a summary on Henry Clay Morrison, see for example, Kostlevy, "Morrison, Henry Clay," 207–8.

role in the transplantation of the Pentecostal meeting revival culture into Philippine Methodism.

Aside from the evangelistic campaigns sanctioned by the bishops, the Methodist holiness impulse also gained a foothold in the resurgent missionary movement as America advanced its colonial interests overseas, which was accompanied by the rise of volunteerism or "interventionism" characteristic of the period known as the Progressive Era.[35] While it is true that holiness revivalism was more concerned with the quality of the church rather than its quantity, it was not at all incompatible with the missionary vision of the MEC.[36] First, we need to realize that missionary recruitment benefited significantly from myriad manifestations of holiness revivalism, broadly conceived, in the life of the church during that same period. Dana L. Robert makes the case by convincingly arguing that holiness piety was the "gasoline" that enabled WFMS missionaries to volunteer and engage in mission work. It was, in fact, through the NHA camp meetings and countless holiness revival rituals woven into the annual WFMS branch or district gatherings that a number of women who had testified to the second blessing also consecrated their lives to the missionary cause.[37] Beyond Robert's thesis, however, we should also take note of the influence of the Keswick-Northfield version of holiness among WFMS missionaries through the work of the SVM. A perusal of the SVM's statistics of "sailed volunteers" from 1906 to 1923 reveals that about five hundred volunteers joined the WFMS, of whom nineteen went to the Philippines. The SVM impetus was also very much alive among MEC regular missionaries, as statistics further confirm.[38]

But holiness revivals were not merely confined to missionary recruitment and inspiration, as they found vigorous application in MEC overseas fields in ways that somehow enhanced and redefined their usual intent

---

35. For an excellent discussion on the relationship of the resurgent missionary movement and American imperial expansion with volunteerism during the Progressive Era, see Chambers, *The Tyranny of Change*, 80.

36. I make a similar argument in Oconer, "Methodism in Asia," in Yrigoyen, *Companion to Methodism*, 160–63.

37. Robert, *American Women in Mission*, 144–48; Robert, "Holiness and the Missionary Vision," 15–27.

38. See list of "Sailed Volunteers" in the indexes of the following SVM publications: Turner, *Students and the Present Missionary Crisis*, 513–32; Turner, *Students and the World-Wide Expansion of Christianity*, 641–70; Stauffer, *Christian Students and World Problems*, 455–533.

vis-à-vis the refinement of the qualitative life of the church. Not only were they utilized to promote higher degrees of Christian experience among indigenous constituencies, they were also employed to reinvigorate zeal among missionaries, and, most importantly, to deliver perceived nominal Christians from inaction or, in some cases, proselytize them from other denominations. These applications would eventually pan out not only in the Philippines, as we will demonstrate later, but also in India, where much of the holiness impetus for Philippine Methodism initially came from. As Robert claims, some "sanctified" WFMS missionaries "disseminated holiness concerns on the mission field into the 1920s, if not longer." One such field which prominently stood out in her study was India.[39] It was through India that Methodism entered the Philippines. We now turn our attention to how holiness culture flourished in that field.

Methodist Pentecostal Revivalism in India[40]

Nothing better captures the state of early twentieth-century Indian Methodist evangelical culture than the observation made by John F. Goucher during a tour of India in 1912. "I heard more about the Holy Spirit in the time I was in India (it was a visit of a few months), than in thirty years from the preaching here in America," remarked the influential MEC minister from Baltimore.[41] Emphasis on the work of the Holy Spirit indeed permeated the life and culture of the MEC mission enterprise in India and this, to some extent, has been alluded to in recent academic forays on Indian Pentecostalism.[42] This was not only indicative of the form of revivalism which found prevalence in Indian Methodism, but also suggestive of the influence of the Holiness movement, broadly conceived, to missionary thought and practice in India. This influence found its way early into Indian Methodist life and, perhaps, if Goucher's claim is to be accepted, with much more intensity and frequency than in mainstream northern American Methodism at that time.

---

39. Robert, "Holiness and the Missionary Vision," 17–25; Robert, *American Women in Mission*, 144–52.

40. A more detailed presentation of this section is found in Oconer, "Keswickfied Methodism," 122–43.

41. As quoted in Badley, *Warne of India*, 17.

42. See for example, McGee, "Latter Rain," 651–52; McGee, "The Calcutta Revival of 1907," 123–43.

We are thereby led back to the influence of the Holiness heavyweight, albeit controversial, William Taylor (1821–1902), who came to India to help induce life to the fledging MEC mission there. Upon his arrival in 1870, Taylor began unprecedented revival campaigns initially within the MEC confines of North India, and further advanced the mission's initial incursion into Cawnpore, and deeper into Bombay (now Mumbai), Poona (now Pune), Calcutta (now Kolkata), Madras (now Chennai) and Bangalore, to the utter disregard of existing comity agreements and much to the embarrassment of the MEC Missionary Society.[43] Unsurprisingly, Taylor's holiness revivalism, which specialized in the conversion of the "already-converted," largely found success among European and British "nominal Christians," mostly Anglicans, who would later form the bulk of MEC membership in what was to become the South India Conference in 1876.[44] Also supporting Taylor, as he moved further south, were a steady stream of "self-supporting" missionaries to continue and oversee the churches he helped establish. These men and women were mostly either recruited from his preaching tours in the United States or Eurasians (mostly Indian-born Britons) awakened through his meetings in India.[45] Among Taylor's recruits were future bishops John E. Robinson, William F. Oldham, and Homer C. Stuntz, who served as presiding elder of the Philippine Islands District. Taylor continued to recruit missionaries for India even after his stint there. Though Taylor left the country in 1875 to assist in Moody's evangelistic tour in England, he continued to recruit "Taylor" missionaries for South India. He was later elected missionary bishop of Africa at the 1884 General Conference.[46]

In the shadow of Taylor's renowned work in India was James Mills Thoburn (1836–1922), a prominent figure in the birth of Methodism in the Philippines, who assumed leadership of the mission after the highly esteemed MEC India pioneer William Butler in 1865. It was Thoburn's vision

---

43. For a comprehensive account of Taylor's self-supporting ministry in India, see Taylor, *Four Years' Campaign in India*; Taylor, *Ten Years*. See also Bundy, "Bishop William Taylor," 3–7; Bundy, "The Legacy of William Taylor," 172–76; Garrett, "James Mills Thoburn," 69–74; Hempton, *Empire of the Spirit*, 168–176.

44. See Ernsberger, "Story of the South Indian Conference," 168; Beal, *Bishop John Edward Robinson*, 7.

45. For a list of pioneering "Taylor" missionaries in South India, see, for example, Taylor, *Ten Years*, 143, 49. Robert also mentions the existence of WFMS "Taylor" missionaries in Robert, "Holiness and the Missionary Vision," 25–26.

46. Bundy, "Bishop William Taylor, Part II," 7–10.

of MEC expansion from what he felt was their "little corner" in Northern India that led him to resort to holiness revivalism by inviting Taylor, whom he first met in a camp meeting in Ohio in 1858.[47] Thoburn also turned to Holiness Methodists for support of the South Indian "conquest" by raising funds through several NHA camp meetings during his furloughs in the 1870s. It was at the 1876 Epworth Heights camp meeting in Loveland, near Cincinnati, where he first met the renowned African-American evangelist Amanda Berry Smith. Smith held a seven-month revival tour in India, mostly within MEC turf, beginning November 1879, which she extensively chronicled in her autobiography, to which Thoburn wrote the introduction.[48] Thoburn was later elected bishop in 1888.

Holiness revival culture was also kept equally alive on the other side of the famed Ganges River even as Taylor, Thoburn, and their band of self-supporting recruits blazed the trail southward. Among a number of MEC camp meetings in the north or Christian *melas*, as they were commonly called in India, the most prominent was the annual *Dasehra* meeting—the flagship of holiness promotion in North India.[49] First launched in 1871, the *Dasehra* meeting was an outgrowth of what one missionary believed to be "a genuine revival movement" inspired by Taylor's work in the north.[50] Held during the popular Indian holiday from which its name was derived, the *Dasehra* meeting is a four or five-day revival gathering every October in Lucknow for the spiritual uplift of missionaries and national workers, and for the promotion of "Higher Life or Full Salvation." The gathering was initially held in a large tent at the Lal Bagh cricket field, but was later moved to the MEC English church sanctuary. Thoburn led almost all of the meetings during its formative years, and was instrumental in their success.[51] MEC

47. Thoburn, *My Missionary Apprenticeship*, 278–79. See also Garrett, "James Mills Thoburn," 69.

48. Smith, *An Autobiography*, v–x, 300–330. For additional details, see *Western Christian Advocate*, 23 August 1911, 9.

49. Dasehra is also spelled "Dashera," "Dussera," "Dussehra," and "Dasara." I am using the spelling used in most MEC literatures. For example, see Hollister, *The Centenary of the Methodist Church*, 96–97. The holiday, having been derived form the words *dash* (ten) and *hara* (kill), commemorates Ramas's slaying of a ten-headed beast. See Warne, *Revival in the Indian Church*, 8–9. The largest MEC camp meeting in north India was the Rohilcund (now Rohilkhund) camp meeting in Chandausi, which also featured holiness preaching. A detailed description is found in Knox, *A Winter in India and Malaysia*, 407–25.

50. *IW*, 19 August 1909, 7.

51. A brief history of the Dasehra meetings is found in *IW*, 15 February 1910, 7–8. See also *IW*, 7 October 1909, 3.

theologian James Mudge, who for eight years was stationed in Lucknow (from 1873–1881), "prominently" helped organize a number of *Dasehras* and claimed to have experienced a "memorable blessing or baptism" at the 1879 meeting.[52] He also extensively defended standard holiness teachings while working as the editor of the MEC weekly *Lucknow Witness*.[53] Other notable personalities who had taken charge, or had made their mark in *Dasehra* included Bishops Francis W. Warne, William F. Oldham, John E. Robinson, Edwin W. Parker, Brenton T. Badley, and Jashwant R. Chitambar, the first Indian Methodist to be elected bishop. Henry Clay Morrison, and popular MEC missionary E. Stanley Jones also spoke at the annual gathering.[54] Lucknow *Dasehra* was also the first annual interdenominational or "united gathering" for holiness promotion in India. It later spurred similar gatherings at Mussoorie, Sialkot, Coonnoor, Jabalpur, Darjeeling, and other mission stations, mostly under the auspices of the SVM.[55]

While the *prima facie* influence of the Holiness movement can easily account for the predominance of "Pentecostal" talk within the MEC mission enterprise in India, this, however, needs to be qualified by two underlying and related themes. First, standard perfectionist Wesleyan terms did not find eminence, at least among prominent MEC figures in India with known links to the Holiness movement. Second, evidence suggests that especially towards the end of the nineteenth century, the MEC Indian mission increasingly turned to non-perfectionist holiness expressions and was, to a degree, on the same trajectory with those whose articulation of moderate holiness piety would later help influence what is now understood as definitive Keswick piety. In other words, the MEC mission in India had been, to a large extent, "Keswickfied." However, this culture did not progress without outside influence given MEC missionaries's interaction with other "Holy Ghost" evangelicals beginning in the 1890s and with growing intensity in

---

52. *IW*, 15 February 1910, 8.

53. A good example of this was Mudge's series of replies to a number of inquiries on the subject of holiness from June to October 1874. See *LW*, 12 June 1874, 82; *LW*, 12 June 1874, 83; *LW*, 3 July 1874, 107; *LW*, 10 July 1874, 114; *LW*, 21 August 1874, 162; *LW*, 11 September 1874, 186–87; *LW*, 18 September 1874, 195; *LW*, 9 October 1874, 218. For more on Mudge's connection with the Holiness movement, see Kostlevy, "Mudge, James," 209–10.

54. Edwin Parker, for example, took charge of the 1899 meetings. See Messmore, *The Life of Edwin Wallace Parker*, 269. For E. Stanley Jones's early involvement, see, for example, *IW*, 15 October 1908, 7; *IW*, 11 November 1909, 4–6.

55. Dyer, *Revival in India*, 24.

the years surrounding the Great Indian Revival of 1905. British India, in a way, became a crucible for American, British, Australian, and European popular evangelicalism as Anglicans, Presbyterians, Methodists, Lutherans, Brethrens, Baptists, YMCAs, Bible Societies, and other Protestants interacted through joint endeavors during that period.[56] It was clear that in the ensuing interplay among evangelicals in India, the non-perfectionist and more moderate Keswick variety of holiness piety was the most dominant.[57]

The predominance of Keswick holiness eventually spilled over the banks of Indian Methodism, and would set the stage for the early character of holiness revivalism in Philippine Methodism. This backdrop not only illuminates the revival ministries of Bishops Thoburn and Warne as they pioneered Methodism in the Philippines, but also that of William F. Oldham, who was elected bishop for MEC work in Malaysia and the Philippines in 1904. It was primarily through Oldham's efforts, as we will show in the next chapter, that *culto Pentecostal* revivalism would find a niche in early Philippine Methodist culture.

---

56. See McGee, "Latter Rain," 651–52; Case, "And Ever the Twain Shall Meet," 6.

57. The important role played by Keswick in India in the outbreak of the Revival is attested in Dyer, *Revival in India*, 24–30. See also McGee, "Pentecostal Phenomena," 114; McGee, "Latter Rain," 651–52.

Figure 1.1. William Taylor, famous Methodist evangelist who helped James Thoburn begin the MEC South India Conference. He was later elected missionary bishop of Africa at the General Conference of 1884. Source: Taylor, *Ten Years* (1882).

Figure 1.2. Bishop James Mills Thoburn, missionary bishop of the MEC in Southern Asia and pioneer of Methodist work in the Philippines. Source: Drew University Methodist Library, Madison, New Jersey.

Figure 1.3. Bishop Francis Wesley Warne, missionary bishop of the MEC in Southern Asia who oversaw Methodist work in the Philippines from 1900–1904. Source: Drew University Methodist Library, Madison, New Jersey.

Figure 1.4. Bishop William Fitzjames Oldham, missionary bishop of the MEC in Southern Asia and the second bishop to oversee Methodist work in the Philippines. Source: Drew University Methodist Library, Madison, New Jersey.

2

Methodist Beginnings in the Philippines

> Since I began to preach the gospel I have felt that the virtue of the Holy Spirit is always in me, and I have never forgotten to pray to God before preaching, begging the presence of the Holy Spirit, and always I have felt his influence.
>
> —Nicolas Zamora, quoted in *Light in the East*

American Volunteerism and Filipino Independence Collide

The last decade of the nineteenth century marked the beginning of what historians call the "Progressive Era," which was a period of great change for the United States. In many ways, writes historian John Whiteclay Chambers II, "it marked the birth of modern America," which he described as having emerged from a national impulse for activism in most sectors of the society.[1] Concomitant with this was the resurgence of the Protestant missionary movement manifested in the significant increase of men and women volunteering for, what William Hutchison phrases as, "an errand to the world."[2] Consequently, it was within this context that the SVM, which we have already pointed out in the previous chapter, was born, and with the word "Volunteer" attached to its name. Other historians, however, ignore the voluntarism aspect of this resurgent missionary activity and instead assess it as a "moral equivalent" of imperialism justified by Protestant clergymen "in terms of the categories of historic destiny and ethical obligation."[3]

---

1. Chambers, *Tyranny of Change*, 274.

2. Hutchison restates the Puritan imagery of "errand to the wilderness." Hutchison, *Errand to the World*, 5; Phillips, "Changing Attitudes," 131.

3. See Hutchison, *Errand to the World*, 91–95; Anderson, "Providence and Politics," 281.

Such understanding of destiny and obligation also helped shape another international role for the United States.

Aside from the resurgent missionary impulse, another dominant feature of the Progressive Era was international activism. America shifted from its traditional policies of isolationism and neutrality as it found the necessity to shape its international environment through diplomatic and military intervention. Moreover, a growing economy, increasing military power, mounting national pride, and developments overseas have all contributed to this shift.[4] In particular, there was also a rising sense of what historians call "manifest destiny" as Americans began to view their nation as a model democracy, a benevolent nation chosen by God to bless neighboring nations.[5] Such a view served as a springboard for American intervention in Cuba as public outcry for the nation's independence from Spanish colonial rule became evident.[6] This also led to the commencement of the Spanish-American War, a conflict that eventually reached the Philippines.

With news of Admiral George Dewey's victory over the Spanish armada at the Manila Bay in May 1898, the United States moved to annex the Philippines in August of that year. Kenneth Mackenzie's survey of the prevailing attitude among representatives of the MEC shows that the majority were in favor of retaining the Philippines based from the framework that "God was acting through the Anglo-Saxon nations to enlighten the world . . . and it was their responsibility to 'take up the white man's burden.'"[7] In light of the positive response of the public and press to the country's role of assuming colonial burdens, and as if to echo the mood of his own church, President William Mckinley, a staunch Methodist, finally came to a decision to retain the Philippines.[8] A few days after the signing of the Treaty of Paris, the fate of the Philippines was sealed as he instructed his military commander in the country to win the confidence of the Filipinos by proving that the United States's mission is one of "benevolent assimilation."[9]

---

4. Chambers, *Tyranny of Change*, 201.

5. Anderson, "Providence and Politics," 280.

6. See Mackenzie, *Robe and the Sword*, 47–67. Mackenzie illustrates the dominant view among representatives of the MEC with regards to American intervention in Cuba.

7. Ibid., 112.

8. See Anderson, "Providence and Politics," 292. Evidences presented by Anderson suggest that McKinley was influenced by the dominant opinion within the MEC.

9. From the letter of President McKinley to Gen. Elwell Otis dated December 21, 1898. Quoted in Salamanca, *Filipino Reaction*, 27.

The Filipinos, nevertheless, rejected McKinley's expressed intention. After all, they had already declared independence from Spain on June 12, 1898, as a result of decisive victories by the Philippine Revolutionary Army under Gen. Emilio P. Aguinaldo in the previous months. Except for the ports of Manila and Cavite, which were still held by Spain, the Filipinos had already liberated the whole of Island of Luzon. However, the arrival of American troops in Manila in August of that year, and the surrender of Spanish authorities solely to the new occupiers meant the transfer of Philippine sovereignty to the United States. The Filipino leaders saw this as a wanton act of betrayal by the Americans for breaking an earlier promise they made with them. This eventually led to the commencement of the Philippine-American War (1899–1903) on February 4, 1899.[10] Meanwhile from India, Bishop James Thoburn was monitoring the developments in the country. About two weeks earlier, the Missionary Society of the Methodist Episcopal Church (hereafter MSMEC) sent him a one-word cablegram: "Go," a coded message to mean that he was to "proceed as soon as possible to the Philippines."[11] On February 28, as the conflict continued to escalate, the bishop fulfilled his mandate as he landed in the battle-scarred city to begin preparations for officially launching MEC work among American soldiers and civilians in the country.[12]

Revival in the Theater and the Birth of a Mission

On Sunday morning, March 5, 1899, a different form of drama unfolded at the *Teatro Filipino* (Filipino Theater), home to Spanish plays and musicals, on Echague Street (now Palanca Street) in the suburb of Quiapo, Manila.[13] Taking center stage this time at the previously famed theater was not a Filipino stage actor, but Bishop Thoburn who had arrived with the intent of fulfilling his long-held vision of establishing MEC work in the

10. See Apilado, *Revolutionary Spirituality*, 19–26. For a comprehensive look at the Philippine-American War, see, for example, Wolff, *Little Brown Brother*. There are, of course, different opinions as to when the war ended, but some historians point to 1903. See, for example, Arcilla, *Introduction*, 102.

11. Thoburn, 23 January 1899, Diary, JTDJ.

12. Thoburn, 28 February 1899, Diary, JTDJ.

13. Thoburn, 5 March 1899, Diary, JTDJ. *Teatro Filipino* was situated in what is now the SM Clearance Store in Quiapo, Manila. I have determined this by carefully analyzing *Teatro Filipino*'s blueprint and descriptions along with an 1898 map of Manila. See Buenaventura, *Theater in Manila*, 17–19, 83–84; De Gamoneda, *Plano de Manila* [map].

Philippines, albeit on the coattails of his country's colonial expansion in the Southeast Asian nation. Oblivious to the ongoing skirmishes between Filipino and American troops in the outskirts of the city, Thoburn, the mission expansionist, proceeded to expand that fateful morning not a political empire, but what we could call an "empire of the Spirit"[14] to underscore his weaving of Pentecostal motifs with his missionary exploits. Recording the occasion in his journal, he wrote:

> At 9:20 A.M. I went to the theatre and found a dozen soldiers at the door and a few others. We went in and somewhat slowly over seventy persons came in and took seats in the main floor while from thirty to 50 Filipinos stood without the railing. Things moved slowly at first but when I began to preach the Spirit wonderfully helped. Seldom in my life have I felt preaching to be such a luxury. We had a collection and got $82, of which $50 were given by one man. Most of the audience were Protestants.[15]

It is interesting to note that Thoburn attributed to the assistance of the Holy Spirit the success of his preaching, even mentioning in a separate account that he felt in "every fibre" of his being that "God was in that place." Similarly, the main content of his sermon was primarily about the third person of the Trinity as he preached "not by might nor by power, but by my Spirit saith the Lord" from Zechariah 4:6, proclaiming the "mercy, and love, and faithfulness, and power of God in this city of Manila."[16] Thoburn's Holy Spirit-centric message and account of that important day were highly consistent with much of his preaching and writing. Incidentally, it was just about the same time that his "magnum opus," *The Church of Pentecost* (1899), a book outlining his holiness theology and robust pneumatology, was being printed.[17]

There were signs that led Thoburn to conclude that the Holy Spirit led the worship service at the theater. In fact, as he was preaching, a certain "Captain Plummer," a Manila resident of twenty years from Albany, New

---

14. I modify David Hempton's phrase "empire of the spirit" in *Empire of the Spirit*, 2, 6. I use the capitalized "Spirit" instead of the lowercased "spirit." Mission expansionism, like the one begun by Thoburn in Manila, appears to be one of the characteristic traits of Methodism. Hempton effectively explores this theme in chap. 7.

15. Thoburn, 5 March 1899, Diary, JTDJ.

16. *IW*, 7 April 1899, 3. Thoburn also used the same text for his first sermon in Singapore. See also Doraisamy, *What Hath God Wrought*, 107.

17. *IW*, 10 February 1899, 1. See Thoburn, *Church of Pentecost*. For more on Thoburn's holiness theology, see Oconer, "Keswickfied Methodism," 130–35.

York, broke down into tears as his "heart warmed toward the Methodists." The stevedoring businessman was also compelled to trade his Presbyterianism to become one of the founding members of the first MEC congregation in the country. While nothing much was expected from the Filipinos who were present given the language barrier, there was at least one who did not leave unmoved, a Filipino *principalía* or upper class of "intelligence and culture" who attempted to invite Thoburn to preach in his home. Though the request was never granted due to the unavailability of an interpreter, it nevertheless underscored the character of early Filipino interest toward Protestant work, which in the few weeks that followed would greatly benefit the nascent MEC mission.[18]

Complementing Thoburn's Pentecost-themed message was the method he employed to conduct the worship service. The event essentially had the hallmarks of a revival meeting—one of the firsts to be held in the country. The handbills distributed and newspaper announcements, which unwittingly positioned Thoburn as a visiting revivalist, certainly got the attention not only of the American soldiers and expatriates who were present, but also of Filipinos eager to experience, perhaps for the first time, a worship service that was different from the Roman Catholic mass they were accustomed to.[19] In the absence of a suitable place, a theater, interestingly, was chosen for this special gathering. We can only speculate whether this was an attempt to replicate the same sacred spaces typically used for urban revivals back in the United States, but the theater setup proved ideal for Thoburn's preaching that morning.[20] The location also served to highlight the contrast in approach between the MEC and the other Protestant missions that came after them. While the Methodists inaugurated their work on a much bigger scale by renting a theater, the Presbyterians, for example, launched theirs in the home of a Filipino family a month later.[21]

After preaching, the bishop appealed that a collection for theater rent be made. While this elicited some awkward smiles from the audience, it nevertheless served as a proxy altar call that helped validate his plans for the mission. The eighty-two dollars, mostly foreign currencies, that filled the two hats that were passed among the audience reassured him that the

---

18. *IW*, 7 April 1899, 3; *GIAL*, February 1901, 59.

19. Ibid.

20. For a study on the relationship between urban revivalism and architecture, see Kilde, *When Church Became Theatre*, 22–55.

21. Rodgers, *Forty Years*, 6.

"people were ready to support the work." To this amount, Captain Plummer chipped in fifty dollars, a small fraction to the one thousand dollars he would give months later.[22] Thoburn's inaugural gathering seemed to foreshadow the revivalistic character of Philippine Methodism in its first year. While Thoburn's visit was the first trip to the Philippines ever sanctioned by the MEC Missionary Society, we must take into account three other MEC pioneers who preceded the bishop. Interestingly enough, these three unrelated pioneers also manifested, to some varying degrees, the influence of the Holiness movement in their work.

Pre-Thoburn Pioneers and the Birth of the Central "American" Church

On August 28, 1898, barely two weeks after the capture of Manila by the Americans, the "evangelistic" Chaplain George C. Stull (1858–1933) of the Montana Annual Conference inaugurated what he claimed to be the "first distinctive Protestant religious service" in the country, which he concluded with an altar call. Attended by soldiers and curious locals, Stull held the service in an old Spanish dungeon in Cavite overlooking the Manila Bay. Describing the event in his journal, he wrote:

> How we sang; how the place was transformed; how the people wondered at our service! My text was, "The power of God." How He showed Himself to us. Eight responded to the invitation at the close of the service to identify themselves with God's people; not to start a Methodist Church, but to band together to honor God. This was the first distinctive Protestant religious service, so the people tell me; for to hold any but the State service heretofore meant death. That the power of God will use this day to make a good Catholic better, any weak American stronger, any backslider ashamed, and the gloomy old dungeon the beginning of wonderful things in these Islands, is my prayer.[23]

22. *IW*, 7 April 1899, 3; *WWM*, December 1899, 6; *GIAL*, February 1901, 59–60. The Filipino could possibly be Don Luis Yangco, a ship captain and one of the first Protestants in Manila. He later opened his home to MEC work. See Stagg, *Teodoro R. Yangco*, 26–27. Another possibility was Don Pascual H. Poblete, editor of a pro-revolutionary newspaper in Manila, who later opened his home for the first Presbyterian services. See Sitoy, *Several Springs*, 41–42, 45.

23. Quoted in Stuntz, *Philippines and the Far East*, 415–16; Stull later retired in Ocean Grove, New Jersey and held a position there. His obituary characterized him as "evangelistic in his message." See *New Jersey Annual Conference* (1934), 353–54; *Montana Annual Conference* (1933), 265–66.

Stull's description of the meeting had some similarities to the service held by Bishop Thoburn in Manila a few months later as we have described in the previous section. Most specifically, his Pentecost-themed message, "the power of God," was strikingly similar to that of the bishop's, not only in its content, but also in its revivalistic bent. It is also interesting to note that although Stull later made the erroneous claim that the gathering "started the Methodist Episcopal Church in the Philippine islands,"[24] his prayers for Filipino Roman Catholics, Americans, and backsliders inadvertently predicted the work that MEC mission would open in the months that followed.

Following Stull, another MEC minister who came before Thoburn was the Rev. Charles A. Owens (1857–1935), a former Taylor missionary from Liberia, who arrived with his wife in the middle of October 1898.[25] Hastily appointed by Bishop Charles McCabe during the Puget Sound Conference to pioneer the so-called "Philippine Island District,"[26] Owens preached "more than forty times" and held "revival services eighteen nights" in a borrowed YMCA tent which was attended by soldiers and some curious locals. The resulting conversions and baptisms led him to organize what he called "a Methodist Church among the soldiers" on November 24. Even though they did not have a permanent preaching place, twenty-four individuals, mostly Methodists from different regiments, "united" with this church.[27] Owens's "Methodist Church," however, proved to be short-lived due to a series of setbacks.

Due to the unpredictable nature of troop deployments, most of his members have been dispatched to the frontlines at the onset of the Philippine-American War.[28] Also, since his appointment in Manila was not sanctioned by the MSMEC, Owens was not getting the necessary support from the denomination. When Thoburn came, Owens bewailed the fact that he had not received any communication from Bishop McCabe, except for a remittance of $300 after writing him an urgent appeal. In addition, he was suffering from ill health due to the recurrence of "African fever," which

---

24. *Montana Annual Conference* (1902), 21–22.

25. *Pacific Northwest Annual Conference* (1936), 71; *WWM*, September 1899, 6.

26. *Pudget Sound Annual Conference* (1899), 23. The irregularity of Owens's appointment stirred some controversy as outlined in Copplestone, *Twentieth-Century*, 177–78.

27. *WWM*, September 1899, 6.

28. *WWM*, June 1899, 6.

he first contracted while in Africa. Thoburn's appraisal of his work did not help either. In a letter to Bishop Edwin Parker of India, he reported: "Owen [sic] is a good man, but not the man for a pioneer. He had not established any regular preaching when I arrived, but was simply preaching to soldiers when he got a chance." He also complained that Owens "discouraged every suggestion" he had made and even "predicted" the failure of his planned meeting at *Teatro Filipino*.[29] Hence, given Thoburn's assessment, Owens and his wife were sent packing home shortly after Thoburn's visit.[30]

On December 17, 1898, three weeks after the founding of Owens's "Methodist Church," another accidental pioneer who arrived in Manila, primarily to cash in on America's "new possession," was businessman Arthur W. Prautch, a former MEC missionary who had worked under Thoburn in Bombay. The son of German immigrants from Wisconsin, Prautch joined Dwight L. Moody's church in Chicago, where he was converted under his preaching in 1882. Two years later, Taylor missionary Dennis Osborne recruited the then eighteen-year-old Prautch under the wings of Taylor's self-supporting missions in South India, where Prautch would become known for his work among the Gujaratis.[31] Prautch's twelve-year missionary career, however, came to an abrupt halt when he withdrew from the Bombay conference in 1897 "under charges or complaints."[32]

But this hiatus proved to be temporary for Prautch. At the prompting of his wife, Elisa Ada, who arrived in Manila on February 1899, the "deacon," as Prautch was fondly called by his peers, was soon thrust back into evangelistic work as he began preaching to passersby at the corner of Escolta and David Streets in the commercial district of Manila.[33] When Bishop Thoburn, who had presided over the same conference that had stripped Prautch of his ministerial credentials, a few days later, it was Prautch who assisted him and organized the gathering at the Filipino Theater. Thoburn reinstated the defrocked minister, but only as a licensed local preacher, putting him and his wife in charge of pioneering MEC work in the city. With the help of Stull, the Prautchs oversaw the congregation that continued to meet at the Filipino Theater. This congregation was initially called the

---

29. Thoburn to Parker, 7 March 1899, Thoburn, James M to EW Parker, BFC.

30. Thoburn, 28 February 1899, Diary, JTDJ; *WWM*, June 1899, 6.

31. Knox, *Winter in India*, 23–26. Additional details on Prautch are also found in Hollister, *Centenary*, 190.

32. *Bombay Annual Conference* (1897), 8, 14.

33. Alejandro, *From Darkness to Light*, 19.

"American Church," and later "Central Church" or Central MEC after moving to a permanent building on December 23, 1901, on the corner of San Luis and Nozaleda Streets in Ermita. By the middle of July, the congregation transferred to "Soldier's and Sailor's Institute" (hereafter Soldier's Institute), a rented hall a few blocks away from the theater at No. 6 Plaza de Goiti (now Plaza Lacson). Started by Prautch, the Soldier's Institute, which began opening its doors on May 1899 was meant as a hub for American soldiers and sailors so they could gather for worship services and have "temperance drinks, meals, games, lodging, and general social enjoyments, free from the temptation of the saloon."[34]

Aside from Stull, there were a number of Methodists who assisted the Prautchs: Jay C. Goodrich, a recent Drew Theological Seminary graduate from the MEC Newark Conference, sent to head the American Bible Society (hereafter ABS) in the country; First Lt. Edward W. Hearne, secretary of the YMCA in Manila;[35] and a number of military chaplains, including Capt. Theophilus G. Steward of the African Methodist Episcopal Church, chaplain of the racially segregated Twenty-Fifth Infantry (Colored) Regiment of the United States Army, who conducted services, marriages, and baptisms at the Soldier's Institute.[36]

Nicolas Zamora and the First Filipino Methodist Church

Although Bishop Thoburn intended to grow MEC work in the Philippines initially around American expatriates who were already in the country, Filipinos entered the picture much earlier than he had anticipated. At the request of five Filipino Freemasons, Prautch opened a Spanish service for them at the Soldier's Institute. After handbills had been handed out, and announcements had been made in the local newspapers, the first service began on Sunday, May 28, 1899, at three o'clock in the afternoon with about fifteen people in attendance. Prautch handed out copies of hymns taken from the South American hymnbook as Chaplain Stull led the singing while

---

34. *GIAL*, February 1901, 58–61; *GIAL*, July 1900, 314.

35. *GIAL*, February 1901, 58–61; Warne, *Light in the East*, 54–55. For additional information on Hearne, see Hearne, *Hearne Family*, 92; Crafts and Leitch, *Protection of Native Races*, 201.

36. Chaplain Steward, who had been present at the first MEC quarterly conference, was listed as "Stewart" in most accounts. See, for example, *PIDC* (1902), 25. Details of Steward's work in the Philippines are found in Steward, *Fifty Years*, 308–52.

also playing the piano. Stull also preached through an interpreter supplied by the Filipinos. Although Prautch lamented that the process of preaching through an interpreter proved to be "tedious and unsatisfactory," the event marked the birth of the first Filipino Methodist congregation in the country or the "First Filipino Church." This Filipino congregation would later find its permanent home in Cervantes Street when it became Knox Memorial MEC. Among the first Filipinos to join these services were Don Paulino Zamora, one of the Freemasons mentioned earlier, and three of his sons, including twenty-three-year-old Nicolas Villegas Zamora (1875–1914). Two months later, on August 6, when the interpreter, who was already deemed ineffective, did not show up, Prautch relied on the assistance of the older Zamora, who in turn ended up urging his son Nicolas to rise to the occasion.[37] Prautch, as if to highlight the providential character of the event, vividly recalled twenty-five years later:

> I therefore went up to him and asked him to take the meeting and preach as there was no interpreter. He arose, spoke a few words of approval of the meeting, and pointing to a young man about twenty-five years of age [sic], said: "My son, Nicolas will speak." Nicolas stood up, declined to come to the front and started to speak in a loud clear tone in Spanish. He never hesitated for words but kept on warming up in earnestness and held the audience spell bound [sic]. After the first few sentences I decided that he was the future preacher and when he sat down and the closing hymn was being sung I asked him. "Will you preach next Sunday?" he said "yes."[38]

Nicolas Zamora's first public preaching was a fitting preview into the prolific preacher he would quickly become. It appears that his preaching, to some degree, already had the hallmarks of what would make for a successful evangelist. His speech was earnest and clear, and even though he declined to go to the front, probably out of modesty, he still exuded confidence and charisma. His effectiveness in preaching could not be overstated since Prautch even testified that Zamora's preaching enabled the young Filipino Methodist society at the Soldier's Institute to attract public interest,

---

37. *GIAL*, February 1901, 60; Prautch, "Beginning of Methodist Work," 38–39; *GIAL*, July 1900, 315. The birth of the Filipino Church is the beginning of what is now Knox Memorial United Methodist Church. Prautch and Warne give conflicting dates as to when the Filipino Church began and as to when Zamora first preached. For consistency, I am following Prautch's dates since he was a direct eyewitness to the founding of this congregation.

38. Prautch, "Beginning of Methodist Work," 39.

and to birth other societies as some attendees arranged for him and Zamora to open similar meetings in their neighborhoods. Soon enough, seven preaching places had been opened in and around Manila, including Pandacan and Malibay, as the two labored with great success.[39] In Pandacan, for example, the work of Zamora had been so effective that the first Filipino MEC chapel was built there, and dedicated by Bishop Warne on August 12, 1900.[40] Additionally, from these endeavors two more Filipinos preachers were recruited, José Bautista and Segundo Sempio, who were licensed as exhorters a few months later.[41]

The young Zamora's emergence as an effective evangelist inadvertently accelerated the MEC's plans for the Filipino ministry. Hence, when Thoburn, together with Warne, arrived on March 6, 1900, for a second visit, he found Methodist work among Filipinos moving full steam ahead. More than six hundred Filipinos had already thrown their lot behind the young evangelist's teachings and, therefore, virtually stood on Methodism's doorsteps, but without any Filipino worker to administer the sacraments to them.[42] Additionally, the Presbyterians had already made headway among some of the prominent families at the Soldier's Institute, including the Zamora family, whom they baptized on October 1899. Filipino Protestants, who were still oblivious to American denominationalism at that time, gravitated between the work of Prautch and Zamora, and the newly arrived Presbyterian missionaries.[43] Therefore, to address the enthusiastic advance of Filipino work, and most likely to outflank the Presbyterians, Thoburn proceeded swiftly to seal Zamora's status within the MEC. Thoburn noted that the two Presbyterian missionaries, James B. Rodgers and Leonard P. Davidson, were "not very happy" with Methodist work among Filipinos.[44]

A few days later, at the first Philippine Islands Quarterly Conference, Thoburn and his small band of Methodists, which also included Warne, three of the four newly-arrived WFMS missionaries and Chaplain Steward, licensed Zamora as local preacher, and after "a very long discussion"

39. Ibid.; *PIDC* (1900), 4; Warne, *Light in the East*, 56–57; *GIAL*, February 1901, 60; *IW*, 4 May 1900, 3; *GIAL*, July 1900, 315.

40. *CA*, 11 October 1900, 1643.

41. *PIDC* (1900), 11, 13.

42. *PIDC* (1900), 4; Warne, *Light in the East*, 56–57; *GIAL*, February 1901, 60; *IW*, 4 May 1900, 3; *GIAL*, July 1900, 315.

43. See Rodgers, *Forty Years*, 32–33.

44. See Thoburn, 6 March 1900 and 13 March 1900, Diary, JTDJ.

agreed to ordain him, although in an unusual manner most likely never done before in the annals of Methodist missions. After a series of cablegram exchanges with MSMEC Secretary Adna B. Leonard and Bishop John H. Vincent, the South Kansas Conference, acting on Thoburn's request, voted to admit Zamora on trial, elect him to deacon's orders under "missionary rule," and transfer him back to the Malaysia Conference, which had jurisdiction over the Philippine mission. Hence, on March 10, 1900, Thoburn ordained Zamora at the Soldier's Institute on the very same spot he had first preached in August, making him the first Filipino to be ordained into the Methodist ministry.[45] "Since I began to preach the gospel I have felt that the virtue of the Holy Spirit is always in me, and I have never forgotten to pray to God before preaching, begging the presence of the Holy Spirit, and always I have felt his influence," Zamora explained to Warne in 1900.[46] Zamora seems to have imbibed a language, if not a precept on preaching, reminiscent of his American guides. Incidentally, Warne was one of them. He took Zamora under his wings, opting to remain in Manila to give the young minister a crash course on Methodism just prior to his election to the episcopacy a few weeks later.[47]

First Wave of Missionaries

Amidst the burgeoning work already started by Zamora among Filipinos in Manila, the first wave of MEC missionaries finally reached the country. On the evening of February 25, 1900, two weeks prior to Zamora's ordination, four missionaries from the WFMS landed on a dock in Manila, namely: Julia Wisner, a missionary from Burma; Mary A. Cody, a teacher from Cleveland; Anna J. Norton, a physician from New York; and Cornelia C. Moots or "Mother Moots," a Woman's Christian Temperance Union (hereafter WCTU) worker from Michigan. Dr. Norton was primarily tasked with medical work, but later pioneered Sunday School and Epworth League work in the city. Cody and Wisner were responsible for establishing a Methodist Girls School, and Moots was to serve as evangelist and temperance worker among American soldiers.[48]

---

45. Thoburn, 6 March 1900, Diary, JTDJ; Moots, 6 March 1900, Diary, CMP; *IW*, 4 May 1900, 3; Warne, *A Filipino Evangelist*, 7–9.

46. Quoted in Warne, *Light in the East*, 57; cf. *GIAL*, July 1900, 315.

47. Warne, *A Filipino Evangelist*, 7, 10–12.

48. See Moots, 26 February 1900, Diary, CMP; Moots, *Pioneer Americanas*, 12–28.

The women's arrival also signaled the coming of missionaries from the MSMEC, the parent missionary board of the denomination. The first to arrive was Thomas H. Martin, a thirty-year-old unmarried graduate of Albion College in Michigan, on March 26, 1900. A licensed local preacher, Martin was briefly tasked to pastor the American Church that met at the Soldier's Institute, and later pioneer MEC work in the provinces of Tarlac and Pangasinan.[49] On May 9, Jesse L. McLaughlin (1870–1952), a deacon from the Upper Iowa Conference, and his wife, Myrtle Ward, arrived. The thirty-year-old McLaughlin became the first presiding elder of the newly formed Philippine Islands District of the Malaysia Mission Conference, which held its first conference on August 20–24, 1900.[50] On January 31, 1901, William G. Fritz (1869–1961) followed. A graduate of Moody Bible Institute and a former missionary to Ecuador with the Christian and Missionary Alliance, Fritz was assigned to begin work in a number of preaching points mostly in Tondo and other suburbs in Manila.[51] Two more missionaries from the Upper Iowa Conference arrived in Manila on April 19 of the same year: Homer C. Stuntz (1858–1924), and Willard A. Goodell (1876–1963). Stuntz, a more senior minister and former Taylor missionary in India, became presiding elder and the new pastor of the American Church, where he led an aggressive campaign to build a permanent home for the congregation. The twenty-four-year-old Goodell, on the other hand, did some work in Manila and later opened work in Bulacan Province.[52]

Revival Work Among The Soldiers

While the warm-hearted appeal of Methodism was never scarce in its first year in the Philippines, holiness revivalism was yet to be manifested. There were, as we have demonstrated earlier, some instances where its application was conspicuous. But just as William Taylor's holiness revivalism in South India was initially intended for Europeans and Anglo-Indians, revivalism in Manila was mostly initiated for the American military as an instant panacea

---

49. Stuntz, *Philippines and the Far East*, 434; *GIAL*, December 1899, 568; *The Intercollegian*, April 1900, 150; *GIAL*, July 1900, 315; Copplestone, *Twentieth-Century*, 189.

50. Stuntz, *Philippines and the Far East*, 434; *The New York Observer*, 6 September 1906, 304; Copplestone, *Twentieth-Century*, 199.

51. *GIAL*, September 1901, 426–427; *The Institute Tie*, January 1902, 159; *Minnesota Annual Conference* (1961), 4:239; Copplestone, *Twentieth-Century*, 189.

52. Stuntz, *Philippines and the Far East*, 434.

to the rising tide of vice and perceived immorality among them. Warne, during his first visit, for example, regretted not being able to hold "evangelistic services" among Filipinos due to the scarcity, if not the steep price tag, of interpreters in the city who were competent enough to know both English and Spanish. Nevertheless, the "equally urgent" effects of alcoholism, which he believed were an embarrassment to "respectable Americans" in the country, led him to direct revival work upon the soldiers instead.[53]

Thus, on March 18–25, 1900, at a series of protracted "Union Meetings" organized by the YMCA where Warne was the featured evangelist, he implored soldiers towards holy living by preaching on the "higher Christian life." Mother Moots's description of one of the meetings in her diary succinctly puts forth a good description of Warne as a revivalist and his message. "Bro. Warne is an excellent evangelist and, surely, there is great hunger among many soldiers for a better, higher Christian life," she wrote. She also reported that twenty-five soldiers signed decision cards that evening, with five of them expressing the desire to join the MEC. These five along with others who signed the cards became members of the first Methodist class meeting in Manila.[54]

Much is to be said about Mother Moots, Cornelia Chillson Moots (1843–1929), one of the four pioneer WFMS missionaries mentioned earlier, since much of the burden of ministering among "soldiers boys," mostly still in their teens, fell on her. A native of Bay City, Michigan, Moots was an evangelist for the WCTU, an organization with recognized links to holiness piety.[55] The WCTU Evangelistic Department, under which WCTU evangelists like Moots worked with, had been superintended by famous holiness advocate Hannah Whitall Smith during its inception.[56] Moots took over duties at the Soldier's Institute not long after Mrs. Prautch left on account of ill health. Despite the tragic loss of her own adopted son Charlie in a Manila hospital, who died from injuries sustained in battle prior to her arrival, Mother Moots found comfort ministering to her new "sons," a job assigned to her by Bishop Thoburn as the so-called "pacification" of the islands dragged on.[57]

53. *IW*, 27 April 1900, 2.

54. Ibid.; Moots, 20 March 1900, Diary, CMP; Moots, MEC Class Book, 1–5, CMP.

55. For more on the influence of holiness piety, broadly conceived, in the history of the WCTU and the life of its founder, Frances Willard, see Warner, *Saving Women*, 146–67.

56. Ibid., 177–78.

57. Moots, *Pioneer Americanas*, 45–49.

In addition to engaging in WCTU activities, she visited the sick, wounded, and dying in hospitals in and around Manila. On March 18, 1900, Warne designated her as class leader of the first Methodist class meeting organized in Manila consisting of soldier boys who were awakened at the YMCA union meetings where Warne preached, as we have mentioned earlier. Meeting at the Soldier's Institute and at the mission home, the class provided opportunities for Moots to kneel with "homesick and sin-sick soldiers" as they "wept and prayed for deliverance from grief, and from the gambling habit, from the drink appetite, and other sins."[58] In addition to class meetings, she also led separate prayer meetings. Her diary entry for March 25, 1901, of one of the prayer meetings she held underscore the fact that she also helped promote experiences beyond conversion, a characteristic feature of holiness revivalism, which she called "greater light" in this instance. She recorded:

> We held our Monday afternoon prayer meeting in our mission home in the fine little hall we have down stairs, and the Holy Spirit was wonderfully with us.
>
> Two souls were saved and a third who was converted last night obtained an added blessing.
>
> The saved are named
>
> Lewis Britenburgh, Battery B 6th art.
>
> Byron Tipton, Battery G 6th art.
>
> And the one [who] came into greater light is
>
> [Harvey A. Jaeger], Battery G 6th art.[59]

Moots did not work alone, however, as she received help, albeit from an unexpected reinforcement. Much of her WCTU evangelistic activities that year were done in collaboration with Genevieve Cutler, who was affectionately called "Sister Ruth" by the soldiers she ministered to. Cutler was a missionary sent by the Peniel Mission, a holiness rescue mission based in Los Angeles.[60] On September 1900, Sister Ruth, who was superintendent of

---

58. Ibid., 52; Moots, MEC Class Book, 1–4, CCMP.

59. Moots, 25 March 1901, Diary, CMP. Moots wrote Byron Tipton twice by mistake. In her class book entry, she identified the third person as Harvey A. Jaeger of Battery B, 6th Artillery. See Moots, MEC Class Book, 32, CMP.

60. Moots, *Pioneer Americanas*, 48. Peniel Mission was founded by Theodore P. Ferguson in 1886. For more on the history of Peniel Mission, see Smith, *Called unto Holiness*, 49–51.

the evangelistic department of a small band of WCTU women in the city, conducted a series of "gospel meetings" or "gospel temperance meetings" for a few weeks at the Soldier's Institute, and at "Seamen's Bethel" (hereafter Bethel). Bethel was a similar hall for sailors in the nearby district of Binondo converted from a recently closed liquor saloon. Located at No. 99 San Fernando Street near *Capitan del Puerto* (Captain of the Port), Bethel was originally started by John MacNeil, an independent missionary, who transferred the hall to the MEC mission for lack of financial resources.[61] Moots, who was on hand to distribute temperance pledge cards and pray with those who responded to the message, described the meetings at Bethel as occasions for the "outpouring of the Holy Spirit."[62] For example, it was in one of the meetings at Bethel where Carl S. Sather, a young Norwegian from the Third Infantry, "knelt in prayer, and when he arose it was with a new heart, and went out to live a new life." After he was discharged from the Army, he decided to stay in Manila to serve as superintendent of Bethel.[63]

Cutler's success may have helped prompt Bishop Warne to officially appoint her as "evangelist," along with Nellie Moody, a newly arrived Peniel missionary, during the second Philippine Island District Conference on May 1, 1901.[64] It is interesting to note that the two Peniel workers were not listed in the official minutes most probably due to the irregular nature of their appointments, even though they were noted by Moots in her diary. This was most likely because prior to 1920 there was no provision in the MEC *Discipline* for the licensing of female preachers.[65] Nevertheless, the bishop's action was indicative of how disciplinary restrictions towards female preaching were circumvented in the mission field to encourage both WFMS missionaries and Filipino workers who were gifted in evangelistic or revival work. As we will see later, this was not uncommon throughout much of the first four decades of Methodism in the Philippines.

61. *GIAL*, May 1901, 228; *The Sailors' Magazine and Seamen's Friend*, November 1902, 348; Copplestone, *Twentieth-Century*, 193.

62. Moots, *Pioneer Americanas*, 52–53; For a brief summary on the inception of WCTU's gospel temperance meetings, see Warner, *Saving Women*, 174–76.

63. Moots, *Pioneer Americanas*, 53; *The Sailors' Magazine*, November 1902, 348–49.

64. See Moots, 9 May 1901, Diary, CMP. The popularity of the gospel meetings, as well as of the two Peniel missionaries who led them was substantiated in "Manilans Bereaved," *Manila Times*, 20 July 1906, in Clippings from Diaries, CCMP. Moots's journal entries are filled with accounts substantiating Cutler and Moody's participation in MEC activities. See, for example, Moots, 9 March 1901, Diary, CMP.

65. See Schmidt, *Grace Sufficient*, 189–96.

Likewise, it is worth noting that the collaboration between the Peniel mission, a holiness organization, and the MEC mission in Manila was a testament to the shared doctrinal and revivalistic commitments embraced by both missions. Furthermore, the fact that Bishop Warne appointed, albeit off-the-record, or at least allowed Cutler and Moody to function as evangelists under the MEC's umbrella showed that he did not have a problem with their message and their methods. The Peniel mission, most likely with the blessing of its leaders in Los Angeles, seemed to have reciprocated the bishop's gesture when they offered, according to Bishop Warne, to transfer their work in Zamboanga, Mindanao, to the MEC mission. Nevertheless, due to the terms the MEC have already agreed to during the comity agreement of 1901, this did not push through.[66] In 1908, the Peniel mission eventually transferred their station there to the Christian and Missionary Alliance, another holiness-related denomination.[67]

When Cutler was recalled to back to Los Angeles a month later, Moody and Moots carried on with the meetings at Bethel. In July 1901, the two traveled to San Isidro, Nueva Ecija, a recently occupied town sixty miles north of Manila, to minister to the soldiers of Twenty-Second Infantry Regiment who were garrisoned there.[68] They conducted a series of evangelistic meetings in a vacant room located in the army hospital and at the surgeon's home where "God's power [was] not so manifest in outward manifestations but in deep solemnity," according to Moody in a letter to Manie Payne Ferguson, co-founder of Peniel Mission.[69] During the first meeting, which was attended by about seventy soldiers, Moots recalled:

> Ms. Moody took charge of singing and the general conduct of the meeting and I gave the first message. When the invitation was given, Co. C 22 inf. Sergeant [Alto V.] Jones and [one unidentified soldier] came and knelt at the chairs, both Christian men the sergeant getting a fuller blessing last evening. The second man told me he had come thinking that very act would enable him to stand more firm. I asked those all who had praying mother or father or both to raise their hand. Think every hand was raised, so our audience was the very best of our land. At times it was almost painful to see the intense play of feeling as expressed in their countenance.[70]

66. Warne, *From Baluchistan*, 6.
67. See Clymer, *Protestant Missionaries*, 50–51.
68. See Moots, *Pioneer Americanas*, 39–43.
69. Quoted in Moots, Diary, CMP: October 1901–November 1902, 60, CMP.
70. Moots, 15 July 1901, Diary, CMP.

Moots's description was consistent with Moody's report of deep solemnity with little "outward manifestations." Only two already "Christian men" responded to Moots's altar call which was most likely an appeal for some deeper form of consecration beyond conversion, as suggested by their testimonies. This was most likely the case for Sgt. Alto V. Jones of Brundidge, Alabama, who had already been converted a few months earlier while reading his Bible in the garrison.[71] Although Moots's call found little response, her appeal to homesick soldiers to remember their praying parents helped create what she described as an "atmosphere of intense play of feelings," nevertheless.

The success of the meetings was further demonstrated when the soldiers paid for the construction of a bamboo "Gospel Peniel Hall" built by Filipino prisoners. Moots later dedicated the building on October 20, 1901, and preached the inaugural sermon.[72] Additionally, at least two soldiers were converted as a result of these meetings, William P. Garvin of Indiana and William T. Gugin of Tioga, Canada. They both decided to stay in the country as missionary colporteurs with the ABS after their discharge from the army. Gugin disappeared, presumed to have died while trekking the trail to Jaro, Leyte.[73] In the absence of any MEC work in San Isidro, Moots also launched a separate work with some of the locals. They would later form the pioneering membership of the MEC in the province a year later.[74]

Filipino Converts at Bethel

While MEC revival work was intended to awaken American soldier boys stationed in the country, it was only a matter of time for this work to reach the Filipinos. For instance, Moots claimed that Filipinos, often attracted by

---

71. See Moots, *Pioneer Americanas*, 54–55.

72. Moots, *Pioneer Americanas*, 48. In her book, Moots, however, ignored Moody's role at Bethel and San Isidro, quite possibly after feeling betrayed by her. Without Moots's knowledge, Moody claimed the gospel hall for the Peniel Mission. See "Gospel Peniel Hall" (37–42), and "All is Not Gold that Glitters" (49–62) in Moots, Diary: October 1901–November 1902, CMP. Moody was recalled, and was relieved by Cutler on November 1901. When she left, Moots wrote, "may she never leave her home land again." Moots, 21 November 1901, Diary, CMP.

73. Moots, Folder # 7, 89, 93, CCMP; *PCA*, 15 July 1907, 15; Barnhart, "Some Philippines Notes," *Bible Society Record*, February 1905, 28.

74. Moots, *Pioneer Americanas*, 41–44; Moots, 21 July 1901, Diary, CMP; *WWM*, January 1904, 6.

the sound of gospel singing at Bethel, usually crowded outside the building during their meetings.[75] But they did not have to wait for long as the enthusiasm generated by the WCTU revival meetings finally spilled over to them when Prautch established two separate services, which also carried some revival character in them. With the assistance of a few of the members from the Filipino congregation that met at the Soldier's Institute, who came to help in the singing, testifying and exhorting in Tagalog, services were opened at Bethel on Wednesday evenings and Sunday mornings. Filipinos singing with "more spirit than tune" attracted passersby; "two soldier ushers invited them in, [and] the place was always packed with thirty or more at the outside door," Prautch recalled of the meetings.[76]

But for some Filipinos, the testimonies proved to be more powerful than the singing. This was the case for Honorio Feliciano, a fisherman, who entered the building one Wednesday evening after hearing the singing as he was passing by San Fernando Street. Prautch recalled: "He was interested in hearing his own people testify in his own language, and this lead [sic] to his conversion." He arranged for a preacher to hold meetings among his neighbors at the fishing village of Bancusay in the suburb of Tondo, and soon after Filipino preacher José Bautista led a congregation that met under the sails of fishing boats by the coast of Manila Bay. On November 5, 1900, less than three months later, a bamboo chapel built and totally paid for by fishermen was dedicated by Presiding Elder McLaughlin and appropriately christened St. Peter MEC, the second Methodist chapel in the country. Tragedy struck, however, a week after the dedication as Feliciano succumbed to tuberculosis and "died triumphant" as Zamora prayed for him while holding his hand. When they buried him, the congregation that gathered by his open grave sung Fanny Crosby's "Close to Thee," Feliciano's favorite hymn and perhaps one of the first Tagalog hymns he had heard at Bethel.[77]

Bethel eventually produced about sixteen other prominent preachers for Philippine Methodism, typically from the working class, who supplemented the work of Zamora in and around Manila. Included among them was Felipe Marquez, a bookkeeper who began preaching in a house in

---

75. Moots, *Pioneer Americanas*, 53.

76. *GIAL*, May 1901, 228–29; *PCA*, 20 December 1902, 9.

77. *GIAL*, May 1901, 228; *GIAL*, September 1901, 427–28; *PCA*, 20 December 1902, 9; Moots, 21 July 1901, Diary, CMP; *Malaysia Mission Conference* (1901), 32; Copplestone, *Twentieth-Century*, 195–96.

Aguila Street in Tondo and, with the help of Fritz, in Dulumbayan Street in Sta. Cruz (now Rizal Avenue). He later became one of the most effective Filipino preachers of Methodism, and was instrumental in its spread in Ilocano-speaking provinces. Another was Luis Ocampo, a washerman, and his wife Nicolasa, who as Prautch attested, was the "better speaker of the two." They organized a Methodist congregation in Gagalangin, Tondo, and later became pioneer preachers in Bulacan Province. The boatman Enrique Cortez and his wife were also among those who were converted at Bethel. The "fiery preacher" soon founded Methodist work in Principe Street and in Parola, both in Tondo. The impact of Bethel would also reach Cavite, a town just south of Manila, through José Salamanca, a druggist by profession.[78]

The MEC evangelistic meetings bear comparison with the seditious nationalist plays in and around Manila which gained popularity between 1903 and 1905. While these plays were popular among Filipino working class and elites who were critical of the American occupation,[79] MEC meetings attracted mostly working class men and women who obviously did not mind lending their ears to American preachers. As in the case of those in the Bethel meetings, they were not hostile to members of an occupying army who ushered them at the door even while a war of attrition against their Filipino "insurgent" compatriots was in full swing. Despite the dissimilar dispositions of their audiences, however, both revival meetings and subversive plays helped create "imagined communities,"[80] to borrow Benedict Anderson's phrase, for their respective audiences. While the subversive plays, according to Vicente L. Rafael, projected "profoundly felt and widely shared social experiences of revolution, colonial occupation, war, and intense longing of freedom (*kalayaan*)" under American rule,[81] the MEC revivals, on the other hand, allowed for both communal expressions of religious freedom, and the repudiation of Spanish colonial rule of the previous years.

The participatory and least structured revival rituals at Bethel, for instance, were obviously in stark contrast with the more subdued and ordered

---

78. *GIAL*, May 1901, 228; *GIAL*, September 1901, 427–28; Copplestone, *Twentieth-Century*, 194–95; Dean, *Cross of Christ*, 205–9.

79. Rafael, *White Love*, 39–51.

80. Anderson, *Imagined Communities*, 6–7. While Anderson's intent was to offer a "more satisfactory interpretation of the 'anomaly' of nationalism," I also find the phrase useful in describing communal religious aspirations.

81. Rafael, *White Love*, 43.

Latin liturgy of the Roman Catholic mass which the converts have been accustomed to and have mostly associated with Spanish colonial oppression. The fact that ordinary men and women were allowed to address the crowd to testify to their experiences and interpret Scripture in the native tongue not only symbolized a defiance of Roman Catholic ceremonies and of any remaining vestiges of Spanish hegemony, but also of self-empowerment without compromising loyalty to Christianity altogether. Although the evangelical message of salvation through personal relationship with Jesus evoked Western individualism,[82] the rituals of singing and testimony in fact helped articulate the collective struggles of these early converts, thereby enabling a sense of belongingness and community among themselves. These rituals also helped provide some semblance of social order amid the rapid turn of events with the onset of American colonial rule. While the old order had seen its day and a new one was emerging, the revival drama not only helped calm the anxieties of its participants but, perhaps, also assuaged their fears about their new colonial masters.[83] These same elements, in addition to preaching, as we will see later would take on holiness motifs for their doctrinal content, similar to the ones disseminated in India.

Early Growth and Expansion

Membership and Territory

The work of Zamora and the other intrepid Tagalog evangelists, like the ones who were converted at Bethel, was pivotal to the spread of Methodism throughout Manila, and the nearby towns of Malabon and Navotas in the Province of Rizal. It is also important to note, that this early expansion was along the coastal towns and villages around Manila Bay. Although there were a few Filipino nobility or *principalía* who would convert to Methodism, most Filipino Methodists came from the middle to lower class families, and mostly from the working class, just like most of the preachers who ministered to them. A description given by Presiding Elder Stuntz in 1901 confirms this:

---

82. See Walls, *Missionary Movement*, 20–21, 45.

83. My analysis is informed by the "social function" model used in explaining revivalism as summarized in McClymond, "Issues and Explanations," in McClymond, *Embodying Spirit*, 40–41.

A large number of the converts are from the middle and lower classes of society. "Not many mighty, not many noble" have yet been called. But they are all sturdily independent. They want nothing but salvation. They are printers, lithographers, washermen, fishermen, clerks, merchants, teachers, and from all the grades of employment in a great city.[84]

On April 26, 1901, MEC growth became more focused as it agreed to concentrate its efforts on provinces north of Manila as a result of its comity agreement with other Protestant bodies to divide the islands into territories.[85] Thus, the MEC mission's efforts naturally followed the Manila-Dagupan Railway, the mass transit that connected *pueblos* (towns) from Manila to the Province of Pangasinan, a route that took twelve hours to traverse. MEC expansion naturally began in towns where there was a train station. Eventually, missionaries and their Filipino counterparts would also branch out from those towns to nearby *pueblos* and *barrios* (villages) that would welcome them.[86] Therefore by the end of 1901, and throughout the three years that followed, Methodist congregations have begun sprouting in the provinces of Bulacan, Pampanga, Tarlac, Pangasinan, Bataan, and Nueva Ecija.

Factors to Rapid Growth

A number of interrelated factors endemic to Philippine society, and not found in other arenas, help account for Methodism's phenomenal advance in the country. First, the almost four centuries of Roman Catholicism in the country had instilled some form of Christianity among Filipinos and, although mostly drawn from Spanish medieval Catholic spirituality of the Iberian-type, admittedly eased the way for Methodism and other Protestant missions to establish their work. The more-than-two-centuries-old annual passion plays known as *sinakulo* and other Holy Week practices,[87] for example, had ingrained into the Filipino consciousness the story of Christ's crucifixion and thereby, without a doubt, helped enhance their reception of the Protestant evangelistic appeal to Christ's crucifixion, or

---

84. *GIAL*, October 1901, 452.

85. Laubach, *People of the Philippines*, 204–6.

86. Devins, *An Observer in the Philippines*, 300–301; *PCA*, 20 December 1902, 10; *GIAL*, February 1901, 63.

87. See Tiongson, *Philippine Theatre*, 1–3.

what David Bebbington calls "crucicentrism."[88] MEC missionaries, in due course, would overcome some of their biases against Roman Catholicism by acknowledging its contributions. "Catholicism with all its errors is vastly better than no God, no Savior, and no Holy Spirit," Daniel Klinefelter once conceded in comparing the conspicuously few conversions seen among Chinese immigrants in Manila with that of Filipino conversions.[89] Oscar Huddleston added: "The barren form of ceremonial salvation and the cold, legal 'Thou shalt not,' spoken by the priest readily gave way to the yearning message: 'come to me all ye that labor and are heavy laden and I will give you rest.'"[90] For Huddleston, Roman Catholic legalism clearly paved the way for Methodist heart religion.

Second, even before Methodism landed on Philippine shores in 1899, a pre-existing Filipino membership and leadership base predisposed to Protestant Christianity was already waiting to be organized. These were a number of Manila-based elite or *ilustrados*, mostly *mestizos* (of mixed Filipino, Spanish, and Chinese heritage), who were no strangers to years of injustice inflicted by Spanish clerics and/or had been awakened against Roman Catholic practices through exposure to the Bible. In 1889, when Nicolas Lallave and Francisco Castells of the British and Foreign Bible Society (hereafter BFBS) came to Manila in a daring, but ill-fated mission, two of the nine bibles they were able to sell were bought by Don Paulino Zamora and Don Luis Yangco, a shipping tycoon in Manila.[91] Zamora, also a nephew of the martyred priest Jacinto Zamora, was later exiled in 1896 to an islet in the Chafarinas in the Mediterranean for conducting Bible studies in his home in Bulacan. He was later released with the help of fellow Freemasons from Spain and Manila right after the signing of the Treaty of Paris in 1898, which formally ended the Spanish-American War.[92] Zamora

---

88. Bebbington, *Evangelicalism in Modern Britain*, 2.

89. *Journal of the PIMC* (1907), 60.

90. *PCA*, January 1908, 8.

91. BFBS agents Nicolas Manrique Alonso y Lallave, a Spanish Presbyterian minister and former Dominican priest in the Philippines and his associate, Francisco de Paulo de Castells were apparently poisoned in Manila. Lallave died and Castells survived, but only to be imprisoned and banished later. See Sitoy, *Several Springs*, 6–7; Canton, *A History of the BFBS*, 5:150–51. For a first-hand account of the events that unfolded during their mission and of Paulino Zamora's role, see *The Christian and Missionary Alliance*, 12 May 1900, 304–5. Castells was affiliated with the MEC in Singapore while working for the BFBS there prior to joining Lallave. See *WWM*, October 1898, 5.

92. Trinidad, *Monument*, 48–52.

and Yangco were among the five Freemasons who requested Prautch to open a Filipino service at the Soldier's Institute in 1899, promising to "fill every meeting with Masons."[93] In addition to the Filipino Protestant intelligentsia, Goodrich, who held a regular preaching schedule at the Soldier's Institute, mentioned that among those who went to the Filipino services were a number of families formerly from a village located in a friar estate which was burned for resisting a cathedral tax levied against them. "THAT WHOLE TOWN IS PROTESTANT!!!," he wrote.[94]

Third, Methodism also found great success in areas where nationalistic sentiments were at a high pitch. For example, it drew its initial membership and a great number of its local preachers from the Manila suburb of Tondo, where revolutionary ideals flourished prior to the Revolution of 1896. The vibrancy of early MEC work in Tondo found its peak with the founding of an indigenous *Ang Katotohanan* (The Truth) Society in 1904 by a group of local preachers who contributed monthly dues to send two self-supporting Filipino missionaries to Bulacan.[95] Consequently, as some sources claim, Nicolas Zamora himself fought as a lieutenant major in the Philippine Army during the Revolution of 1896 under General Gregorio del Pilar.[96] This nationalistic sentiment fostered by *Katotohanan* and Zamora, however, would later backfire when it evolved into a major schism in 1909. When Methodism expanded northward beginning in 1900, its preachers were most successful in towns where the Aglipayan movement (later to become the Philippine Independent Church), a revolution within the Roman Catholic Church led by disillusioned Filipino clergy, was strong. Methodism found a large following in northern Tarlac, where the religious revolution was initially conceived.[97] Thus, reflecting on the movement's contribution to MEC growth, Stuntz, who also served as presiding elder of

---

93. Laubach, *People of the Philippines*, 180–81. Filipino Freemasons in Spain greatly supported anti-friar activities in the Philippines, and aided the ill-fated mission of the BFBS in Manila on 1889. See Schumacher, *Propaganda Movement*, 144–53; Sitoy, *Several Springs*, 7–8.

94. Goodrich to Haven, 1 December 1899, Folder 1, Philippine Agency, American Bible Society Archives, New York, NY.

95. *PCA*, October 1904, 2–3.

96. See Trinidad, *Monument*, 53–54; *Ang Ilaw*, January–September 1975, 4.

97. The movement was largely strong in most of the provinces north of Manila—the same areas designated to the MEC by the Evangelical Union. To understand the "geography" of the Aglipay movement, see Doeppers, "Philippine Revolution," 163–69. For a comprehensive history of the movement, see Schumacher, *Revolutionary Clergy*.

the Philippine Island District in 1901, acknowledged that the movement "loosens this fruit from the tree, and we gather it."[98]

Finally, the above factors were further augmented by the homogenous nature of Philippine community life. The individual-centered message of salvation by evangelical Protestantism had to make way for the more communal "mass movement" or mass conversion to Methodism in a number of *barrios* or small communities. This came as no surprise, given Philippine MEC missionaries's relationship with Indian MEC work, where the much-celebrated mass movement strategy involving the mass baptism of lower caste Hindu groups, was highly employed.[99] In the Philippines, however, much of the *barrio* mass movement pivoted mainly around the conversion or anti-Roman Catholic sentiments of the *principalía* class. These were chiefs or elite members of the community, mostly *mestizos* who carried the title "don" or "doña," or those belonging to the few landed elite, as was the case in Central Luzon. They were also sometimes called *caciques*, a Spanish term mockingly applied to people of influence and affluence.[100]

The conversion of the people in Malibay (now part of Pasay), a *pueblo* (town) about five miles south of Manila, illustrates this point. When the *presidente* (mayor) and other officials welcomed Methodist work through the efforts of Zamora, almost the whole community of about three to four hundred people followed suit. Initially, Methodist services began in the *presidente*'s home, but as the attendance grew, they moved to the local cockpit, and finally, upon the *presidente*'s recommendation, on the old stone Roman Catholic church their ancestors built. Damaged by storms, and gunfire from clashes between Filipino and American troops, the congregation renamed the corrugated-roofed sanctuary, "Iglesia Metodista Episcopal." Roman Catholic friars came four times to reclaim the old church, but only to be escorted out of the town and told that the building was owned by the people. As Presiding Elder McLaughlin testified at the Malaysia Annual Conference in 1901: "Each time the plucky President has informed the

---

98. Stuntz, *Philippines and the Far East*, 495. See also Deats, *Nationalism and Christianity*, 127.

99. For more about the MEC Indian mass movements, see Copplestone, *Twentieth-Century*, 787–833. A recent related study can be found in Taneti, "Dalit Conversions," 204–13.

100. An insightful study of the Central Luzon *barrio* is found in Fegan, "Central Luzon Barrio," 97–98. It was also this form of "cacique democracy" that has pervaded Philippine politics since American colonial rule and up to the present. See Anderson, "Cacique Democracy," 3–33.

emissary of the scarlet woman that that is now a Protestant church and if Rome wants it she must repay the people all the money they put into it."[101]

MEC's feat in Malibay would also be repeated in Atlag, a fishing village in the town of Malolos, Bulacan, where Methodism was established primarily through the labors of Doña Narcisa Dimagiba. The sixty-five-year-old Dimagiba experienced conversion in early 1901 at a service in Bancusay, Tondo, when Nicolas Zamora preached the need to "approach God spiritually, without forms or ceremonies." Recalling the event, she later testified: "a great peace came into my heart, like a great light in a dark place." She returned to Atlag in July of that same year and began preaching to her neighbors. She later opened her house for worship services. This congregation grew and, by January 1902, began meeting in an old fish hall where fishers stored their nets and traps. By Easter of that same year, when MEC preachers Luis and Nicolasa Ocampo arrived to visit them, there were already more than a hundred attendees to the Dimagiba-led congregation. When Willard Goodell came a month later, he baptized ninety-two converts and organized them into a Methodist society. On August 23, 1902, the Atlag MEC chapel became the first Methodist chapel dedicated in Bulacan.[102]

Nevertheless, Methodism scored its biggest coup in Central Luzon, in the town of Mexico, Pampanga, where *principalía* brothers Don Vicente and Don Mariano Cunanan, and José and Pacifico Panlilio became Methodists along with Mayor Tomas Lazatin, most of the town's political scions, and about a thousand people. The Cunanans, the Panlilios, and Lazatin were among the first licensed local preachers of Pampanga Methodism. Converting their large theater, which stood just across the Roman Catholic church building, into an MEC chapel, the Cunanans would later help bring their new-found religion to their tenants and sharecroppers in *Hacienda Cunanan* (Cunanan Estate, now named San Vicente), a predominantly Methodist village to this day, and to Panipuan, where "every family in the barrio but one" joined the MEC.[103]

---

101. *Malaysia Mission Conference* (1901), 32; Stuntz, *Philippines and the Far East*, 442–45; Copplestone, *Twentieth-Century*, 196–97.

102. *The Epworth Herald*, April 4, 1903, 11; Stuntz, *Philippines and the Far East*, 445–446; *Christian Herald*, 22 July 1903, 610; *WMF*, January 1909, 14.

103. *PCA*, 1 August 1903, 9; *PIDC* (1903), 40; *PIDC* (1904), 29–30.

Presbyterian Missionaries, ABS Colporteurs, and American Soldiers

In addition to the foundational work laid down by *principalía* converts, it is important to note there were also a few congregations that sprang from seeds sown by Presbyterian missionaries, ABS colporteurs, and even American soldiers who ministered to them even before MEC representatives reached them. For example, the congregations in Hagonoy in Bulacan Province, in San Fernando, Mexico, and Lubao in Pampanga Province were initially organized through the efforts of James Rodgers, Leonard P. Davidson, and Benigno Dayao of the Presbyterian mission in early 1901 prior to the comity agreement that forced them to cede these congregations to the Methodists.[104] The congregation that was to become Bancal MEC in Guagua, Pampanga came about through the efforts of Ed A. Matthews, a colporteur of the ABS. Through the aid of a stereopticon to project illustrated images from the Bible, Matthews, as MEC missionary William Brown acknowledged, led the people to "find for themselves the truth that makes men free."[105] It is also interesting to note that the groundwork for what was to become the MEC congregation in Mexico, Pampanga came about through the work of an American soldier and the Presbyterian mission. A young man from Mexico was converted in prison through one Corporal Wright of the Forty-First Volunteer Infantry, a prison guard, who "preached Christ" to him. Upon his release, he returned to his hometown and preached the "wonderful tidings of the Gospel of Jesus Christ," inspiring many, including the town mayor, justice of peace, and other prominent men to embrace the gospel. They later arranged for Presbyterian missionaries to conduct worship services in the town's cockpit.[106]

The Birth of the Philippine Islands Annual Conference

Hence, given these unique conditions, it is not hard to imagine why by 1904, the MEC in the Philippines after five years of existence, had already outpaced MEC membership rolls in Japan, Korea, Mexico, South America,

---

104. For MEC congregations that trace their beginnings to the Presbyterian mission, see, for example, T. Valentino Sitoy, *Several Springs*, vol. 1, 96–98; cf. *GIAL*, September 1901, 432.

105. Quoted in Goodrich, *Bible Work*, 12–14; *ABS Annual Report* (1904), 191–92.

106. *The Assembly Herald*, July 1901, 96–97.

and Africa, which had all been established decades earlier.[107] Recognizing this, the 1904 General Conference passed an enabling act organizing the Philippine Islands District of the Malaysia Annual Conference into the Philippine Islands Mission Conference. Bishop William F. Oldham, missionary bishop for Southern Asia presided over its first session on March 15, 1905. With fourteen full members, eleven missionaries, and three Filipinos, the conference was also divided into two districts: the Manila District, which covered Manila, Rizal, Bulacan, Pampanga, Nueva Ecija and Bataan; and the Northern District, the predominantly Ilocano-speaking region in the country, which bordered from northern Tarlac, Pangasinan and all the way to Ilocos Sur and Abra.[108]

Philippine Methodism continued to grow exponentially, and consequently, after nine years since the first MEC worship service held in Manila, it reached another important milestone. On March 3, 1908, after having attained the required conditions set forth in the MEC *Discipline* of 1904, the Philippine Islands Mission Conference unanimously voted to become the Philippine Islands Annual Conference. By this time, there were already twenty-six clergy full members, eight of whom were Filipinos; sixteen probationary Filipino ministers; 536 local preachers; 120 chapels; and a constituency of 12,850 full members, and 15,502 probationary members from Manila to Vigan and Aparri in the north.[109] By 1913, Filipino MEC members had already exceeded the combined membership of all the other Protestant denominations by more than ten thousand, despite being supervised by a much smaller missionary workforce.[110]

---

107. Stuntz, *Philippines and the Far East*, 453–54.
108. Alejandro, *From Darkness to Light*, 59–60.
109. *PIAC* (1908), 85–96; cf. ibid., 87–88.
110. See Kwantes, *Presbyterian Missionaries*, 152–54.

Table 1. MEC membership, chapels, and workers in the Philippines in 1908

Province/ Area	Membership (Full & Probationary)	Chapels	Local Preachers & Women Workers	Filipino Elders/ Deacons/ Probationers	MSMEC & WFMS Missionaries
Manila	8,438	42	130	8	15
Bulacan	2,001	11	60	1	2
Pampanga	4,397	16	66	2	2
Nueva Ecija	1,484	9	36	0	2
North Tarlac	1,572	55	55	5	2
South Tarlac	203	0	9	0	1
West Pangasinan	1,548	9	29	0	4
East Pangasinan & Nueva Vizcaya	5,074	14	72	3	4
Cagayan & Isabela	1,736	6	18	0	2
Ilocos Sur & Abra	1,449	8	89	2	2
TOTAL	27,902	120	564	19	36

Training Workers and Other Endeavors

As it continued its advance, the MEC also sought to consolidate its evangelistic push through the recruitment and training of indigenous workers. Hence, on August 25, 1903, the first Manila Bible Institute, a month long training institute, was launched. About fifty licensed male local preachers from Manila and as far as Pangasinan participated.[111] This later paved the way for other Bible Institutes in the provinces, and was continued as an annual training event in the many years that followed. These Bible Institutes, as we will demonstrate later, were common venues for holiness revivals, as they would typically incorporate Pentecostal meetings in the evenings to accommodate the public. While Bible Institutes per-

111. *PCA*, 1 September 1903, 3–4.

sisted for years, clergy education was eventually institutionalized with the establishment of the Florence Nicholson Training School on October 11, 1905, at the mission house in Cervantes Street, Manila, adjacent to the First Filipino MEC. Opening with three faculty members and five students, the school would later operate cooperatively with the Presbyterian mission's Ellinwood Seminary in 1907, and subsequently in the years that followed, with other seminaries to form the Union Bible Seminary (now Union Theological Seminary).[112]

The training of women workers was also of paramount importance to the blossoming mission, which, therefore, led the WFMS to open the Deaconess Training School in 1903, to prepare young women for evangelistic work. Recruited from various MEC congregations in Manila and the provinces, ten teenage girls matriculated during the first school year, a modest beginning for what would later become the Harris Memorial Deaconess Training School (now Harris Memorial College, hereafter Harris).[113] Aside from Harris, the WFMS also established a similar and yet simplified version of Harris in the north, the Bible Woman's Training School (later, Lingayen Bible Training School for Women) in Lingayen, Pangasinan. Founded by WFMS missionary Louise Stixrud, the school formally opened its doors on January 3, 1908, to students who were called to serve as "Bible women," mostly to support the expanding evangelistic work in the northern provinces.[114] As we will show later in the subsequent chapters, the work of both deaconesses and Bible women were also integral in the dissemination of holiness revival culture in Philippine Methodism.

The emergence of training institutions meant to reinforce the evangelistic thrust of the denomination was not the only sign of its growth and advance, however. Methodists also actively engaged in social projects as part of their efforts to build rapport with the masses and, subsequently, reach them with the gospel. On December 10, 1906, WFMS missionary Dr. Rebecca Parrish opened the Bethany Hospital and Dispensary, which occupied five rooms on the first floor of Harris in Sta. Cruz, Manila. The hospital was renamed the Mary Johnston Hospital when it relocated to Tondo on August 18, 1908. It also opened a School of Nursing that same year.[115]

---

112. See *Florence B. Nicholson*, 4–5; *PCA*, November, 5; Alejandro, *From Darkness to Light*, 125.

113. *PIDC* (1904), 64; cf. Robledo, "Gender, Religion," 72–74.

114. Alejandro, *From Darkness to Light*, 95.

115. Ibid., 96–97; *WCPIAC* (1907), 10–11.

Aside from hospital work, another important area of MEC ministries in the country was its dormitories for high school and intermediate students. We should note that the MEC did not endeavor to provide education for the masses in the Philippines, as it typically did in other fields, because the American colonial government was already providing free education to the public. The first dormitory to emerge was at Lingayen, Pangasinan in 1907, which served as "Christian home" for boys attending the provincial high school. That same year, Harris also opened its facilities to seven girls attending schools in Manila, but was later discontinued. Several dormitories were later organized mostly in major centers in the north, in the towns of Tarlac, Lingayen, Dagupan, Aparri, Tuguegarao, and Ilagan, which further attracted more converts to Methodism. Manila would follow suit in 1912 with the construction of a boys dormitory, which later became Rader Hall, on Isaac Peral Street (now U. N. Avenue), and a girls dormitory on Nozaleda Street (now Gen. Luna Street), which later transferred to Sampaloc to become the Hugh Wilson Hall.[116]

---

116. Alejandro, *From Darkness to Light*, 109–10.

Figure 2.1. Nicolas Zamora, pioneer Filipino preacher and the first Filipino to be ordained in the MEC. Source: Devins, *An Observer in the Philippines* (1905).

Figure 2.2. Pioneer Methodist workers in Manila, Philippine Islands District Conference, August 20–23, 1900: (top, left to right) Edward W. Hearne, Jay C. Goodrich, Arthur W. Prautch, John MacNeil; (middle, left to right) Nicolas V. Zamora, Julia Wisner, Bishop Francis Warne, Mary A. Cody, José Bautista; (bottom, left to right) Dr. Anna J. Norton, Presiding Elder Jesse L. McLaughlin, Myrtle W. McLaughlin, Cornelia Moots. Source: *GIAL*, February 1901.

Figure 2.3. WFMS missionary Cornelia C. Moots and Peniel Mission missionary Genevieve Cutler, Manila, 1901. Mother Moots partnered with Sister Ruth (Cutler) in conducting evangelistic and revival work among American soldiers stationed in Manila. Source: Moots, *Pioneer Americanas* (1903).

Figure 2.4. Felipe Marquez, pioneer Filipino preacher, preaching outdoors in one of his circuits in Northern Luzon, c. 1903–04. Source: The United Methodist Church Archives—GCAH, Madison, New Jersey. Mission Photograph Albums—Philippines #1, 39.

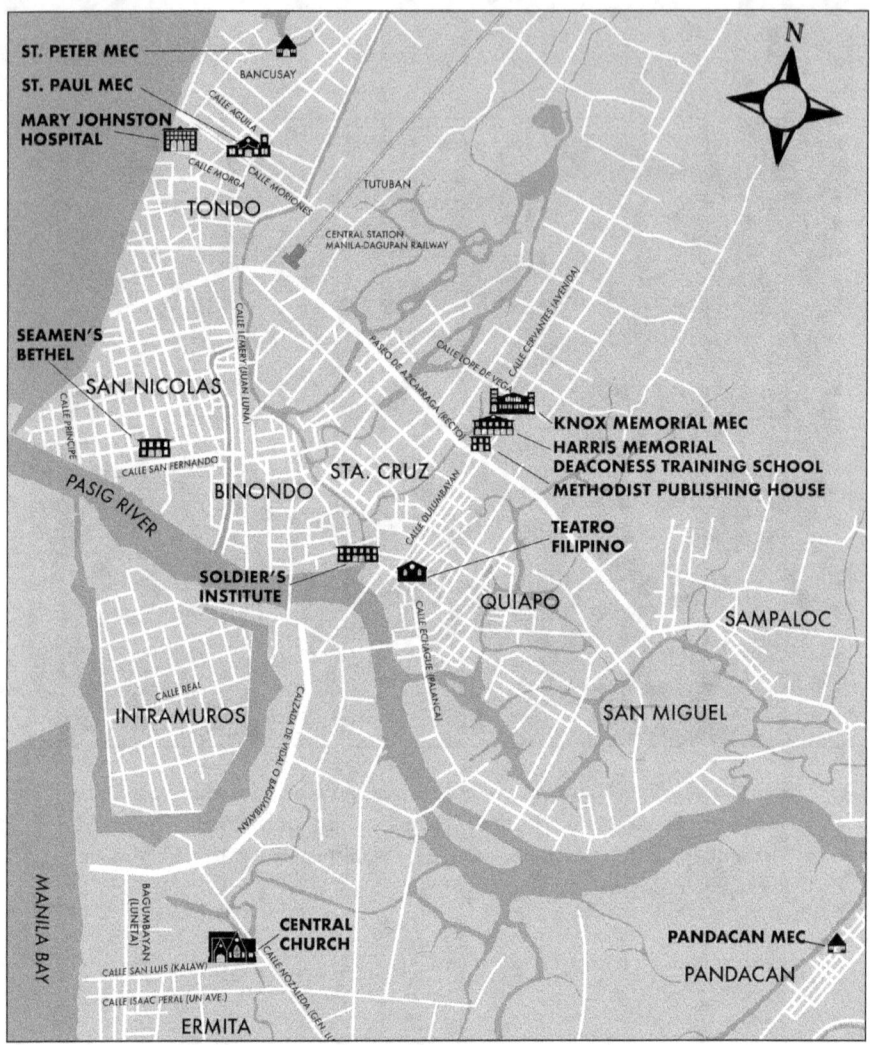

Figure 2.5. Key MEC sites in Manila, 1899–1910: (top to bottom) 1) St. Peter MEC, Bancusay, Tondo (location unknown); 2) Mary Johnston Hospital, Quesada St. (now J. Nolasco), Tondo; 3) St. Paul MEC, Plaza Moriones, Tondo; 4) Knox Memorial MEC, Cervantes St. (now Avenida), Sta. Cruz; 5) Harris Memorial Deaconess Training School, Cervantes St., Sta. Cruz; 6) Methodist Publishing House, Cervantes St., Sta. Cruz; 7) Seamen's Bethel, San Fernando St. (near Captain of the Port), Binondo; 8) Soldier's Institute, Plaza de Goiti (now Plaza Lacson), Sta. Cruz; 9) Teatro Filipino, corner Echague St. (now Palanca) and San Roque St., Quiapo; 10) Central Church, corner San Luis St. (now Kalaw) and Nozaleda St. (now Gen. Luna), Ermita; 11) Pandacan MEC, Pandacan (location unknown). Map based from De Gamoneda, *Plano de Manila* (1898). Illustration by author.

METHODIST BEGINNINGS IN THE PHILIPPINES

Figure 2.6. Narcisa Dimagiba, pioneer female preacher and founder of Methodism in Atlag, Malolos, and Willard Goodell, missionary in charge of Bulacan Province; Atlag, Malolos, Bulacan, 1902. Source: *The Epworth Herald*, 4 April 1903.

Figure 2.7. The congregation of Mexico MEC, Mexico, Pampanga, 1902. Methodism found phenomenal success in Mexico where many turned Methodists, including a number of town officials and elites. Behind them is a mural of the Ten Commandments and two open bibles, most likely referring to the Old and New Testaments, adorning the exterior of the former theater. This was a recurring motif for most Methodist chapels at that time to distinguish them from Roman Catholic chapels. Source: *PCA*, 1 August 1902.

Figure 2.8. The first session of the Philippine Islands Mission Conference, Central Church, Manila, March 11–15, 1905: (seated, left to right) Nicolas V. Zamora, Arthur E. Chenoweth, Presiding Elder Homer C. Stuntz, Bishop William F. Oldham, Ernest S. Lyons, Harry E. Farmer; (standing, left to right) Felipe Marquez, George A. Miller, Marvin A. Rader, R. V. P. Dunlap, Berndt O. Peterson, Willard A. Goodell, Daniel H. Kleinfelter, William H. Teeter, Teodoro Basconcillo. Source: The United Methodist Church Archives—GCAH, Madison, New Jersey. Mission Photograph Albums—Philippines OP #1, 31.

Figure 2.9. Women's Conference of the Philippine Islands Mission Conference, Central MEC, Manila, February 17–23, 1907: (left to right) Marguerite Decker, Mary Klinefelter, Edna Teeter, Karla Rayner, Alice Peterson, Myrtle McLaughlin, Blanche Klinefelter, Gertrude Dreisbach, Olive Farmer, Jean Rader, Rebecca Parrish, Leona Huddleston, Louise Stixrud. Source: Courtesy of Rita A. Owen, granddaughter of William and Edna Teeter, missionaries to the Philippines (1904–1909).

Figure 2.10. Central District Bible Institute, San Fernando, Pampanga, 1908: (seated on bench) unidentified, Pearl S. Housley, Edwin L. Housley, Juan Macaspac, William and Lilian Teeter, unidentified, Gonzalo Canda, unidentified, Pedro Sison, unidentified. Source: Courtesy of Rita A. Owen, granddaughter of William and Edna Teeter, missionaries to the Philippines (1904–1909).

3

Culto Pentecostal Revivals Begin

Your coming has practically fixed the holiness idea as the birthright of every man in the Methodist Church, and I desire these revival bands to move through the country not only for the sake of sinners, but that we might have sincere saints.

—Bishop William Oldham to Henry Clay Morrison, 1910

The Crusade Against Roman Catholicism

Methodist rapid growth was complemented by an evangelistic strategy consistent with Methodist heart religion, but which was, in most cases, engulfed in classic Reformation themes. This dynamic was fittingly captured by Warne's description of the interior decoration of Pandacan MEC, the first MEC chapel built in the Philippines, when he dedicated it on August 12, 1900:

> The pastor, Nicholas [sic] Zamora, and the people did the decoration and ornamentation of the interior without a suggestion from one of the missionaries, and I think a brief description of it will convey a clear idea of their Protestant evangelical ideas: On the inside wall above the entrance door are the words, "El Alma no Puede ser Com prado" (The soul cannot be bought). On a screen just inside the door hung the Ten Commandments, neatly framed. On one side of the wall above the windows were the words, "Nuevo Testamento," and on the other side, "Antigua Testamento." On the pulpit were the words, "Dios es Amor" (God is love). I visited the church several days before the dedication, and on the wall behind the pulpit on one side the people had tastefully painted, "Dios justo Salvador" (Just God and Saviour), but on the other side they had painted a cross. As soon as we entered Nicholas Zamora, the pastor, saw it, and in emphatic tones said, "Roman Catholic! No!

no! no!" and ordered it taken off. On the morning of the dedication instead of the cross behind the pulpit we saw in beautiful letters a Spanish translation of John 4. 24: "God is a spirit, and they that worship Him must worship in spirit and in truth"—a good selection for any church—and underneath these two was a Bible, and on it the words, "La Santa Biblia" (The Holy Bible).[1]

The fact that the Pandacan sanctuary was adorned with Scripture texts is a testament to Protestantism's emphasis on the Bible and its proclamation. The texts selected were meant to repudiate common Filipino Roman Catholic practices or understanding of salvation. For example, the notion that salvation can be gained through good works was countered by the words *El alma no puede ser com prado* (The soul cannot be bought) on the inside wall above the entrance door. Also, the framed Ten Commandments hanging by the door was most likely meant to remind the visitor of the third commandment which warns against idol worship or, when applied to the Philippine setting, the veneration of religious images. Hence, it was for this reason that Zamora vehemently ordered the removal of a painting of the cross at the center of the wall behind the pulpit. Instead, taking its place was an inscription from John 4:24 proclaiming that "God is a spirit" and must therefore be worshipped in "spirit and truth," and a Bible with the words *La Santa Biblia* (The Holy Bible). Ironically, as Zamora and other Filipino Methodists took pains to rid themselves of anything that may constitute as idol worship, they might have inadvertently elevated Scripture texts and murals of the Bible to the same veneration status Roman Catholics accorded to saints.

Anti-Roman Catholic motifs like the ones used in Pandacan helped define early Filipino Methodist self-identity as they continued to adorn other MEC chapels that have been built during the period. In a country that never knew any form of Christianity except Roman Catholicism, Methodist missionaries pragmatically allowed their converts to behave more like Protestants than distinctively Wesleyans as they encouraged it even through their early publishing endeavors. For example, the first Tagalog tract published by the mission was "What do Protestants Believe" (1900) by Paulino Zamora.[2] When it launched its official newspaper, the *Philippine Christian Advocate* in 1902, one of the first articles featured was "Baquit Aco Protestante? [Why I Am A Protestant?]" by his son Nicolas.[3] It was also

1. *CA*, 11 October 1900, 1643.
2. *GIAL*, September 1901, 428.
3. *PCA*, 1 February 1902, 4.

not an accident that in 1905 the first major Tagalog book published by the mission was the 120-page *History of Protestantism*, written by Thomas Martin to complement booklets on Methodist basics issued a year earlier.[4] As standard staples encouraged among their preachers and adherents, Protestant principles co-existed with, if not surmounted, Methodist essentials.

Though Methodists retained their zeal for evangelism by heavily relying on street preaching, they vigorously preached, in most instances, the Reformation message of *sola fide* or salvation by faith alone to counter long-held beliefs and customs of Roman Catholics. This was precisely what Harry Farmer and a band of Filipino preachers did in a town in Pangasinan in 1905 when they preached "salvation and pardon through faith in Jesus Christ only" or "direct religion without the mediation" of saints or priests.[5] Other Methodists even took this as far as imploring people to renounce their "idols" as three Filipino preachers traveling with William Fritz did in 1901 when they preached one evening to hundreds of devotees in five makeshift chapels setup throughout Tondo during Holy Week.[6] Recalling their exploit in one of the chapels, Fritz reported:

> The first place visited was a big tent building holding seven hundred to eight hundred people, and securing the consent of the owner, we stationed ourselves in front of the altar with backs to their wooden gods, and after our first song the idol worshipers stopped and listened to us, and the Filipinos, as brave as a Peter and a Paul, told them about their idolatry and its wrongs and how much God loved them and he gave Jesus Christ to save them from their sins, and they could have salvation without money and without price. It was a new story to them, some murmured at it first, others felt chagrined at the way they had been deceived in worshiping these false things, and when the invitation was given for all those that desired to receive Jesus as their personal Saviour and leave their idols to kneel with us, the majority knelt before God, seeking mercy and forgiveness. The next day these idols were taken away.[7]

It is interesting to note the coalescing of revival and anti-Roman Catholic themes in this account given how the common evangelistic call

4. *PCA*, August 1905, 7.

5. *PCA*, October 1905, 11; *PCA*, 1 July 1904, 4. A similar point is found in Maggay, "Early Protestant Missionary Efforts," 32–33.

6. *GIAL*, September 1901, 426–27.

7. Ibid., 426.

to "receive Jesus" as "personal savior" was appropriated by the Filipino preachers and Fritz in a predominantly Roman Catholic setting. Genuine profession of faith in Jesus, they taught, must result in one's renunciation of the age-old practice of devotion to religious images, statues, and iconography. Simply put, as the account suggests, to be rid of such "idols" was sufficient proof that one has truly received Jesus as personal savior. Early Filipino Methodist identity, as well as that of other Protestants, seems to have hinged on this practice, a sort of rite of passage for many Roman Catholic converts to Methodism through the years.

Methodists's bellicose attacks against Roman Catholicism did not only find expression through their publishing endeavors and their preaching, but also through verbal confrontation with Roman Catholic clerics by using a battery of proof texts from the Bible as their weapon of choice. This happened, for instance, in Malibay when one Methodist class leader sat at a confessional with a visiting priest. Instead of confessing his sins, he read from his Bible James 5:16 to point out that the hearing of confessions is not the monopoly of the priest, but that the Bible admonishes believers to confess their sins with one another.[8] Another incident took place at an evangelistic meeting held by Zamora in a theater in Caloocan in June 1902. When the local priest Valentino Tangog allegedly barged in at the conclusion of his sermon and accosted him in front of about one hundred fifty listeners, Zamora quickly turned the occasion into a debate by arguing against "the inutility of prayers to the saints," supported by several verses from the Bible. The ensuing discussion, which as Zamora claimed he single-handedly dominated, purportedly led the audience to applaud the young preacher while ridiculing Tangog for his inability to come up with a sound biblical argument.[9]

In addition to debates, Filipino Methodist preachers, to the amazement, if not amusement, of their missionary backers, also attracted hearers at the expense of the Roman Catholic *padre* whom they compared to the Pharisees in the New Testament for their supposed lack of morality. This was precisely what one preacher did in Ilocos Sur in 1906 when he regularly preached in front of the town's Roman Catholic church, drawing his text mostly from Matthew 23, echoing Christ's denunciation of the Pharisees, while a "great many go out to hear him, following mass."[10]

8. *GIAL*, October 1901, 476–77.

9. *Christian Herald*, 22 July 1903, 610; *PIDC* (1903), 42–43; Trinidad, *Monument*, 76–78.

10. *PCA*, April 1906, 5, 7.

In reality, though MEC spokespersons in the country constantly denied it,[11] their brand of evangelism was proselytism since most, if not all, of their converts were former Roman Catholics. This stems from the understanding that Roman Catholics are not Christians, but "heathens." In fact, taking such notion further, some missionaries even defined Filipino conversion from Roman Catholicism as tantamount to deliverance from a litany of vices, immoralities, superstition, ignorance, and even the lack of industry.[12] Methodists essentially understood the solution to many social ills of the country as being connected to winning the battle against what they derisively called the "Romish Church." Although anti-Catholic polemics would persist among Filipino Methodists for years, Kenton Clymer has suggested that Methodist missionary attitudes towards Catholicism, to some extent, improved over time.[13]

The Crusade against Sin Begins

Relative to the growing détente was an increasing realization among missionaries of the need to shift from a crusade against Catholicism to a crusade against sin. In 1901, for instance, Stuntz complained that "the social life of the convert is beset with difficulties. Smoking is a universal habit. Women, men, and children all smoke. It is hard to convince that it is either wrong or injurious. It will require line upon line to deal with that social custom alone. Cockfighting is as much a national game as baseball is with us," and one affluent convert, most likely referring to Simeon Blas of Malabon, who built an MEC chapel with a 300-seating capacity at his own expense, was the owner of a local cockpit. "The remainder of the Sunday he spends at the cockpit gate taking his entrance money from the crowd that throng the place," he lamented. Stuntz further predicted: "In my opinion this man who is interested in the cockpit will not continue studying his Bible and attending the services very long before he will drop the objectionable business."[14] Stuntz's lack of optimism for Blas's future with Methodism proved to be wrong, nevertheless, as we will see later.

11. See, for example, *PCA*, February 1906, 3.
12. See, for example, *PCA*, December 1904, 2–3; *PCA*, February 1905, 2; *PCA*, June 1907, 3.
13. Clymer, "Methodist Missionaries," 177.
14. *GIAL*, October 1901, 452.

But in the years that followed, there was an increasing concern to raise the standards of membership from that of merely enrolling converts to that of "building them up towards righteousness."[15] One of the earliest signs of this emerging new direction was manifested by Bishop Warne when he preached "the deepening of their spiritual life" to over fifty Filipino preachers at a service during the 1903 District Conference in Manila, which led to their "seeking a baptism of the Holy Spirit."[16] Despite the commitment to spread holiness doctrine, Warne's influence within Philippine Methodism was, however, minimal on account of his limited visits to the country.

The shift was further institutionalized that same year with the launching of the first Bible Institute, an important training venue for Philippine Methodists for years to come, which was intended not only for practical study but for a "deepening of spiritual life" among local preachers.[17] The exhorters's class in Malabon also followed suit, which eventually compelled Simeon Blas to shutdown his cockpits, contrary to Stuntz's prediction, after experiencing "full salvation from sin" in one of its sessions that same year.[18] A year later, the same emphasis was manifested with the inclusion of a "Higher Life" section in the *Advocate*, which featured short articles that celebrated "workers of righteousness" and instances of deepened spirituality and advancement towards higher moral standards among Philippine Methodists.[19] There was also a growing "confident and gratified" sense that "Methodism means no more cock-fighting."[20] Accordingly, membership requirements were made rigid during the same period that persons going through the probationary period of membership must show evidence that they have "given up gambling, drinking, smoking, *buyo* [betel leaf] chewing, and other forms of sinful habits."[21] Efforts to encourage holy living were further supplemented by attempts to promote Pentecostal experience and revivals happening outside the country. In 1905, the *Advocate* expressed the need for translated editions of William Arthur's *Tongue of Fire*.[22] Then,

---

15. *PCA*, November 1904, 2.
16. *PCA*, 15 March 1903, 6–7.
17. *PCA*, October 1905, 11; *PCA*, 1 August 1903, 9.
18. Farmer, *Philippine Mission*, 53–54.
19. See, for example, *PCA*, October 1904, 3; *PCA*, January 1905, 5.
20. *PCA*, 1 March 1904, 6.
21. Alejandro, "From Roman Catholicism," 31.

22. *PCA*, May 1905, 3. For connections between holiness doctrine and Bunyan's *Pilgrim Progress*, see Jones, *Perfectionist Persuasion*, 35–37.

a year later, it also kept Philippine Methodists abreast of the Welsh Revival, as well as of the spreading revival in India, and hoped that a "revival may come to Manila and the Philippines in all its power."[23]

Despite these rather sparse attempts and indicators to promote holiness-Pentecostal spirituality among Filipino Methodists, we need to understand that Methodist anti-Catholicism was still very much around and remained a distraction for the mission. As Isaac Harper, the editor of the *Advocate* complained in January 1908:

> We would say that nine-tenths of the Filipino people need the Gospel of Christ; they need true religion and undefiled; they need to know the renovating power of the Holy Spirit. The Christian Missionary has a big job on his hands in the Philippines, and he has little time to fight the errors of the Romish Church. He must fight sin and unrighteousness in high places; he must raise the standard of morality; he must enthrone Christ in the hearts of the people instead of on a pedestal; he must teach the people to love the God of the Bible and the Christ-Saviour of the world.[24]

The editorial marked a peak on the call for a shift in Filipino Methodist identity—that from mere anti-Catholics to a holy people empowered by the Holy Spirit. The appeal could have not come at a better time as it coincided with the direction that was about to be aggressively espoused by Bishop William F. Oldham that same year as he began to set his sights on leading a more conscious and concerted effort to disseminate holiness teachings in the country.

Bishop William F. Oldham

Bishop William Fitzjames Oldham (1854–1937) was among the many Anglo-Indian converts of William Taylor's famous revival work in South India, having been converted in Poona in 1873 through the preaching of Daniel O. Fox, one of Taylor's self-supporting associates. Born in Bangalore, India, and a son of a British military officer who commanded Indian troops, Oldham would later pioneer the MEC's advance in Singapore and Malaysia. He was later elected bishop for South India, Malaysia, and the Philippines at the 1904 General Conference. Despite the overwhelming

---

23. *PCA*, January 1906, 3–4; *PCA*, March 1906, 10. See also Bishop Oldham's report on the Indian revival in *PCA*, July 1906, 4.

24. *PCA*, January 1908, 3. See also a similar call in *PCA*, October 1907, 9.

influence of holiness piety among his predecessors and colleagues in India as we have pointed out in a previous chapter, Oldham initially held a more reserved attitude towards holiness due to a radicalized form that divided his home church in Poona in 1876.[25] Nonetheless, as early as 1898, while taking charge of a church in Columbus, Ohio, he began a friendship with Iva Durham Vennard, then traveling revivalist for the Woman's Home Missionary Society and later founder of the Chicago Evangelistic Institute and the National Holiness Missionary Society. She preached holiness in his church, which was composed of "many wealthy and aristocratic members."[26] Despite his close association with Vennard, it was not until November 1907, while temporarily taking charge of the English Church in Singapore, that Oldham began to profess sanctification, or what he called "the most significant experience of my life" since his conversion. This took place while lecturing on the "Higher Christian Life" at an interdenominational "Tuesday meetings" held at the Town Hall,[27] which Oldham detailed in his autobiography:

> The fourth Tuesday [November 5, 1907] meeting came. The prayer room was full. I closed my brief Bible reading and then said to the people that fairly as I had been trying to set forth the teaching I was void of the experience, and then I proposed that all those who felt with me that they must find this fullness of salvation should bow with me in yielding consent and in earnest supplication. What happened for the next several minutes I do not know. I only know I threw myself upon my knees and I saw a movement among the people towards me. When I came back to my conscious self my little wife was bowed against me raining tears upon my cheek, while on the other side of me knelt old Mr. Haffenden, the seventy year old agent of the Bible Society, as Godly and as true a man as I have ever known. And next to him I saw a Chinaman, and then several of my own teachers, Tamil, Englishmen, Eurasians, Chinese, people of several denominations, and no denominations

---

25. Doraisamy, *Oldham*, 20–21.

26. Bowie, *Alabaster and Spikenard*, 83. For more on Vennard, see Pope-Levison, "Vennard, Iva May Durham," 302–3; Pope-Levison, *Building the Old Time Religion*, 1–10.

27. Although Oldham did not give the date in his autobiography, his sanctification most likely took place after being "compelled" to return to Singapore on account of an unspecified crisis there shortly after coming to Manila in August 28, 1907. See *PCA*, September 1907, 6. Oldham arrived in Singapore on October 1, 1907, and there, after his second Sunday, started the Tuesdays meetings. See *The Malaysia Message*, September 1907, 96; *The Malaysia Message*, November 1907, 14; *CA*, 29 November 1917, 1266.

at all, all of them earnestly praying for complete deliverance from the belittling and harassing power of sin.²⁸

Oldham called his experience "fullness of salvation," another phrase use to refer to entire sanctification which, in his case, was accompanied by a lost of consciousness or awareness of what was happening around him. This could well be very similar to accounts of people falling or fainting in early Methodist revivals in England and America, or being "slain in the Spirit," as it was later referred to in Pentecostal circles.²⁹ Regardless of what truly happened to Oldham, there is no doubt that he regarded this "second crisis experience" as pivotal to his own spiritual formation. In as much as it marked a "new day" in his life,³⁰ it also signaled a new era for the Methodist Church in the Philippines beginning in 1908.

Newly organized in 1908, the Philippine Islands Annual Conference in Manila proved to be a watershed moment for Philippine Methodism. It was, according to a report in the *Advocate*, "the most spiritual Conference session since the opening of the Mission" as Oldham literally turned the morning devotional meetings into holiness revival meetings. Speaking before American missionaries at the Conference, Oldham spoke on the "higher life" all throughout the six morning meetings. He was also accompanied by Bishop John Edward Robinson (1849–1922), who, in 1874, was plucked by William Taylor from his studies at Drew Theological Seminary to join his self-supporting project in South India. Robinson, similarly exhorted the Filipino preachers to a series of talks on the "higher life" as well, and had an "affecting altar service" on the sixth morning. Although working with the aid of an interpreter, Robinson was reported to have deeply affected them, as one even testified: "I am daily overcome with weeping while he speaks."³¹ A day after the conference, the tandem also went on a brief holiness revival tour to MEC congregations outside Manila. Highlighting the outcome of his Pentecostal-themed messages, Robinson narrated that in Malolos, Bulacan, "not a few earnestly sought the fullness of the Spirit,

---

28. *CA*, 29 November 1917, 1266; Doraisamy, *Oldham*, 72–73. See also *PO*, April 1932, 16–17.

29. For an explanation of "slain in the Spirit," see Poloma, *The Assemblies of God*, 27. For examples of the occurrence of such phenomena in early British Methodism, see, for example, Heitzenter, *Wesley and the People*, 111–12; Kent, *Holding the Fort*, 47–48. For early American Methodism, see Wigger, *Taking Heaven by Storm*, 104–24.

30. *CA*, 29 November 1917, 1266.

31. *PCA*, March 1908, 3–5; *PIMC* (1908), 16–22. For more on Robinson, see Robinson and Robinson, *In Memoriam*, 10–11.

and mother[s] and fathers in Israel received spiritual uplift." Also, in the town of Mexico, Pampanga, there were "manifest tokens of the presence of the Spirit," and one young man from the affluent Cunanan clan received the "blessing" and testified of his conversion.[32] Months later, just after the 1908 General Conference ruled that he officially reside in Manila, Bishop Oldham admonished the missionaries that the shift to holiness spirituality should define the rest of the quadrennium:

> Let none of us live below the high level of the full privileges of Christian men and women. There is a full salvation which lifts men to the highest plane of personal worth and effectiveness . . . If with this we seek to earnestly cultivate the affection and respect of our Filipino brethren, God will abundantly bless our labors, and I trust we may reach the end of the quadrennium with increased number and a deeper tide of religious life.[33]

Oldham vigorously led a holiness revival movement that promoted a "deeper tide of religious life" throughout the remainder of his term. It would not be an exaggeration to say that it was during his leadership that the concept of sanctification, an experience subsequent to conversion, including its Pentecostal derivatives, found its place in the vernacular of Philippine Methodism. Oldham's policies and programs essentially helped create the environment and stimulus whereby holiness revivalism could flourish in the country. The best example that highlights this was the coming of Henry Clay Morrison, the famous Holiness evangelist from Kentucky, who by Oldham's invitation conducted a series of Pentecostal meetings in Manila in 1910.

However, Oldham's intentions for the mission abruptly ended in 1912, when he was appointed secretary of the Board of Foreign Mission in New York. In 1916, upon his return to the episcopacy as MEC bishop for South America, he continued his holiness advocacy in the Philippines by bringing E. Stanley Jones, who conducted revival meetings in Manila in 1917.[34] In 1920, he also arranged to have his long-time friend Iva Vennard for a three-week revival campaign in the city. Upon his retirement, Oldham remained an active holiness advocate and a "staunch friend" of the Chicago Evangelistic Institute and Vennard.[35] In addition to Oldham's contributions, a

32. *IW*, 16 April 1908, 247.
33. *PCA*, October 1908, 17.
34. See Klinefelter, *Adventures with God*, 67.
35. Bowie, *Alabaster and Spikenard*, 223. Oldham also wrote materials for CEI. See, for example, Oldham, *Christian Motive*.

long line of American and Filipino revivalists supplemented Oldham's call in 1908 in the months and years that followed. The first among them was Charles W. Koehler.

Charles W. Koehler: Missionary Revivalist

The official sanction for holiness spirituality was accordingly met with support and complemented first in Manila through several revival meetings conducted by Charles William Koehler (1875–1955), who arrived at the close of 1907. A graduate of Iowa Wesleyan and a former "conference evangelist" of the Southern Illinois Annual Conference,[36] Koehler conducted "Pentecostal services" for the YMCA at Fort McKinley, a military base near Manila, resulting in hundreds of conversions early in 1908. Koehler also led Pentecostal meetings in half a dozen points in and around Manila as well as in the Bible Institute and District Conference that year. Summing up the year, his district superintendent claimed that the Filipino ministry had entered into "deeper personal religious experiences and witness to the saving power of the Gospel and the indwelling of the Holy Spirit."[37]

Koehler's work clearly typified that of an itinerant professional revivalist, which was conspicuously absent among the missionary force during the first eight years of Methodism in the country. Also known for his proficiency in Tagalog, Koehler, a son of German immigrants, quickly gained a reputation among his Filipino counterparts for his evangelistic skills and piety. By 1910, he reported that Filipino preachers were conducting their own Pentecostal services by "faithfully" copying his mannerisms, his movements, and the same songs sung in his meetings, albeit with little success.[38] Although this was no cause for celebration on Koehler's part, the popularity of his work marked a point in the development of Filipino preachers from that of being recipients to practitioners of *culto Pentecostal* revivalism. Holiness revivalism had finally seeped through the liturgical patterns of Filipino Methodists.

By combining revival measures with the message of holiness or Pentecostal baptism through his Pentecostal meetings, Koehler was

36. See Koehler's obituary in *Iowa-Des Moines Annual Conference* (1955), 138. See also *Southern Illinois Annual Conference* (1906), 15.

37. *PIAC* (1909), 35, 39. See also Eveland to Cooke and Hughes, 28 April 1914, Eveland, William Perry (Bishop and Mrs.) 1912–1914, MFUMC.

38. *PCA*, July 1910, 9.

quintessentially the first MEC Holiness evangelist in the Philippines. While we cannot find detailed accounts describing his meetings, Harry E. Farmer's letter to Oldham in 1912 seems to provide a clue by commenting that Koehler was "versatile, humorous and inspiring at all times" in reference to his preaching work in the Sunday School conventions.[39] Although Koehler's methods enamored him to his audience, his deep piety perhaps explains more why Filipinos were receptive to his message—the messenger was the message. At a reception held prior to his departure in 1914, Farmer intimated that the nationals found Koehler to be "the most brotherly missionary, that he understood them better, that he had helped them so much spiritually and they knew they could depend upon him; many of them wept at parting." Thus, it would not have been unimaginable that when the Zamora schism broke out in 1909, it was Koehler's work that stemmed the tide of schism and saved MEC work in Manila, Farmer asserted.[40] Koehler's preaching prowess was further recognized through the annual "Koehler Oratorical Contest" at Florence Nicholson Seminary in Manila, where he was a faculty member.[41] Ironically, in 1913, Koehler fell out of the grace of the current bishop and Oldham, who by that time was Board of Foreign Missions secretary in New York, for over-extending his furlough by conducting revival meetings in a number of churches in Illinois at a time when he was badly needed in the Philippines.[42]

As revivals began sweeping churches in Manila beginning 1908 as a result of Koehler's work, the *Advocate* acknowledged that the conversions or the "thronging of multitudes" of the early years that had "meant little more than a new method of registering a protest against Spanish misrule and friar oppression" was no longer seen.[43] Membership quality had taken precedence over quantity. Such spirit, however, proved to be too late to prevent a major schism that was to take place the following year.

"Revival Spirit" to Quench the Fires of Schism

The Philippine Methodist "revival spirit" of 1908 took an unexpected turn a year later when, barely a week before the start of the Annual Conference

39. Farmer to Oldham, 20 November 1912, Farmer, Harry, MFUMC.
40. Farmer to Oldham, 26 August 1914, Farmer, Harry, MFUMC.
41. *PIAC* (1913), 81; *PO*, November 1911, 6.
42. See Koehler to Oldham, 22 January 1913, Koehler, Charles W., MFUMC.
43. *PCA*, May 1909, 3; *PCA*, May 1909, 3.

in Manila, the highly esteemed Nicolas Zamora, together with most of the preachers from Tondo belonging to the *Katotohanan* Society, announced their defection from American Methodism and established an independent Filipino Methodist Church, *La Iglesia Evangelica Metodista en las Islas Filipinas* (The Evangelical Methodist Church in the Philippine Islands, or hereafter IEMELIF). Although the church intended to be free from foreign control and leadership, it retained much of the polity and doctrine of the parent church. Of the estimated 30,000 Methodists in the country at that time, about 1,500 from Manila and nearby provinces joined the secession.[44]

Not only did the missionary leadership downplay the Zamora disaffection as misplaced jingoism in line with the growing nationalist independence impulse in the country at that time, it also chose to respond to it solely on spiritual terms. The editor of the *Advocate*, for example, predicted that the schismatics were bound to fail because their message, they alleged, lacked spiritual substance. "Another fatal weakness of the Zamora movement will doubtless be found in its failure to feed the spiritual cravings of the people. Its gospel is 'Independencia' [independence] rather than salvation," he argued.[45] Regardless of the criticisms expressed by some missionaries, some of them did acknowledge that the painful schism of 1909 proved to be a blessing for the mission. For example, reflecting on the effects of the crisis two years later, Ernest A. Rayner admitted that it brought about "a change of emphasis" or, in other words, it served as a catalyst for them to shift their emphasis to holiness revivalism. He echoed: "We were suddenly called to turn our attention from the work of swelling membership to the more vital problem of deepening the spiritual experience of our reduced numbers."[46] Quality had to take precedence over quantity as holiness promotion was to play a key role in preventing, if not countering, the devastating toll of the secession.

First to react to the crisis was the Manila District, the most affected by the schism. By August, Koehler was leading the charge with his Pentecostal services. At St. Paul MEC in Tondo, supported by District Superintendent Marvin Rader and Bishop Oldham, and with the aid of a stereopticon projector, he conducted several evening meetings where the "altar was soon

44. See *PCA*, March 1909, 3; Clymer, "Methodist Response," 426–27; Deats, "Nicolas Zamora," 336; Trinidad, *Monument*, 116–24.

45. See for example, *PCA*, April–May 1909, 3. For more on this issue, see Copplestone, *Twentieth-Century*, 228–32.

46. *WWM*, December 1911, 12.

filled with penitents."⁴⁷ Thus, interpreting the success of Koehler's "great meetings" in Manila, Bishop Oldham, in his report to the New York Board, exclaimed: "This is God's answer to the Zamora defection."⁴⁸ What happened in Tondo also began to spread to other churches as Koehler doubled his efforts within the district. As Rader summarized:

> We are greatly impressed by the fact that all of the churches are praying for a deeper work of grace and show a real hunger for spiritual food for their souls. There is a lingering in prayer, a reaching out of faith to God for his abiding presence. There is noticed a growth of marked purpose in the sermons preached. Here-to-fore many have preached without a clear idea of what they wanted to accomplish. Now the appeal comes out clear and strong for a new life full of righteousness and the Holy Ghost.⁴⁹

Rader's report of the impact of Koehler's revival work in Manila acknowledged a marked shift in the content of the preaching of their Filipino colleagues as they have begun admonishing their audiences towards "new life full of righteousness and the Holy Ghost" or, to put it differently, towards holiness and Spirit-filled living. In a separate report, Koehler himself echoed a similar sentiment: "Our pastors and people are beginning to realise more and more the need of this kind of work. We believe that we are on the eve of a great revival among this people. They are beginning to realise the need of a salvation that saves from sin."⁵⁰

While much of Koehler's work was confined in Manila, small signs of this "revival spirit" also began to emerge in the provinces of Nueva Ecija, Pampanga, Tarlac, and as far as Ilocos Sur and Abra. In Vigan, for example, District Superintendent Oscar Huddleston reported a "deepening of the spiritual life among all members."⁵¹ In Tarlac, Rex R. Moe, a missionary from Nebraska, further attested: "We can almost draw a distinct line between Christians and mere Protestants. The Filipino is coming to recognize the difference. The Christians are definitely converted and have a religious experience. The Protestant may be simply joining against Romanism."⁵² For Moe, the MEC's emerging shift towards holiness spirituality had given Fili-

---

47. *PIAC* (1910), 34; cf. *WPIAC* (1910), 109.
48. Oldham to Leonard, 7 September 1909, Oldham, W. F., MCUMC.
49. *PIAC* (1910), 33.
50. Ibid., 37.
51. Ibid., 62.
52. Ibid., 49.

pino Methodists an increasing sense of self-identity that would differentiate them from other Protestant groups and, most likely given the timing of his comment, from Zamora's IEMELIF movement.

Koehler's earlier pronouncement that they were on the "eve of a great revival" could not have been truer as his revival efforts served as precursors to a much bigger and comprehensive revival wrought about by a widely-known visiting American Holiness evangelist at the next annual conference.

H. C. Morrison's Pentecostal Meetings in Manila

Invited by Bishop Oldham, Henry Clay Morrison (1857–1942) visited Manila from March 1–8, 1910, for a series of Pentecostal meetings as part of his "world tour of evangelism" which had previously taken him to India and to Rangoon, Burma (now Yangon, Myanmar), and Singapore.[53] The Kentucky-born Morrison was ordained in the Methodist Episcopal Church, South, but left the pastorate in 1890. Known as a powerful orator, Morrison also devoted his life to evangelistic work, coordinating holiness revival work in the South, and editing the Louisville-based weekly *The Old Methodist*, which later became the immensely popular *Pentecostal Herald*.[54] Also, Morrison's influence extended to other holiness groups, including holiness advocates within the northern MEC. MEC bishops supportive of the Holiness movement, for instance, invited him to conduct Pentecostal meetings during the General Conferences of 1904 and 1908 in Los Angeles and Baltimore, respectively.[55]

Morrison's tour was financed by the Board of Missions of the Holiness Union, which appointed Morrison in the fall of 1908 to "to make an evangelistic tour around the world" by "preaching full salvation," among its objectives.[56] Morrison's coming to the Philippines effectively exemplifies how the Holiness movement had engendered a robust transpacific relationship between Methodist missionaries in Asia and some prominent Holiness evangelists from the United States. It is therefore not hard to understand why other well-known Holiness evangelists would visit the country years later. Shortly after completing his evangelistic tour, Morrison became the

53. Morrison, *World Tour*, 78–202.
54. Kostlevy, "Morrison, Henry Clay."
55. Morrison, *Some Chapters*, 191–92.
56. Morrison, *World Tour*, 7–9.

president of Asbury College, a holiness school in Wilmore, Kentucky.[57] Asbury would later play a significant role in the development of holiness revival culture in the Philippines as we will show later in the next chapter.

In Manila, Morrison spoke in all of the morning services during the six-day conference at the Knox Memorial "First Filipino Church" MEC, with the aid of an interpreter, and at the special evening meetings at Central "American Church" MEC.[58] Morrison documented his Manila visit in a three-article series published two months later in the *Pentecostal Herald*. Summarizing the results of his hour-long morning devotional meetings at the conference, Morrison wrote: "The altar was filled every morning with people seeking the Lord for pardon, restoration or full salvation. Missionaries and natives flocked together to the mercy seat and prayed and sobbed out their heart longings into the ear of our compassionate God and he blessed them."[59]

The conference minutes also captured the essence of Morrison's description on a day-to-day basis. For example, during the fifth morning of the conference, since God, as Morrison recalled, came upon them in a "very gracious and melting way" during devotions, Bishop Oldham pronounced: "We will not break into this revival spirit with the transaction of Conference business." They therefore deviated from the already-approved schedule by dedicating the whole morning for a Pentecostal meeting where, as noted by the conference secretary, "the Holy Ghost was present in great power."[60] Morrison recollected:

> The Spirit was present and we had a gracious time. Almost the entire body of the native ministry was at the altar seeking holiness of heart; quite a number of the missionaries, also several of the young Filipino women. There were tears, prayers, songs, heart searching and crying out to God. Quite a number of persons, I think four missionaries, gave clear testimony to the fulness [sic] of the blessing of Christ and a number of the native ministers rejoiced in a new found grace. We put the doctrine of regeneration, the remains of sin, and the sanctifying power of Christ's blood before them as clearly as we could, and believe it went into their heads and hearts.[61]

57. Morrison, *Some Chapters*, 231–38; Kostlevy, "Morrison, Henry Clay."

58. Detailed accounts of these meetings are found in *PIAC* (1910), 11–21; Morrison, *World Tour*, 203–13; *PH*, 4 May 1910, 8; *PH*, 18 May 1910, 1.

59. *PH*, 4 May 1910, 8; cf. Morrison, *World Tour*, 205.

60. *PIAC* (1910), 16; Morrison, *Some Chapters*, 219.

61. *PH*, 18 May 1910, 1; cf. Morrison, *World Tour*, 211–12.

It is worth noting that "almost the entire body" of Filipinos responded to Morrison's altar call. As a result, a number of Filipino preachers were entirely sanctified or, as Morrison described, "witnessed to the belief that they were cleansed from all sin," while others manifested "great desires for deliverance from all the carnal nature and the baptism with the Holy Ghost."[62] While the meetings helped a number of Filipino workers experience or seek sanctification, missionary Isaac B. Harper, the editor of the *Advocate*, on the other hand, recognized the therapeutic effect of the revival upon the Filipino workers as it helped them deal with the wounds caused by the schism of the previous year. "Their hearts had been made sore by the experiences of the year. Never had they been so tired. It was pathetic to listen to their prayers as they poured out their hearts to God. Their forms would shake with emotion and tears would stream down over their faces," he observed.[63]

Correspondingly, Morrison's meetings also had an effect on "quite a number" of missionaries. As he reported, four out of the thirteen who were present also professed sanctification or what he called "the fulness [sic] of the blessing of Christ," while the others "witnessed to a gracious refreshing in grace," according to a separate account.[64] This goes to show one of the ways holiness revivalism functioned in the mission field. It was also meant for missionaries who have not experienced the second blessing back home to finally experience it. But beyond the promotion of the experience of sanctification, holiness revivals also served to revitalize missionaries and infuse in them a renewed sense of enthusiasm for their work. For example, District Superintendent Marvin Rader tearfully testified that "he was anxious for the conference to close that he might hasten out with the gospel."[65] Oldham's letter to Morrison after the conference also effectively illustrates this:

> When I cabled you, I did not know how marked a step forward your coming would bring. I called the mission together yesterday to discuss especially the matter of revival and I found the men's heart are all aglow, but they all feel that we must organize Revival bands in which Americans and Filipinos shall go together all over our territory to call the people to repentance and the Christians to a deeper life of holiness. Your coming has practically fixed

---

62. *PH*, 4 May 1910, 8; cf. Morrison, *World Tour*, 206.
63. *PCA*, March–April 1910, 4.
64. *PH*, 4 May 1910, 8; cf. Morrison, *World Tour*, 206.
65. *PH*, 18 May 1910, 1; cf. Morrison, *World Tour*, 212.

the holiness idea as the birthright of every man in the Methodist Church, and I desire these revival bands to move through the country not only for the sake of sinners, but that we might have sincere saints.[66]

Morrison's visit inspired Oldham and his associates to mark out a new revival strategy intended for two different audiences: first, the unconverted towards repentance, and second, the already-Christian towards holiness. That same month, he clarified this in an open letter in the *Advocate* to his American and Filipino co-workers by calling for a "direct revival movement" primarily directed to their Methodist constituents who have not been genuinely converted yet or as Oldham implied have not yet a clear conception of "immediate repentance" and "a true faith in Christ as Saviour and Lord" or the evangelical experience known as justifying faith. The Filipino, he surmised, had gotten so familiar with the Roman Catholic practice of auricular confession before a priest that they do not understand what true repentance means. Also, "many of those who were in revolt against the old order and were therefore willing to be enrolled as 'Protestants,' had yet but little conception of Evangelical Christianity." "I trust, therefore, that utmost attention will be given to the making of wide revival plans for the year and for their close working," he further exclaimed.[67] Morrison's Pentecostal meetings in Manila have effectively solidified MEC's shift from its anti-Catholic crusade to a crusade against nominal Christianity.

Indeed, the appeal did not fall on deaf ears as "revival meetings of the Holy Spirit type," as one missionary labeled them,[68] persisted in Manila and northward to other provinces for decades, although in varying intensities and frequencies—a fact later substantiated by Bishop Dionisio Alejandro, who, at various points, was one of the prominent players in the revival movement. Morrison's visit, he wrote, had made the term *culto Pentecostal* the "watchword" in early Philippine Methodist life and culture; services lasted "from one week to ten days and continued until the outbreak of World War II."[69]

---

66. Quoted in Morrison, *World Tour*, 213.
67. *PCA*, March–April 1910, 3.
68. *PIAC* (1910), 45.
69. Alejandro, *From Darkness to Light*, 106–7.

Figure 3.1. Pandacan MEC chapel, the first MEC chapel built in the Philippines, dedicated August 12, 1900. Methodists also claim that it was "the first Protestant chapel" in the country. Source: *CA*, 11 October 1900.

Figure 3.2. Procession Preaching, Mexico, Pampanga, 1912. This was one of the ways Methodists contextualized their mission in the Philippines. Instead of parading religious images and icons, as the Roman Catholics did, they often paraded floats adorned with Scripture texts, open bibles, or even preachers on carts like the one shown here. Source: The United Methodist Church Archives—GCAH, Madison, New Jersey. Mission Photograph Albums—Philippines #3, 115.

Figure 3.3. Pentecostal Procession, San Fernando, Pampanga, 1907. Methodist processions were also called "Pentecostal processions" and were meant as a show of force. The original caption for the image boasts that the mayor, the chief of police, and provincial secretary, all Methodist local preachers, participated in the procession. Source: Farmer, *Philippine Mission* (1910).

Figure 3.4. Charles W. Koehler and his wife Ida Koehler (left) with WFMS missionaries Mildred M. Blakely (seated) and Orilla F. Washburn (right) of the Bible Woman's Training School, Lingayen, Pangasinan, 1914. Charles Koehler, highly regarded for his revival work, was the first MEC missionary to conduct Pentecostal meetings in the Philippines. Source: The United Methodist Church Archives—GCAH, Madison, New Jersey. Mission Photograph Albums—Philippines #2, 64.

Figure 3.5. Pentecostal meeting, St. Paul MEC, Tondo, Manila, August 1909. Led by Charles Koehler and Bishop William Oldham, the gathering was intended to counter the effects of the Zamora Schism at St. Paul, the church where the schism began. Source: Farmer, *Philippine Mission* (1910).

Figure 3.6. Philippine Islands Annual Conference, Knox Memorial MEC, Manila, March 2–8, 1910. Famous Holiness evangelist Henry Clay Morrison (center, holding boy) conducted Pentecostal meetings during the conference. Morrison reported that most of the Filipino delegates were "at the altar seeking full salvation" and about four missionaries experienced sanctification during the meetings. Source: *PIAC* (1910).

4

Seasons of Pentecost, 1911–1924

The prayer lasted about an hour, then we felt the forgiveness of our sins, received the baptism of the Holy Ghost and obtained the victory over our difficulties, troubles and temptations. When we came back to our seats we were entirely changed.

—Arcadio de Ocera, *PIAC* (1919)

It may not be an exaggeration to say that Holiness revivalism was the most distinctive characteristic of Philippine Methodism that set it apart from other Protestant denominations in the years following Morrison's visit. This will be fleshed out as we examine the individuals who either supported or conducted Pentecostal meetings and engendered its various manifestations in the field from 1911 to 1924, Methodism's twenty-fifth year in the country.

Bishop William P. Eveland

Bishop Oldham's departure in 1912 did not weaken the holiness revival policy he had launched in 1910 since it was sustained by Bishop William Perry Eveland (1864–1916), who was elected missionary bishop for the Southern Asia field at the same General Conference which appointed his predecessor to the missionary board in New York. Although Oldham's exit may have marked a weakening of Indian Methodist holiness impulses within Philippine Methodist life, the religious experience and theological orientation of the relatively unknown educator from Pennsylvania did not drift far from that of Oldham, Warne, and Thoburn. In fact, Eveland, who was president of Williamsport Dickinson Seminary (now Lycoming

College), was converted at a revival meeting at Cumberland Street MEC in Philadelphia under the preaching of famed MEC female evangelist Maggie Van Cott, who, as one scholar argues, operated "on the fringes of the Holiness movement."[1] Upon his arrival in 1912, Eveland's first decree to the missionaries and Filipino workers echoed not only insights about his religious experience, but also his aspirations for the mission, in a manner strikingly similar to Oldham's 1908 mandate for the mission:

> The very best thing that has come into my own life is the consciousness that God, for Jesus Christ's sake has forgiven me my sins and sent his Holy Spirit into my heart. I know that Jesus is my Friend and helper and this knowledge makes me strong and happy. Jesus does help me gain the victory over temptation and sin. He does help me grow in cleanness and righteousness and goodness.
>
> To teach these things to men is our real task. It is what you and I working together must try to do.[2]

Eveland framed his own spirituality around the Wesleyan soteriological themes of justification, assurance, and sanctification by affirming God's forgiveness, the infilling of the Holy Spirit, and how Christ enabled him to have "victory over temptation and sin" and to grow deeper in holiness. He then reminded the missionaries and Filipino pastors that it was their "real task" to teach these same principles to people.

Evidence of Eveland's commitment to his mission manifesto is abundant since he also functioned as a professional revivalist like Oldham. For instance, he clearly manifested this skill on his first ordination service in the Philippines during the Annual Conference of 1913 at Knox Memorial MEC in Manila:

> As we finished our impressive ordination service, the impulse came upon me to ask both the newly consecrated elders and deacons to kneel at the altar, and one after the other to pray first for themselves and then for those who knelt with them, that the Lord would then and there so baptize them with his Spirit that they should go forth to be good ministers of Jesus Christ. As one who was close to that altar I can testify that we were consciously certain that God had answered that prayer. Then I tried to preach an ordination—no, that is not the way to state it—I did not need to

---

1. *Central Pennsylvania Annual Conference* (1917), 121–22. For Van Cott's connection to the Holiness movement, see Everhart, "Maggie Newton Van Cott," 312–13, 317.

2. *PO*, August 1912, 23.

try. It would have required real effort to refrain from preaching at that time and in that place. At the close of the sermon an invitation to men to come and seek salvation seemed the only thing. And they came. The altar was filled. Six o'clock came, and then seven, and still that congregation lingered. The evening meeting was only one hour off and we felt that we must close.[3]

What is interesting here is how Eveland creatively incorporated revivalism into what was supposed to be a standard ordination ritual by admonishing the ordinands to pray for a "baptism of the Holy Spirit," first, individually and then for their fellow ordinands. After preaching, the bishop then proceeded with an altar call for those who were seeking salvation. About twenty professed conversion from among those who occupied the altar, according to the official minutes. Although they had to close the service, it sparked another altar-filled meeting at Knox, and a series of revivals in three nearby churches led by Filipino preachers.[4]

The bishop's revival work was not merely confined to the annual conferences, however, but also made an impact in the provinces. In 1914, for example, Eveland preached to a very large crowd at a revival meeting for two straight nights in Peñaranda Town in Nueva Ecija. Joshua Cottingham's recollection of the event five years later, further illustrates the life-changing effects of the bishop's preaching. Cottingham recalled:

> An old man of sixty was converted. A gambler, cock-fighter, beetle nut chewer, living with a woman to whom he was not married. That night his gambling and his rooster went out forever but what to do with the woman he did not know. She too was old. Both were very religious. They had not married because they were very poor and the padre had not urged them to marry... But God spoke and the old conscience was renewed. The next night he came back and brought his old wife, and she too came to the front and was wonderfully converted. That night the old couple decided to marry and make a public confession of their sins.[5]

Bishop Eveland further took seriously the goals he had stated in 1912 when he requested the mission board for a new missionary for the Cagayan

3. *CA*, 24 April 1913, 563.

4. Ibid.; *PIAC* (1913), 29. Bishop Eveland similarly "turned the ordination service into a consecration meeting" during the Malaysia Conference in February 1915. See Eveland to Oldham, 24 February 1915, Eveland, William Perry (Bishop and Mrs.) 1912–1914, MFUMC.

5. *PIAC* (1919), 48. See also *PIAC* (1915), 61.

Valley field in 1915, and noted one of the traits this missionary should have in order to produce better results in the country. "He ought to be a Kansas man; full of the evangelistic spirit," Eveland insisted.[6] His request did not come to fruition, though. The fifty-two-year-old bishop's life was tragically cut short in a fishing accident on July 24, 1916, when his steel rod hit a poorly insulated power line while vacationing in Mt. Holly Springs, Pensylvannia.[7] This left the Philippine MEC mission without permanent episcopal supervision for four years. Eveland was eventually succeeded by Bishop Charles Edward Locke, who also made revivalism one of his priorities during his tenure (1920–1924), although to a lesser degree. Just like his predecessor, Locke, in his first letter to his Philippine constituents underscored the place of revivalism for his term. "I am confident that all of our pastors, with the cooperation of their Congregations, will take advantage of their opportunities and conduct special revival meetings," he maintained.[8]

Missionary Men and the Transmission of *Culto Pentecostal* Spirituality

The overwhelming amount of missionary support for *culto Pentecostal* spirituality starting from 1910 and up to the first quarter-century of the Philippine MEC mission cannot be overstated. Of the twenty-eight missionaries who were present at some point during the period (an average of thirteen every year),[9] a significant subset promoted revival meetings in their respective stations and, to a degree, found common ground on Pentecost or holiness-themed revivalism. This is not to suggest that all of them preached with the same skill and intensity that Charles W. Koehler had, but they did express their support of *culto* Pentecostalism in various ways and various degrees, most often articulated through holiness revival-associated parlance.

Pioneer missionaries who were present during Morrison's Manila visit in 1910 evidently served as agents in the dissemination of holiness-Pentecostal piety in their respective stations in the years that followed. Farmer

---

6. Eveland to Oldham, 6 March 1915, Eveland, William Perry (Bishop and Mrs.) 1912–1914, MFUMC.

7. *CA*, 3 August 1916, 1029.

8. *PO*, December 1920, 2. He also participated in a number of revival gatherings. See, for example, *PIAC* (1921), 57; *PIAC* (1922), 15.

9. See Conference rolls from *PIAC* (1911) to *PIAC* (1924).

himself, who claimed conversion in an MEC revival meeting in Cedar Rapids, Iowa,[10] explicitly took on this role as he supported the work of Koehler, even inviting him to conduct Pentecostal services at the seminary, which enabled the students to attain the "highest New Testament experience for themselves."[11] In 1913, he even complained to Oldham, who by that time was already serving as mission board corresponding secretary, that there was no one to lead the revival movement given Koehler's absence, and that for his part he was trying all that he could to keep the emphasis alive by leading seminary students into "deep religious experience."[12] Marvin A. Rader, the district superintendent of Manila who, Morrison wrote, had broken down into tears during his Manila meeting, celebrated the condition of Methodists in his district in 1911 for living a "higher plane religiously and morally than the Romanists."[13] In the ensuing years, Rader, who held different administrative posts for the mission into the 1920s, still figured in a number of revival meetings.[14] Daniel H. Klinefelter, district superintendent of Central District, a graduate of Moody Bible Institute, and a native of Audubon, Iowa, noted in 1911 that leading his constituents to a "knowledge of righteousness, peace and joy in the Holy Ghost has been the goal of the year's work."[15] In 1915, while serving the Manila District, he argued that any preacher who "does not believe in revival meetings" "has no place in the Methodist Ministry."[16] A year later, he rejoiced to "see people turn from Satan to God, sin to righteousness, old neighborhood quarrels settled at the altar of the Church with many tears."[17]

Other pioneer missionaries who operated in the provinces north of Manila were also similarly supportive of *culto* Pentecostalism. In Central District, which was comprised of several provinces in Central Luzon, Edwin L. Housley of the North Ohio Conference reported that "Revival power" characterized their work in 1911. "We are persuaded that revival

10. See Farmer's "religious experience" in Farmer to Missionary Society of the MEC, 29 December 1903, Farmer, H., MCUMC.

11. *PIAC* (1912), 73.

12. See Farmer to Oldham, 1 August 1913, Farmer, Harry, MFUMC.

13. *PIAC* (1911), 48.

14. *PIAC* (1921), 57.

15. *PIAC* (1911), 35. For Klinefelter's autobiography, see Klinefelter, *Adventures with God*.

16. *PIAC* (1915), 74; *PIAC* (1917), 74.

17. *PIAC* (1916), 44. "Old quarrels," for instance, were settled at a revival meeting in Bagumbayan, Navotas. See Klinefelter, *Adventures with God*, 44–46.

fire must burn off these heart-fields before system and spiritual fruit can result, and "the desert blossom as the rose," he concluded.[18] In 1915, after serving as superintendent of the newly formed Pampanga District for a year, he reported that "deep consecration and revival power have prevailed in the whole district and characterized the workers on every circuit."[19] Rex R. Moe, a native of Nebraska, who was in-charge of the Tarlac Province reported that in the months following Morrison's campaign, they had turned the platform in the Tarlac chapel into an altar for revival meetings, where "God poured out new blessings upon us. Some of our members learned for the first time to pray aloud. Some got a new vision of the Christ and a new idea of conversion."[20] A year later, he summed up the work in province as a "real revival season," stating that the preachers had the "fire from on high."[21] Moe further carried with him the same emphasis when he was stationed deeper north, to head the Cagayan District in 1918.[22] Berndt O. Peterson, a native of Salina, Kansas, had consistently welcomed *culto* Pentecostalism, mostly led by Filipino ministers and revivalists missionaries, in the Pangasinan District, where he served as Superintendent for more than ten years (1911–1921).[23] A similar direction was taken in the Northern District under Oscar A. Huddleston. Formerly of the Southwest Kansas Conference, Huddleston reported during the Conference of 1915: "We believe in the new birth and the renewal of the Holy Ghost, and 'to them that believe He is precious.'"[24]

We need to reiterate, however, that the majority of these pioneers did not function as revivalists *per se*. But most of them did encourage and relegate this type of work to a rising number of Filipino revivalists, and on some occasions, to Filipino women and a few WFMS missionary evangelists who operated within their charge, which we shall demonstrate later. Koehler also did occasional *culto Pentecostal* work, mostly reviving preachers in the evening revival services held in the annual gatherings such as Bible Institutes, lyceums, Sunday School conventions, and district conferences held

18. *PIAC* (1912), 58. For more on Housley, see Housley, E. L., MCUMC.

19. *PIAC* (1915), 71.

20. *PIAC* (1911), 43. For more on Moe, see Moe, R. R., MCUMC.

21. See *PIAC* (1912), 62–63.

22. See, for example, *PIAC* (1918), 40.

23. See, for example, *PIAC* (1912), 49, 53; *PIAC* (1913), 55; *PIAC* (1914), 59; *PIAC* (1921), 53–54. For more on Peterson, see Peterson, B. O., MCUMC.

24. See *PIAC* (1915), 50. For more on Huddleston, see Huddleston, O. A., MCUMC.

in their stations. But in the few years that followed, Koehler's special status as Holiness evangelist was increasingly supplemented, and eventually supplanted by a new batch of missionaries, who we will appropriately label "Post-Morrison missionaries."

Joshua Cottingham and Other Post-Morrison Revivalists

A number of post-Morrison missionaries also helped perpetuate Bishop William Oldham's holiness vision for the MEC mission in the Philippines. The most famous among them was Indiana native Joshua Frank Cottingham (1874–1939), who arrived with his wife, Bertha deVer, a month after the Conference of 1910 to begin work in Nueva Ecija Province.[25] It was Cottingham, aside from Koehler, "who could really bring things to pass in a revival meeting," Farmer once mused.[26] After Koehler's premature return to the United States in 1914, Cottingham increasingly emerged as the foremost Holiness revivalist for the entire mission. Born in Butler County, Kansas, Cottingham moved with his parents to Milan, Indiana, in his youth and completed his education at Moores Hill College (now University of Evansville) in Moores Hill, Indiana. Cottingham also attested to receiving a post-conversion sanctification experience together with his wife on January 14, 1905, but theirs was accompanied by a call to foreign missionary work.[27] His biographer added that it was "while he was praying at the altar and consecrating himself to God he received his Pentecostal blessing and the call, 'Go ye into the world and preach the gospel to every creature.'"[28] This experience later led him and his wife to mortgage their house in Milan and enter Taylor University in Upland, where they would eventually sign SVM pledge cards to go to the mission field.[29] The small college was named after Bishop William Taylor and known for its close ties with the MEC's holiness wing.[30] Consequently, Cottingham's ties with Holiness Methodists

25. *PCA*, March–April 1910, 12.
26. Farmer to Oldham, 26 August 1914, Farmer, H., MFUMC.
27. Cottingham to Leonard, 22 November 1909, Cottingham, J. F., MCUMC.
28. *North Indiana Annual Conference* (1939), 377–78.
29. Cottingham to Leonard, 22 November 1909, Cottingham, J. F., MCUMC. See also SVM records in Turner, *Students and the World-Wide Expansion of Christianity*, 642. Assorted biographical information is also found in Cottingham, Joshua F., and Mrs. Cottingham, MBUMC.
30. For more on Taylor University, see, for example, Kostlevy, "Taylor University," 291.

in Indiana is demonstrated by the fact that he was able to secure from them almost five hundred dollars in annual pledges for Filipino preachers while on furlough in 1913, even though he initially resented them for contributing more to independent Holiness faith missions.[31]

Thus, given holiness revivalism's formative role in Cottingham's ministry and his close proximity with Indiana Holiness Methodism, it would not be difficult to imagine why he would later become the linchpin of *culto* Pentecostalism in the Philippines. Essentially following in the footsteps of Koehler, Cottingham headlined as Holiness revivalist in special evening services during several Bible institutes, Sunday School conventions, lyceums, and even in district conferences in Manila and in the provinces until his recall in 1933.[32] Unlike Koehler, however, Cottingham quickly found favor with Bishop Eveland, and thus in 1914, four years after his arrival, he became Superintendent of Central District, an area which comprised the Central Luzon provinces of Bulacan and Nueva Ecija. Accounts of Cottingham's meetings are ubiquitous, but the one he held during the Pampanga District Conference in 1919 showed that much of his popularity stemmed not mainly from his preaching, but from his ability to make things happen afterwards as apparent from this account by Pampanga District Superintendent Arcadio de Ocera:

> At the close of the spirit-filled message, invitation to come to the altar was announced in which all of us came and knelt. While kneeling and praying earnestly the fear and holiness of the Lord caught us, and everybody trembled and cried much tears. We fervently asked the Lord to forgive us our sins, mistakes and failures. The prayer lasted about an hour, then we felt the forgiveness of our sins, received the baptism of the Holy Ghost and obtained the victory over our difficulties, troubles and temptations. When we came back to our seats we were entirely changed.[33]

Cottingham's holiness revival work was not merely confined to the Philippines, however, but also found a place during his furlough in Indiana in 1919 where some preachers and laymen "had their Pentecost" in a

---

31. Cottingham to Oldham, 9 September 1913, Cottingham, Joshua F. (Rev. & Mrs.), MFMUMC.

32. Accounts of Cottingham's revival ministry are numerous. These are excerpted in Laubach, *People of the Philippines*, 221–22, 229–30. For a brief profile on Cottingham, see Rousselow and Winquist, *God's Ordinary People*, 201–3.

33. *PIAC* (1919), 57–58.

meeting he conducted.[34] Then, a few months later, in what was obviously an acknowledgement of their success in the Philippines, Cottingham's Pentecostal meetings were imported to Mexico following an urgent request from the MEC missionary board in New York. It was former Philippines missionary Harry Farmer, who was then corresponding secretary for South America under the administration of MEC social gospeler Frank Mason North, who facilitated Cottingham's four-month revival campaign in several MEC churches and districts in Mexico.[35] In Pachuca, for example, Cottingham's preaching account for one day brought to fore the very same Pentecost and holiness-themed sermons that pervaded his revival preaching in the Philippines. "In a Preacher's Meeting in the afternoon I spoke on 'Baptism for service' that night I spoke on 'Sins that are weights,'" he wrote.[36] Cottingham later assumed the leadership of the Manila District in 1921, which further reinforced his revival legacy even among young people. He introduced the first Epworth League Christmas Institute in the "beautiful resort" of Sibul Springs in San Miguel, Bulacan as a religious leisure and revival event for young people—"for rest, study and prayer."[37] Much will be said about this annual youth gathering in a separate section below.

Another Indiana native to arrive with his wife along with the Cottinghams in 1910 was Samuel H. Armand (1879–1913), who immediately headed to Aparri, the northernmost province in the main island of Luzon. After mastering the local dialects, the Madison, Indiana native began conducting several "successful revivals" in Pangasinan Province.[38] Just like Cottingham, Armand also claimed to have had a post-conversion "baptism of the Holy Spirit," which he experienced while attending Moores Hill College, the same school that Cotingham went to. Thus, as in the case of Cottingham, it would not be farfetched to see the importance of this experience in Armand's involvement with holiness revival work in northern

---

34. Cottingham to Farmer, 15 October 1919, Cottingham, Joshua F. (Rev. & Mrs.), MFMUMC.

35. Farmer to Cottingham, 16 October 1919, Cottingham, Joshua F. (Rev. & Mrs.), MFMUMC.

36. Cottingham to Farmer, 20 January 1920, Cottingham, Joshua F. (Rev. & Mrs.), 1912–1922, MFMUMC.

37. *PIAC* (1922), 49. Religious leisure and the appeal to nature are also hallmarks of the Holiness and Keswick movements. See, for example, Troy Messenger, *Holy Leisure*; Bebbington, *Holiness*, 80–81.

38. See, for example, *PIAC* (1913), 55; *PIAC* (1913), 58.

Luzon. Armand's revivalism, however, came to an abrupt end when he succumbed to diphtheria barely three years after his arrival.[39]

Among the other post-Morrison missionaries who actively helped disseminate *culto* Pentecostal spirituality, aside from Cottingham and Armand, was Archie Lowell Ryan (1881–1955). Arriving in 1914 to cater to the growing demand for Sunday School work within the MEC mission, Ryan supported and lauded Cottingham's Pentecostal meetings, even integrating them in the Sunday School conventions he organized for the districts. Given his mobile status, Ryan essentially functioned as a revivalist in most of the Sunday School gatherings he organized.[40] Another popular missionary evangelist was Arthur Lawrence Beckendorf (1884–1975) of St. Paul, Minnesota, a recent graduate of Drew Seminary when he became the missionary in charge of Nueva Ecija Province in 1918. After a year, Beckendorf became Superintendent of the Central District, where he continued the revival policies of Cottingham, who went on furlough that year. Beckendorf, who was known for his mastery of Tagalog, was also a favorite preacher in the Epworth League Christmas Institutes during the 1920s.[41]

Along with its noted success in the provinces, *culto* Pentecostalism was also evident among Manila-based missionaries. At the English-speaking Central Student Church, Otto Houser of Northeast Ohio, who had arrived in 1919, emphasized revival work among his congregants, mostly students from surrounding colleges. Rader, Superintendent of the Manila District, wrote in 1920, just months after Houser's arrival: "Central Church has had its best year. A revival Spirit possessed us all."[42] Another missionary who came to Manila a year later was Raymond E. Marshall (1888–1940) of New Jersey, who was also known for his revival preaching. For example, the Drew Seminary graduate stirred up a "pentecost" among preachers and deaconesses during the consecration service for the Sunday School Convention in Malolos. As District Superintendent Beckendorf recalled:

> Bro. Marshall preached following with a call for consecration. The preachers and deaconesses of the province came forward in a body.

---

39. See *Indiana Annual Conference* (1913), 194–95. For more on Armand, see Armand, Samuel H., MCUMC.

40. *PO*, April 1916, 12–14. See also *PIAC* (1917), 91. For more on Ryan, see Ryan, Archie L., MBUMC.

41. See, for example *PIAC* (1920), 51; *PIAC* (1925), 37; Candelaria, interview. See also Beckendorf, A. L., MBUMC.

42. *PIAC* (1920), 60–61.

They called upon God and He answered. There was heart searching and tears. There was confession and restoration. One pastor who had spoken harshly to another the day before showed by his tear stained face that all was well. A young pastor later testified that during those moments of waiting before God he was for the first time truly converted. Another who had contemplated leaving the ministry, at least for a time, stated that God's claim and grip constrained him to remain. A former deaconess there informed us that she would accept an assignment at this Conference.[43]

In as much as the years following Morrison's visit saw the emergence of missionaries who functioned as revivalists, it was not until the annual conference session of 1923 that a fulltime "conference evangelist" was appointed for the first time. This responsibility fell on the shoulders of Joseph Clemens (1862–1936), an ordained elder from the Central Pennsylvania Conference and a retired army chaplain previously stationed in the Philippines. Clemens's brief, yet fruitful, revival tour of churches in the Manila-West District early that year led him to express before the Conference his desire to be appointed for "special services."[44] His consequent appointment led him and his wife, Mary Knapp Strong Clemens, to more than six years of revival work in the country's capital and in the provinces. The results of their labors had been widely celebrated in conference reports and resolutions for the numerous conversions that accompanied them. For example, in 1923, he baptized more than two hundred adults in Pampanga after conducting his famous Pilgrim's Progress stereopticon presentations for seven successive nights in Angeles, Camp Stotsenburg (now Clark Field) and Porac. He was also credited for more than four hundred professions of faith for conducting the same in a number of churches in the Cagayan District.[45] A year later, District Superintendent Lorenzo Tamayo reported that Clemens's revival services led to the baptism of 892 people, including children that year.[46] By combining preaching with technology, particularly through the use of a stereopticon projector, Clemens's revival ministry was not only effective in awakening non-believers, but also in the promotion of holiness among existing members. As District Superintendent Joseph Moore summarized Clemens's campaigns in the Ilocos District in 1929:

43. *PIAC* (1921), 39.
44. *PIAC* (1923), 14, 29, 47.
45. *PIAC* (1924), 38, 57.
46. *PIAC* (1925), 58–59.

"Wherever the Chaplain goes there is a stirring of dead men's bones, and old sinners in the church are made to quake and repent by his preaching of righteousness and salvation."[47] Throughout his evangelistic career in the Philippines that spanned more than six years, it is estimated that he had baptized more than 16,000 people.[48]

A Religious Fiesta: *Culto Pentecostal* in Focus

While we have established the personalities involved, we are now compelled to focus on the practice itself. While general descriptions of revivals have been abundant in the reports and some hints have been given in the previous sections, nothing surpasses the imagery provided by Archie Ryan in his article, "A Gracious Filipino Revival," in the *Philippine Observer* detailing the revival meetings that were held during the Bible Institute in San Leonardo, Nueva Ecija on February 8–17, 1916. Ryan's article illustrates what he claimed to be a "typical" revival meeting in the Philippines:

> The evenings during the nine days were entirely given over for evangelistic meetings. I wish some of our friends in America, especially any who are lacking in enthusiasm for Foreign Missions, could have been present at the meetings Saturday night and Sunday morning. Saturday night there was a short sermon by Bro. Housley of Pampanga District. Then Bro. Cottingham took charge. First there was a ten minute testimony service. And how they do testify! No urging required. Then they made the bamboo chapel ring with "Nothing but the blood of Jesus" in Tagalog, interjected by occasional Hallelujah, which is the same in both languages. About 350 people were present in the little crowded chapel, and during the invitation nearly every one was on his [sic] knees, on the dirt floor, praying. Yes even outside the chapel people were kneeling in prayer. Pastors and others were doing personal work meanwhile. What a passion some of these people seem to have for souls! In the midst of that wonderful spectacle I said to Brother Cottingham, "My, I wish we could reproduce by phonograph and moving picture the sound and sight of this wonderful manifestation of Divine Presence and Power. What an inspiration it would be to our people at home!" Twenty people were converted and joined the church that night, ranging in age from twelve to seventy. It was a sight to make the angels rejoice. While these things were going on, a band

---

47. *PIAC* (1929), 50–51.
48. Hanners and Webb, "Joseph Clemens."

concert was running in competition two blocks away, with about twelve people making up their audience. Truly the gospel has not lost its drawing power.

Sunday morning witnessed a continuation of the religious fiesta. A splendid Sunday School session began at 8:30 am. And even though the cock-pit, the great national evil of the Philippines was in session, the chapel was crowded, so that some of the classes had to meet outside in the shade. How does that sound for February? A professional cock-fighter, on previous evening had come to church carrying his rooster according to the custom. But during the service the Lord got hold of him. And the man was forthwith converted, gave his rooster away, and thus broke with his most besetting sin. He was also at Sunday School that morning.

Well, after the S. S. service, I was asked to take charge and conduct a Decision Day service. It had been planned that I should preach the morning sermon, following the Decision service. But the Lord took charge of things, and we didn't interfere. We let the service take its own course, and even if I did have to put my sermon back in the barrel, what is that to getting the people saved? This, we constantly insist, is the goal of all Sunday Schools.

The S. S. lesson happened to be the "Call of Samuel." We took this as our start and spoke briefly of our duty to respond quickly when God calls, and that God calls everyone of us now to take Jesus as our Saviour and Master, to make Him our Friend, Counselor, and Helper, to crown Him King in our lives. Then we called for testimonies again, asking them to tell what Jesus had meant to them as Saviour, Friend, etc. Sometimes two or three were on their feet at once. There were about fifty testimonies in ten minutes. It was inspiring! Then the Superintendent of the S. S. led in prayer, after which the invitation was given. We sang, "I surrender all." The personal workers started. The altar began to fill up. Everything was spontaneous. The Lord was wonderfully leading. There was one visiting pastor whose face is a benediction to watch in such a meeting, Victorino Jorda. While the young people were coming forward, his face was shining, and he would say, "O Lord, save some more," and when another would come, he would shout, "Hallelujah." Well, I can't tell it all. Two more songs were sung, "Fill me now," and "Take me as I am." Prayers followed. And before the service closed twelve more joined the church, and twenty-five were baptized, both children and adults. Then we sang "He will hold me fast," and in response to the question, "How many believe he does and will hold you fast," practically every hand was raised in that large congregation. After the benediction, it was suddenly remembered that the collection had been forgotten. So while it was being taken someone started, "Shall we gather at the river," which was interjected by many hallelujahs. The Lord was wonderfully outpouring his spirit.[49]

Although the event itself was a Bible Institute, an annual district gathering of lay workers and ministers held mostly during the dry seasons, the evenings provided opportunities for a protracted revival meeting for the delegates and the community—underscoring one of the ways *culto Pentecostal* revivalism was woven into the fabric of Philippine Methodist life. The fact that the meetings lasted for nine evenings essentially contributed to the release of pent-up emotions in the last two days, as vividly captured in Ryan's account. It should be noted, however, that preaching was not at all central in the narrative. Instead, it was the drama that followed that defined its success in the eyes of the missionary. Although Housley preached on Saturday evening, it was the ensuing testimony time, with a little help from Cottingham's ability to work up the crowd, that enabled the meeting to transition into an altar service.

On the same Sunday morning, testimonies followed by an impromptu altar call so overwhelmed the schedule that Ryan was forced to defer his sermon. The spontaneity, if not lack of order, was a break from the more restrained regular Sunday worship services introduced by the MEC mission. The occasional "hallelujahs" from the audience during the service was not a typical feature of Philippine MEC worship life either. *Culto Pentecostal* revivalism therefore allowed for a different expression of worship where usual conventions of religious hierarchy and social orders of class, gender, and even color were broken, albeit temporarily. In a way, they implicitly signified at best Methodism's antithetical opposition to the intricacies of the Roman Catholic mass and the hierarchical structures they represented while providing ritualized expressions for religious freedom. This very dynamic, for instance, was implied by Cottingham in his description of a similar revival meeting he led in Peñaranda in 1915:

> One feature was the closing consecration service. The District Supt. as leader could witness it all. Such a sight as were the one hundred and fifty men and women kneeling on the dirt floor while more than half of them were making their offering to God, orally as is their custom, and asking God to seal the offering with a Baptism for service, and in the midst our bishop Eveland kneeling

---

49. *PO*, April 1916, 12–13.

with them; what a contrast in culture, education and office, and yet he was one of them. It was no wonder that God honored and sent his Holy Spirit into the hearts of the petitioners.[50]

Whereas we cannot help but speculate whether Cottingham's "contrast" alluded to some racial stereotyping, the scenario itself brings to fore egalitarian aspects mostly associated with Pentecostal-themed revivalism.[51] To have both Filipinos and Americans, in the case of both the Peñaranda and the San Leonardo revivals, in the same sacred space and intimately going through the same motions together conjures powerful images of solidarity and egalitarianism, at least in that moment of bliss, and most unlikely seen in other settings. Truly, it would be not farfetched to claim that *culto Pentecostal* rituals helped create for its participants a temporal heaven where aspirations for equality became a reality. This same dynamic may have also been at work when Filipino ministers, as we have mentioned in the previous chapter, intimated that Koehler was "the most brotherly missionary."[52]

The absence of preaching in the San Leonardo account did not necessarily mean the absence of theological content, however. The spontaneous singing that erupted seems to make up for the lack of preaching as they underscored the themes that were at the heart of the meetings. None of the songs can be found in the 1914 edition of the official American *Methodist Hymnal*.[53] Popular gospel composer Robert Lowry's "Nothing But the Blood of Jesus" (1876) captured best the theme for the evening meeting. The singing of Winfield Weeden's "I Surrender all" (1896), Ocean Grove's Elwood H. Stokes's "Fill Me Now" (1879),[54] Eliza H. Hamilton's "Take Me as I Am" (1880), Robert Harkness's "He Will Hold Me Fast" (1906), and Lowry's "Shall We Gather at the River" (1864), respectively, also highlighted the drama sequence for the Sunday service—consecration, sanctification/Pentecostal baptism, assurance, and heavenly bliss were the order of the day. Although Ryan did not specify whether the songs were sung in the dialect during the Sunday meeting, evidence suggests that this was most likely

50. *PIAC* (1916), 58.

51. The breaking of racial lines was a typical feature in the more intimate and highly ecstatic gatherings of the Azusa Street Revival. See, for example, Robeck, *Azusa Street Mission*, 141.

52. Quoted in Farmer to Oldham, 26 August 1914, Farmer, Harry, MFUMC.

53. See *The Methodist Hymnal* (1914).

54. For more on Stokes, see Brown, "Stokes, Elwood Haines," 285.

the case. None of the songs except "Shall We Gather at the River" were in the MEC Tagalog hymnbook of 1910.[55] But in the Pampango hymnbook of 1913, all of the songs had already been translated in Pampango,[56] which thereby strongly suggests that they were already available in Tagalog and were popular among Tagalog Methodists by the time of the aforementioned revival. Furthermore, although not present in the official American Methodist hymnbook, most of the songs were available in the unofficial revival-oriented gospel collections published by the Methodist Book Room beginning 1905.[57] This again reinforces the fact that the MEC mission work in the Philippines was more willing to draw from popular American evangelical sources than what the denomination's intellectual elites, purists, and policy makers back in the United States would allow.

The emergence of these hymns in 1913 also reinforces our earlier argument that a shift to revivalism for the Philippine MEC mission was already in place right after Morrison's visit in 1910, and with it came the influx of more popular gospel tunes—perhaps, the very ones that may well have been part of Koehler's repertoire of revival hymns that were being "copied" by Filipino preachers and disseminated to the provinces. Their popularity is further attested by their continued inclusion in the most recent version of the Tagalog hymnal.[58] Corporate hymn singing had been an integral part of Methodist life and had proved its drawing power early on when Filipinos first began to gather at Seaman's Bethel in 1900. We also need to remember that the gospel hymns also owed their appeal to a preceding indigenous Filipino musical culture "enriched" by the presence of Iberian Roman Catholic sacred music.[59] But the gospel hymns offered something more than what their Catholic predecessors had offered, nonetheless. Despite their reference to American or Western evangelical experience, the "heart religion" motifs of the hymns, which were mostly sung in the subjective or first person obviously appealed to the Filipinos, who sang them with great fervor during the meetings. The hymns, especially when sung in the local vernacular, articulated not only their communal aspirations, but also their personal longings even while allowing them to connect to a higher power. But for all their enthusiastic singing in the nocturnal meetings, one does

55. See *Ang Himnario* (1910).
56. See *Ing Himnario* (1913).
57. See Vernon and Pilkington, *United Methodist Publishing House*, 199–201.
58. See Reyes, ed., *Ang Imnaryong Ebangheliko* (1946).
59. See Rempola, "Christian Missionaries," 3–4.

not have to wonder why Methodists were derisively compared to toads by their irritated neighbors. "Frogs have many friends, they sing quack, quack, quack all the time but who cares to hear them," complained one Roman Catholic to her Methodist husband.[60] Thus, in addition to the testimonies, hymn singing helped make *culto Pentecostal* a ritual of community.

It is also significant that one noted result of the meetings suggests that they were designed not only to bring about conversions, but also to promote holiness, which in this case involved a deliverance from the "besetting sin" of gambling. Ryan suggested that a professional cock-fighter who got converted the night before returned a changed man—that is, after he gave up his rooster—that Sunday morning. Thus, given the outcomes of other similar meetings, like the public confession and wedding of an elderly couple at the revival meeting led by Bishop Eveland in Peñaranda in 1915, it is no wonder that Tagalog Methodists also called them "*culto ng pagbabagong buhay*," the literal translation of which is "life-changing worship service."[61] While what happened in San Leonardo suggests the prominence of holiness themes during the meetings, it is important to note that the very sight of a "converted" professional cock-fighter publicly demonstrated the ability of early Philippine Methodism to "re-order" or discipline the lives of its adherents and, therefore, its appeal.[62] Such appeal was also very much at the crux of what one sympathetic politician in 1924 shared with Pampanga Superintendent Arcadio de Ocera: "I hate the Roman Catholic Religion very much and I cannot swallow the Aglipayan Church; so my great inclination is toward the Methodist church for I have observed in it the righteous manner of living of its ministers as well as their followers."[63]

Nevertheless, the very thing that attracted would-be members to Methodism also appeared to be the cause for some of the most virulent attacks against it. For instance, when Conference Evangelist Joseph Clemens conducted a series of revival meetings for a new church-planting project in Floridablanca, Pampanga in the summer of 1925, it is not difficult to discern the nature of the opposition placed against him. According to de Ocera in his report:

---

60. Quoted in *WCPIAC* (1912), 124.

61. See *PIAC* (1916), 44.

62. This particular analysis is informed by a similar argument for the appeal of American Methodism as provided in Wigger, *Taking Heaven by Storm*, 98–103.

63. Representative Pablo Angeles David as quoted in *PIAC* (1924), 55.

> From the very beginning the Roman Catholics of that town did everything they could to oppose the Chaplain in his work. During the second evening the service was seriously disturbed by noise and disrespect which finally resulted in the Chaplain being forced to oppose a young man who deliberately smoked during the service and went so far as to come forward and blow smoke in the face of the evangelist in order to disturb the meeting. This trouble maker with some of his friends then threatened to strike the Chaplain and would have done so had not Pastor [Prudencio] Tuason intervened. On the third night another form of persecution took place in the form of a vaudeville performance which was deliberately planned and carried out a short distance from the scene of the evangelistic meeting in order to disturb and detract attention from the Protestant service. This uncalled for procedure was brought to the attention of the Municipal President but this official was unwilling to take action against the guilty parties for the reason that the initiator of this lawlessness was a personal friend and very influential in local politics whose ill will would stand in the way of the President's reelection.[64]

It would not be farfetched to surmise that the smoking incident and the parallel vaudeville shows, which were meant to disrupt Clemens's meetings, were also intended as a direct affront to the holiness values that these meetings represented. They, however, failed to stop the meetings since the provincial governor quickly intervened on behalf of the Methodists. He reprimanded the town *presidente* and ordered him to shutdown the shows. While de Ocera assessed the seven-night meetings as a "success," they only produced thirty-seven new members, which was a far cry from the usual hundreds of conversions that usually accompanied Clemens's work.[65] Regardless of their outcome, the Floridablanca incident demonstrates how *culto Pentecostal* revivalism were less successful in areas where there was no established Methodist presence. They simply created a sense of uneasiness to communities where vices and practices, which Methodists deemed immoral, have been left relatively unchallenged for a long time.

Hence, whether they attract more people or invite opposition, it is clear that the seasonal Pentecostal services served as periodic reminders to Methodists to observe high moral standards and were recurring demonstrations to the public of the price one had to pay to become a Methodist. The altar call time, in particular, was not only an initiatory ritual (prior to

---

64. *PIAC* (1925), 54.
65. Ibid.

baptism) for those who wanted to enter a life of moral rectitude, but also a venue for the already-Methodist or the so-called "backslider" to recommit his or her life to the same standards. The altar call also carried with it a sense of optimism about the possibility of self-improvement through the power of the Holy Spirit, which runs diametrically opposed to the common Filipino concept of *kapalaran* (fate), the fatalistic tendency to explain everything as irreversible and predetermined.[66] The power of the divine being, the Holy Spirit, to miraculously enable people to attain some degree of Christlikeness was quite liberating and empowering for Filipinos to hear. This was very much the expectation, if not understanding, when they sung the chorus of "Fill Me Now" in the vernacular:

Puspusin, puspusin [Fill, fill]

Jesus ako'y puspusin [Jesus fill me]

Anyo mo ako'y puspusin [Your presence fill me]

Lapit ako'y puspusin [Come fill me].[67]

The altar call, with its heavy emphasis on the work of the Holy Spirit accompanied by emotional ecstasy was also not without cultural antecedents, as it found affinity with elements of supernaturalism—the belief in the miraculous, spiritism, and interaction with indigenous spirit beings—present in pre-Hispanic Philippine folk religions, which had persisted as "folk Catholicism" in most parts of the country for more than three centuries.[68] Simply put, rather ironically, the American-imported *culto Pentecostal* rituals became venues for Filipino Methodists to express some elements of their indigenous spiritual culture. It helped provide institutional legitimacy to religious expressions that would have been considered taboo in the official rituals of Roman Catholicism.

---

66. *Kapalaran*, according to Palugod has been misconstrued as fatalistic, but in reality the original intent behind it was the opposite. See Palugod, "Filipino Religious Consciousness," 35–36.

67. Reyes, ed., *Ang Imnaryong Ebangheliko*, 21.

68. See Abinales and Amoroso, *State and Society*, 59–60. See, also, Maggay, *The Gospel in Filipino*, 3–4; Maggay, "Early Protestant Missionary," 33. I do not claim, however, that Filipinos or Asians or "third world" people are the only ones who are "right brained" or have cultural precedents in folk religion that would make them more attracted to Pentecostal-type rituals.

Filipino Holiness Revivalists

As we have suggested in the previous sections, a great number of "spirit-filled" Filipino preachers also conducted their own *culto Pentecostal* in the immediate years following Morrison's visit. While most missionaries did supervisory work and few functioned as revivalists, it was the often-maligned Filipino foot soldier preachers who, despite their lack of education, were at the forefront of revivalism in the local churches. Nowhere else was this more evident than in Central Luzon. Pedro B. Cruz, for example, who according to Oldham was among those who "called upon God for the blessing of which Mr. Morrison spoke," began conducting his own Pentecostal meetings in the town of Gapan in Nueva Ecija Province six months later. Oldham, who had witnessed Cruz's preaching in the small MEC chapel, related that Cruz spoke "with such power and in such demonstration of the Spirit that a large and effectual door was opened, hundreds were soundly changed in heart and life, and the whole community lifted to higher conceptions of conduct."[69]

A year later, after experiencing their "Pentecost" in a Pentecostal service conducted by Koehler in a Bible institute in the same province, a number of Filipino pastors went to conduct "gracious revivals" in several towns, where "old habits and vices were given up." One minister who conducted these revivals was purportedly offered financial support by the Roman Catholic *municipal presidente* for helping "clean up" his town.[70] Local preacher Pablo Roque, after confessing at a revival held by Cottingham in 1913 that "his work had been fruitless because he was a servant of cigarettes and *buyo* [betel leaves]," "began a revival in his barrio, received 37 new members, organized a church, bought a house and made it into a chapel, organized a Sunday School and now promises five pesos per month for a pastor."[71] In 1914, pioneer Tagalog preacher Candido Magno conducted "a weekly Pentecostal meeting in every circuit" in his charge, which even compelled an Aglipayan Priest in San Antonio Town to leave his parishioners, as he "seemed he was all the time surrounded by these meetings."[72] Ulpiano de Pano and Victorino Jorda, according to Cottingham, were "especially filled with the Holy Spirit and evangelistic zeal," and they saw a total of 270

---

69. Oldham, *India, Malaysia, and the Philippines*, 61–62.
70. See *PIAC* (1912), 65.
71. See *PIAC* (1913), 66–67.
72. *PIAC* (1914), 68.

conversions in their circuits in 1915.⁷³ For 1916, he noted that "the best work in revivals" in nearby Bulacan Province was by Esteban T. Cruz.⁷⁴ In nearby Pampanga Province, Filipino preachers were also at the forefront of revival meetings. "Sunday evening we were with Bro. Arcadio de Ocera at San Vicente, Mexico, where in a Spirit-filled meeting sixty-eight adults and four children were baptized, and the Lord's Supper administered to the large congregation. Fifty adults were baptized in the same congregation the Sunday before in this same revival," wrote Housley in 1912.⁷⁵

Further north in the Cagayan Valley region that same year, pioneer minister Felipe Marquez, one of the first converts at Bethel in 1900, conducted "successful pentecostal services in every congregation with splendid results" in Nueva Vizcaya Province. In the town of Solano, Victorino Lapitan, fresh from seminary for the summer break, also began promoting MEC's brand of morality through a series of meetings which prompted some young men to "not like him because the young women of the church will not dance on account of his opposing it."⁷⁶ However, not all boys who were interested in Methodist girls resisted Methodist preaching as shown in the conversion by Calixto C. Sanidad more than a year before. What happened to him in a Methodist chapel in Narvacan, Ilocos Sur, on December 25, 1910, offers a very good glimpse into the passionate preaching of one Filipino pastor. Writing about the event years later, he reminisced:

> One Christmas night in the Philippines I wandered into the Methodist chapel in our town. I had come to slip a note to a pretty girl. Presently I forgot all about her. With all the intensity of my being I was leaning forward toward the man who was speaking, now on fire, now in tears. I felt he was speaking to me. When the invitation was given, I was the first to rush forward. Upon my knees I surrendered to Christ. From that night I never missed kneeling in secret with God, especially when I was away from home.⁷⁷

Sanidad's encounter with passionate Methodist revival preaching left an indelible mark in his life. He later ended up studying in Presbyterian institutions in the United States and was ordained by the Chicago Presbytery

---

73. *PIAC* (1916), 61–62
74. *PIAC* (1917), 65.
75. *PIAC* (1912), 59.
76. *PIAC* (1912), 49.
77. Quoted in Laubach, *Seven Thousand Emeralds*, 133–34.

of the Presbyterian Church. He returned to the Philippines in 1922 to serve as a student evangelist in Cebu.[78]

In 1912, in the province of Pangasinan, returning seminarian Roman Calica's revivals in Rosales Town were so effective that, even "Eugenio Caretativo, a backslidden exhorter was so revived that he called in some of the brethren to help him eat his fighting rooster. This matter was brought up at the District Conference. I informed our preachers that there was no rule in our Discipline which forbids eating fighting roosters," Peterson testified.[79] In 1916, in Paniqui District in the Ilocano-speaking part of Tarlac Province, pioneer Filipino Superintendent Lorenzo Tamayo exclaimed: "There has been a hallelujah time in most places, as the souls have been redeemed and the lives of our members have been renewed and become strong by the power of the Holy Spirit."[80] By 1918, this holiness revival work had also become so prevalent in Cagayan Province that one WFMS missionary reported that some officials informed her that "the revival spirit of our workers has changed the moral standing in some towns."[81]

Aside from their prevalence in the provinces, the same "revival spirit" was not without evidence among Filipino ministers in the nation's capital and its neighboring towns. Although Superintendent Klinefelter initially complained that preachers in the Manila District "take little interest in revival meetings, some even opposing them," he lauded seminarian Agaton Pascual for branching out from Marikina to the town of Taytay, located east of Manila, where he had "a sort of continuous revival all year, and a chapel site has been bought and a chapel is soon to be built."[82] The chapel at Taytay would later become the nexus of a Pentecostal schism in 1954, as we will demonstrate in chapter 6. The following year, Klinefelter's efforts to encourage his pastors to engage more in revival work eventually paid off. "Most of our Pastors are definitely committed to revival work and those who have made it the big thing on their work bring the largest returns in all lines of church work," he reported.[83]

---

78. Ibid; Sitoy, *Several Springs*, 216.
79. *PIAC* (1913), 55.
80. *PIAC* (1916), 69.
81. *WCPIAC* (1918), 39.
82. *PIAC* (1915), 77.
83. *PIAC* (1916), 42.

Dionisio Alejandro and Other Asburians

Perhaps the most notable among the league of Filipino evangelists who blazed the trail with the holiness message was future bishop Dionisio Deista Alejandro (1893–1972). Alejandro's life illustrates not only the pervasive influence of Morrison in the dissemination of *culto* Pentecostalism, but also that of Cottingham's direct role in the transfer of American holiness thought to a number of Filipino preachers. In 1910 the Cabanatuan, Nueva Ecija, native formed bonds with the newly arrived Cottingham, for whom he worked as an interpreter. With Cottingham's help, the self-described "disciple" of the missionary eventually sailed for the United States in 1911 to study at Asbury College in Wilmore, Kentucky, under a program launched by Morrison, with Oldham's support, to educate "Filipino young men who were intending to enter the ministry."[84] Another Filipino who arrived together with Alejandro was Cornelio D. Julian, a local preacher from Sta. Maria, Ilocos Sur Province, who later "made a fine speech which elicited applause" at the National Holiness Convention in Cincinnati.[85] Although Alejandro had already been exposed to the message of "the baptism of the Holy Spirit and the deeper Christian experience" through earlier discussions with Cottingham,[86] it was not until during his final year at Asbury that Alejandro attested with clarity to what he called his "Canaan Land" experience. In his January 8, 1915, diary, Alejandro wrote:

> For some time I had walked in faith concerning my sanctification, but I had not the witness of the Spirit. This morning I went before Him in prayer, seeking to know His will concerning me. There was a deep consciousness that I was fully cleansed and that my poor heart was flooded with joy unspeakable, and full of glory. Amen! Glory to His name! Praise the Lord! I am sanctified![87]

Alejandro's sanctification eventually thrust him into holiness revival territory in a manner reminiscent to that of his American mentor. Upon returning in August 1915 and with an undergraduate degree in Philosophy,

---

84. Alejandro, "From Roman Catholicism," 36–37.

85. See *Asburian 1915 Yearbook*, 39. Julian stayed in the United States to pursue medicine, and then returned to his hometown in Sta. Maria, Ilocos Sur, as a physician. He was later elected lay delegate of the Philippine North Annual Conference to the 1940 General Conference. See *General Conference* (1940), 198.

86. Alejandro, "From Roman Catholicism," in Nee, *Voices from Many Lands*, 36–38.

87. Quoted in ibid., 38. It is also worth noting that while he had a definite date for his sanctification, Alejandro did not have one for his conversion. See page 27.

the twenty-two-year-old Alejandro was appointed district evangelist for Cottingham's Central District, where he began conducting "successful revivals" in a number of towns in Nueva Ecija.[88] It was also about this time that he translated Morrison's seminal work, *The Baptism with the Holy Ghost* (1900). By 1920, Alejandro had quickly risen through the ranks to become the editor of the Tagalog monthly *Mabuting Balita* and an instructor at Union Theological Seminary, Manila, (hereafter UTS), and in 1924 pastor of the English speaking congregation of Knox Memorial MEC. That same year he was elected clergy delegate, along with Cottingham, to the General Conference in Springfield, Massachusetts. Among the impressions he had, it was the holiness part—the address of Evangeline Booth, the head of the Salvation Army—that he found to be most significant. Her plea for "a deeper Christian experience and higher life," Alejandro observed, "saved the conference from many a haggling and wrangling about non essentials."[89]

But despite Alejandro's buoyed-up hopes at the august body, troubles awaited him in Manila regarding the work of the District's Domestic Missions Board, which he headed. After experiencing unfair treatment at the hands of the newly installed Bishop Charles B. Mitchell, who was "very stern with him," and Ernest Lyons, his district superintendent, the promising minister eventually withdrew from the ministry. "In all the controversy I was not approached in the spirit of a brother, it was always paternalism instead of fraternalism," Alejandro complained. Cottingham, who sided with his former protégé, surmised that if his "real son" were the "same type of a man as was Nicolas Zamora, he could have taken most of the Tagalog pastors with him. He left quietly."[90] While Alejandro pursued a successful career in the Bureau of Education in Nueva Ecija, several attempts by Cottingham and others to draw him back would eventually bear fruit, albeit fourteen years later. At the 1939 Conference, just a month after Cottingham's death, this became a reality as Alejandro's former colleagues welcomed him back when he applied for readmission.[91] Five years later, at the height of the Japanese occupation, and as if indicative of his unrelenting popularity among them, they unanimously elected him bishop, thus making him the first Filipino MEC minister to be elected to such a position.

88. *PIAC* (1916), 61. See also *PIAC* (1917), 65.
89. Leete, *Methodist Bishops*, 12–13; *PO*, September 1924, 7.
90. Cottingham to Diffendorfer, 3 September, 20 October 1925, Cottingham, Joshua F., MFUMC.
91. See *PIAC* (1939), 32.

Even after his retirement, Alejandro continued to uphold the doctrine of sanctification, although with some qualifications, as we will demonstrate in the next chapter. In 1967, the retired bishop maintained: "It is therefore an important part of the divine economy of salvation that each believer should have his Pentecost; unless he does his Christian experience cannot very well be considered full and complete."[92]

Aside from Alejandro, there were also other Filipinos who went to Asbury and participated, to some varying degrees, in the spread of *culto Pentecostal* culture. Among them was Pedro B. Cruz (1885–1934), Cottingham's assistant in a number of Pentecostal meetings in the outskirts of Nueva Ecija in 1912,[93] who went to Asbury in 1916. After his sophomore year, Cruz transferred to northern California, where he ministered among Filipinos and in time completed his studies at the Pacific School of Religion in 1919. The Cabanatuan native later became the first Filipino Superintendent of the Manila District in 1930.[94] Nicolas C. Dizon also matriculated at the college in Wilmore, Kentucky, and completed his studies there in 1917.[95] Shortly after his return to Manila in 1920, after briefly ministering among Filipino plantation workers in Honolulu, Hawaii (1918–1919), the native of Orani, Bataan, began assuming the role of an evangelist by engaging on an extensive revival tour of churches mostly within Tagalog territory, essentially continuing the type of work pursued by Alejandro who had moved to Manila.[96] Dizon later became the pastor of Knox MEC beginning in 1921. He returned to Honolulu in 1924, where he later pioneered an independent Filipino church and became a staunch advocate for labor rights.[97]

Another Asburian was Eugenio Fernandez, a *balikbayan* (returned Filipino immigrant) who was converted while en route to the United States shortly after joining the Navy. After being discharged in 1923, he arrived in Wilmore just about the time a revival broke out from the town's Methodist church which eventually spread through the campus. Fernandez was sanctified with the help of Wilmore Methodists. Upon completion of his studies

---

92. See Alejandro, "The Holy Spirit," 71. Cf. Cunningham, *Holiness abroad*, 206. See also Alejandro and Valencia, *Episcopal Address*, 7.

93. *PO*, June 1913, 24.

94. *PO*, January 1934, 4. See also, *Asburian 1917 Yearbook*, 41.

95. *PO*, November 1920, 20. See also Alex Vergara, "Filipino Ministry in Hawaii," 25; *Asburian 1917 Yearbook*, 26, 30, 70.

96. *PO*, February 1921, 17–19.

97. *PIAC* (1921), 10; *PIAC* (1925), 90; Vergara, "Filipino Ministry in Hawaii," 154; *Honolulu Record*, 26 May 1949, 5.

in 1928, Fernandez returned and enlisted to work with the MEC in Pangasinan, where he later reported holding revivals. He was ordained in 1935.[98]

Female Assistants and Revivalists

WFMS missionaries, missionary wives, and Filipina deaconesses not only welcomed the spread of holiness revival culture during the period, but also served at its forefront in many ways. Filipina deaconesses, for example, reported helping in revivals as a general feature of their work in their *destino* (church assignment) right after they graduate from Harris.[99] But this type of work was not merely limited to their official assignments, as suggested by Pampanga Deaconess Mercedes Alabado's report in 1915:

> Candaba is my appointed destination, but most of the time I have been in other places assisting in revivals. Among these were Saligsig, San Vicente, Mexico, Talba, Magalang, and Arayat. In these places it was a joy to see many hearts turned to the Lord. Upon my return to Candaba I tried to give my people some of the inspiration that I have received. Then we started a revival in my own town, to which we invited Mr. Housley, Miss Thomas, Mr. Alabado, Mr. Sison, Sister Inocencia, and Brother de Ocera. The result of this special effort was 69 new members. Besides this the spirit of the Lord stirred up the hearts of the people throughout the whole community.[100]

Some deaconesses also served as interpreters for missionaries in the revivals[101] and, as Bishop Eveland suggested, proved to be better than men, like the pastor who did "fairly well" at a revival but could not get the results he wished. But then a "little deaconess" came to assist him. "She is little, if any, over five feet in height. She will weigh less than a hundred pounds. But she has the strength that cometh from God, and before she and the Lord had finished with that congregation, seventeen new-born souls had entered the Kingdom," Eveland gladly attested.[102] Similarly, it was the "linguist" Deaconess Victoria T. Santos who translated for Morrison before an

---

98. Fernandez, "On a Stormy Sea," 57–69; *PIAC* (1935), 36.
99. See *WMF*, June 1919, 206.
100. *WCPIAC* (1915), 32.
101. *WCPIAC* (1915), 30.
102. *WMF*, September 1914, 313–14.

audience of national workers and missionaries during the Annual Conference in Manila in 1910.[103]

While the young deaconesses proved to be indispensable helpmates for Filipino ministers and visiting missionary evangelists not familiar with the vernacular, it was mostly the women missionaries who provided the much-needed musical accompaniment to the meetings. This was the role mostly assumed by Bertha Cottingham during her husband's revival meetings. "We took the organ along with us and at almost every place held revival services, for one or two nights," she wrote.[104] In some instances, it was the sound of an organ playing that helped lure people into the nocturnal gatherings. For example, WFMS missionary Wilhelmina Erbst of the Minnesota Branch who assisted Filipino preachers in the Manila District testified: "I wish you could see these crowds coming through the moonlight from all directions to the little palm leaf tent out in a potato field or a rice plantation. They gather so closely about me and my little organ that I can scarcely breathe, but how they do sing and pray!"[105]

But while music was an integral part of the revivals that the missionary women skillfully took charge of, for some, however, their involvement continued even after the revivals. Central District worker Louise Stixrud, who came from the Minneapolis Branch of the WFMS, for instance, reported that when "Cottingham or Filipino preachers have a revival meeting at a place, soon after, Fidela [de Jesus] and I go and hold an institute there to teach the new members and strengthen them with the old ones in the faith."[106] But in this case what was supposed to be an institute paved the way for another responsibility rarely, if not vaguely, acknowledged in the official reports:

> At Guiguinto we arrived at six o'clock at night. We were tired and did not plan to hold a meeting the first night, but while we were unpacking our things the small hut filled up with people. They sat on the window sills and everywhere so we could hardly arrange ourselves. While we ate supper, I could not complain of being alone as thirty seven faces stared at every bite I ate. There was no way out, and we had to hold a meeting. So we opened our little organ and held our services with them.[107]

103. *WFMSAR* (1910), 137; Robledo, "Gender, Religion," 122.
104. *WCPIAC* (1915), 28.
105. *WCPIAC* (1912), 124.
106. *WCPIAC* (1917), 34.
107. Ibid., 34–35.

While Stixrud's account clearly illustrates that the presence of an *Americana* (American female) also helped attract people to their meetings perhaps out of curiosity, it also suggests that women's role in the revivals were not merely confined to supporting roles, but also involved preaching. Obviously, the fact that the Norwegian-born Stixrud and De Jesus held a service, although out of expediency, suggests that they preached. It is also important to point out that even though this was done in the absence of Filipino pastors and male missionaries, WFMS missionary evangelists often held revival meetings at the invitation of Filipino clergy and, most likely, with the sanction of the American district superintendent and even the bishop. In Baliuag, for example, where the new pastor "was about ready to pack his box and leave," Stixrud, who came with her colleague J. Edna Thomas of Pampanga, recalled: "Every night we had a revival meeting. The last Sunday we had a testimony meeting and I have never attended a better one. The pastor, local preachers and members were all blest and filled with the spirit of God."[108] The fact that Filipino ministers and local preachers were willing to entrust their spiritual uplift to these missionary women suggests that they had no problem accepting them as authority figures deserving some level of esteem.

Although the lack of details in Stixrud's report may still leave one wondering as to whether she really preached in revival meetings, a number of accounts sent by Philippine missionaries in the WFMS official monthly *Woman's Missionary Friend* and other periodicals support the fact it was not uncommon for WFMS missionaries, particularly those assigned to evangelistic work, to preach in the field, mostly in revivals. Erbst perfectly illustrates this when she held a revival at a remote station in Cagayan Valley in 1918:

> This was Sunday and people came to call on the missionary even before the seven-thirty service. The scene when we reached the little church compensated me for the hardships and the comforts of the previous day and night. The people had crowded into the church until there was not room for a single one more, and many outside peeping through the cracks of the woven bamboo.
>
> The eager faces were all the inspiration I needed, for it is easy to speak to hungry folks. I talked on the resurrection life, and the people responded to the gentle influence of the Holy Spirit. There was no room for an altar service, but every one knelt and, with all

---

108. *WCPIAC* (1917), 34.

those black heads bowed, the Bible woman poured out her heart in prayer.[109]

Culto Pentecostalism was neither a monopoly of the male missionary nor of the Filipino male evangelist, as Erbst's account suggests. At a time when MEC women in the United States were still not allowed to be licensed as local preachers,[110] their WFMS colleagues like Stixrud, Thomas, Erbst, and others were preaching without restrictions to both male and female audiences across the Pacific. While the rituals of *culto Pentecostal* proved liberating to the Filipinos who participated in them, they also helped accommodate the aspirations of the women who led them. Victorian norms of gender and denominationally prescribed limitations to women were suspended, if not lost, in a ritual which enabled its participants to submit to the will of the "Spirit" rather than to human conventions.

Unsurprisingly, Filipina deaconesses followed in the footsteps of their American mentors and the pioneer Filipina women preachers who blazed the trail before them, like Narcisa Dimagiba, pioneer preacher in Bulacan and Bataan who died in 1906 due to fatigue on a trip to the mountains to preach among the Aetas. She was generally welcomed as preacher in many churches, except in Malolos, where there were objections to female preaching.[111] Even as Victorian notions of domesticity were promulgated to fill the student life at Harris, it was the revival spirit, also promoted by their WFMS teachers that allowed its graduates to transcend Philippine gender mores that had long been Hispanicized. We need to be reminded that Filipino women in pre-Hispanic society had more social status, prominently as "ritual specialist with power to access and influence the spirits existing in nature," but this was eventually "reordered" by the friars to "conform to Hispanic Catholic norms."[112] Although such a role survived through folk religious practices for many years during the Spanish era, MEC *culto* Pentecostalism inadvertently lent institutional legitimacy to it by serving as a venue for Filipino women to become ritual specialists, but this time, with access to the one "Spirit" of the Christian Bible. Beyond the Bible woman "who poured out her heart" in Erbst's meeting, as mentioned earlier, or

---

109. *WMF*, November 1918, 383. For other examples of Erbst's preaching tours, see *PCA*, August 1910, 9–10.

110. It was not until 1920 that MEC women regained their right to be licensed as local preachers. See Schmidt, *Grace Sufficient*, 272–75.

111. *WCPIAC* (1906), 79–80. See also *PCA*, April 1906, 8.

112. Abinales and Amoroso, *State and Society*, 22, 58–59.

Fidela de Jesus taking prominent role in Stixrud's revival services, there were others who functioned as ritual specialists, but without the guidance of the missionary. The young Tita Umengan, for example, led worship and preached at the invitation of a town *presidente* and his wife during a pioneering mission at a town in Aparri Province in 1911.[113] Another deaconess also made this apparent in her account of a revival she helped lead with two other deaconesses in the summer of 1918. "We just came from a revival at . . . [name of place was omitted]. We were only three girls. We did our best even if it was a rainy time. We felt that the Holy Spirit was with us because the people gave their hearts to Christ, specially the members became stronger in their faith in Christ," she wrote.[114]

The Christmas Institute

The revival work of Filipina deaconesses illustrates how *culto Pentecostal* culture allowed Filipino women to break social conventions of their time and empowered young people for ministry. Philippine Methodism was in fact, for the most part, a youth movement during its first two decades in the country. However, it was only in the 1920s that the need to integrate a growing group of second generation Methodists became a growing concern. As a result, there was a move to ensure that Methodist youth, who had been born into the denomination or had been received as children, would be able to follow in the footsteps of their parents and be able to make personal faith decisions. Hence, it was no accident that Methodist youth ministry began much more intensified and institutionalized during the decade. A prime example of this was the launching of the Epworth League Christmas Institute (hereafter CI) in 1921.

The origins of the CI can be traced back to the first "Christmas Epworth League Institute" held for four days after the Christmas of 1921 in Sibul Springs, San Miguel, Bulacan. It was organized, as mentioned earlier, by missionary Joshua Cottingham, district superintendent of the Manila District, and was attended by sixty-two young people from Manila and the neighboring provinces of Bulacan, Nueva Ecija, Pampanga, Bataan and Zambales.[115] Sibul Springs, which was home to the historic Biak na Bato mountain caves, was already a designated vacation spot for Filipino MEC

113. Tita B. Umengan's letter as quoted in *WMF*, July 1912, 236.
114. Quoted in *PO*, September 1918, 11.
115. See *PIAC* (1922), 49.

workers and their families at that time. Although Cottingham specifically added the word "Christmas" to the name of the Institute in his first report, he, as well as others in 1921 and in the years that followed, also alternately called it the "Epworth League Institute" (hereafter ELI) as it was called in the United States.[116] In fact, there were already eighty-seven ELIs administered by the Epworth League in the American mainland by 1921. First begun in 1906, ELIs in the United States, unlike the ones in the Philippines, were typically held during summer.[117] To further discern the way ELIs developed in the Philippines, let us now probe deeper into Cottingham's description of the first CI:

> We often feel like challenging other fields to produce a finer, more eager and earnest group of young people than our own in the Philippines and never did we feel prouder than we recently did at the *first Epworth League Institute* at Sibul. Organized along the same lines as the great institutes at Lakeside [Lakeside, Ohio] and Geneva [Lake Geneva, Wisconsin], we journeyed to that beautiful resort for rest, study and prayer. Sixty-two students and workers were there. From the very beginning the Spirit of God was there in power. Hearts were melted and remade. Consecrations were deep and only eternity will show how lasting. There was recreation and rest but it was so consecrated that the presence of Jesus was manifest always. Sibul must be continued. We must have some rest houses and a chapel. Next year we should have no less than 150 of our young people there. Out of Sibul will come consecrated workers that will win these fair Islands to Christ.[118]

While the American ELI was obviously the main fountainhead of the Sibul Springs CI, it is worth noting that Cottingham cited the "great institutes at Lakeside and Geneva" as its inspirations. This was a reference to the renowned Chautauqua Institute in Lakeside, Ohio and the YMCA workers retreat and training camp in Lake Geneva, Wisconsin, both famous summer training retreats and popular spots for ELIs. The Chautauqua Institute in Lakeside was an outdoor center for training Sunday School teachers while the YMCA camp in Lake Geneva was a summer retreat and

---

116. *PIAC* (1922), 49. The Manila District comprised the greater Manila area including Bataan and Zambales. Central District (Bulacan and Nueva Ecija churches) and Pampanga District (Pampango speaking churches in Pampanga and Tarlac) were part of the Sibul Springs CI.

117. A brief history of the Epworth League Institute is found in Diffendorfer, *World Service*, 559–61.

118. *PIAC* (1922), 49.

educational facility for leadership training.[119] Thus, when Cottingham cited the two famous summer retreats as the templates for the first CI, he was in effect highlighting the successful interplay between nature and Christian youth formation back home, which he believed he was able to replicate at Sibul Springs. But as for the timing of the event, however, the first CI did deviate from its American counterparts. The much cooler breeze of December was obviously more idyllic than summertime for the CI's intended purpose of "recreation and rest," thereby giving it a unique Christmas twist in the Philippines. It was this same unique feature that also evidently led to the renaming of the ELI to CI by Philippine Methodists.

However, while Lakeside and Lake Geneva today scarcely represent their rich religious past, and ELIs had ceased to exist in the United States, it is interesting to note that the CI they helped inspire continues to persist as an integral part of Philippine Methodist life and culture today. One contributing factor to its persistence deserves our attention here—the "religion of the heart" or revivalistic nature of CI. This was very implicit in the following generalized descriptions of the first Sibul Springs CI made by Cottingham: "the Spirit of God was there in power," "hearts were melted and remade," "consecrations were deep," and "Jesus was manifest always." Likewise, at the Women's Conference held in parallel with the sessions of the Philippine Islands Annual Conference in 1922, Cottingham's wife, Bertha, gave a similar description, but with a few additional details:

> In the busy days after Christmas and just before Conference we went to Sibul for the first Epworth League Institute. So very full was our time that over and over we said, "This is one task too many." We did not see how another institute [in reference to Bible institutes] was possible this conference year. But duty called and we left all and went. What a time of joy and blessing those days were. There was not a single service or class that the presence of the Spirit was not there in power. Jesus indeed walked in our midst those days and the last day under the leadership of Bishop and Mrs. Locke many life decisions were made some of which are now being carried out in active Life Service.[120]

---

119. Lakeside and Lake Geneva were popular venues for ELIs. See Diffendorfer, *World Service*, 288–89. See also Schmitz and Flanders, *Chautauqua Institution*, 7; Smeltzer and Cucco, *Lake Geneva*, 77. For the most recent scholarly treatment on the beginnings of the Chautauqua movement, see Rieser, *Chautauqua Moment*, chap. 1.

120. *WCPIAC* (1922), 15.

Hence, from its inception, the CI was already a setting for the revival or renewal of Methodist young people. It is not difficult to see this in light of the prevalence of revivals within Methodism during its early years in the Philippines. Accordingly, the CI can also be understood as one of the ways Philippine Methodists extended and institutionalized this revival culture among their young people. The CI was to serve as a venue for Methodist youth to experience conversion or to publicly profess faith in Jesus Christ, just like their parents before them, and to consecrate their lives to God by becoming pastors or deaconesses. These public professions of conversion or consecration to the ministry took place in the nightly evangelistic meetings and in the climactic consecration service during the last day of the institute. Many Filipino workers who became pastors and deaconesses in the years that followed trace their first public profession to enter the ministry at the altar calls of CI. For example, referring to the first CI in 1921, Central District Superintendent Arthur Beckendorf, also a favorite speaker in the CIs, noted how Gerardo Samson, a young supervising teacher from Bulacan, "dedicated himself" to "active Christian service" during the Sunday consecration service.[121] The revival rituals of the CI not only proved to be central to its early attendees, but also helped insure its growth and vitality.

Hence, given the success of the 1921 CI, the Conference Committee on Sunday School and Epworth Leagues recommended: "We rejoice in the success of the first Epworth League Institute as recently held at Sibul Springs, and recommend that it become an annual affair, embracing other leagues of the Conference as well as those in and near Manila."[122] The recommendation was eventually heeded and, thus, three years later the second CI was born—the North Central Luzon ELI—which was held in Lingayen, Pangasinan from December 19-23, 1924.[123] Other districts followed suit in the ensuing years. The five-day gathering still persists to this day as a quasi Chautauqua-holiness revival event for Filipino United Methodist youth throughout the country and for the Filipino diaspora in the United States.[124]

---

121. *PIAC* (1922), 42. Conference records in the immediate years beyond 1922 do not indicate that Gerardo Samson became a pastor.

122. *PIAC* (1922), 63.

123. *PIAC* (1925), 57.

124. For a brief history of the Christmas Institute in the United States, see for example, Pacific Northwest Christmas Institute Web site, "CI-PNW History," http://www.ci-pnw.org/history.html (accessed January 7, 2016).

From Crusade Against Sin to Crusade Against Social Evils

In addition to youth work, the influence of *culto Pentecostal* also found expression through the official pronouncements of the denomination. This fact is substantiated by annual conference reports from 1911 to 1924, which either celebrated the rise of revivalism and a marked advance in holiness and deepening spirituality among Filipino Methodists, or addressed the need for the church to further engage in revivals, rid its ranks of immorality, and condemn perceived public "evils" such as cockfighting and other forms of gambling, liquor saloons, tobacco use, dance halls, boxing, prostitution, and the heavily-disdained *cine* (movie theater). These themes are repeated so often in the numerous reports of both missionaries and Filipinos, as articulated in the district reports or committee resolutions, that one can scarcely doubt their importance not only in discerning the warp and woof of Philippine Methodist life, but also in understanding Filipino Methodist self-perception and aspirations in light of rapid social change under American colonial rule.

Among the many reports during the annual conferences, the ones presented by the Committee on the "State of the Church"—tasked with diagnosing or summarizing the general condition of the church on an annual basis—best evince these recurring motifs and serve to provide a preview of the place and function of holiness promotion and Holy Spirit-themed revivalism during the period. In its 1911 report, a year after Morrison's visit, the Committee acknowledged that "revival is coming out of the experimental stage" and beginning to occupy a "definite and all important place" in the life of the church.[125] In 1912, the Committee noted that "many hearts have been cleansed as shown by the outward signs. Many have left the gambling table, the cock-pit, the drink, and the cigarette, for the Master's sake."[126] The following year, the Committee wrote that "evangelistic methods which have brought good results in the States, bring equally good results here," and that "our preachers are cleaner, and the members of the church have given up their vices for the better life."[127] Similarly, the 1916 Committee observed that "each year marks an advance in holiness" while reiterating the need for

---

125. *PIAC* (1911), 77.
126. *PIAC* (1912), 80.
127. *PIAC* (1913), 91.

preachers to "be sure of their own spiritual experience, in order that they may lead the people into deeper waters."[128]

By 1917, more than four months after President Woodrow Wilson signed the Jones Law into effect, which cleared the path for Philippine independence and pushed for further "Filipinization" of the colonial government, including the establishment of the Philippine Senate and House of Representatives, the Committee similarly encouraged "Filipinization" of revivals while attuning them to indigenous conditions. It recommended that each pastor should "be his own revivalist" and that local churches should "specially set apart" a month each year for revival meetings, preferably during dry seasons.[129] Two years afterwards, as the Committee acknowledged that "deeper spiritual life is found everywhere," it not only asserted the need to further address "deeply rooted sins," promote "family altars," and conduct "children's revivals," but also called for unity against "all evils menacing to public welfare."[130] In 1921, a shift was beginning to take shape as the Committee began to direct its attention from a crusade against sin among MEC constituents to a crusade against social evils. Even as it rejoiced that the church stood "stronger and purer," the Committee called on it to channel such character in the public sphere by dethroning "king Alcohol" and "stamping out other vices."[131]

Consequently, Filipino Methodists in the public sphere responded to the call for a crusade against social evils. Chief among them was Justo Lukban (1863–1927), mayor of Manila from 1917–1920. A staunch Methodist and member of the committee that helped raised funds for the construction of Mary Johnston Hospital in 1909, Lukban had stood for "the cleanest city possible," according to Manila District Superintendent Marvin Rader. Lukban curbed down the operation of dance halls to only once a month from 7:30 to 10:00 in the evening. He also tried to curtail cockfighting by imposing higher taxes but was prevented by the city council. But what helped Lukban gain the admiration of his fellow Methodists was his uncompromising, yet controversial, approach to prostitution. From October 16–25, 1918, he had the police round up about 170 women of "ill repute" from the city's red light

---

128. *PIAC* (1916), 101.

129. *PIAC* (1917), 100. For additional details on the Jones law and its relationship with "Filipinization," see Abinales and Amoroso, *State and Society*, 140–41.

130. *PIAC* (1919), 85. The restoration of "family altars" was one the aims for the "propagation of holiness in the General Church," as mentioned by Methodist Holiness evangelist E. S. Dunham at the National Holiness Convention in Denver in 1914. See Dunham, "Propagation of Holiness," 3.

131. *PIAC* (1921), 68.

district in Gardenia Street in Sampaloc. Then, he had them hustled into two coastguard steamboats, and shipped to Davao in the Island of Mindanao, supposedly with the intention of providing them employment in hemp farms. While Rader conceded that the move was "a little drastic," he, nevertheless, expressed support for the mayor's move since it "meant freedom of the girls from a life of slavery and vice, and a chance to start life anew."[132] Yet the press and the public saw it differently. The consequent uproar eventually reached the Supreme Court through the landmark case, Villavicencio vs. Lukban. While the country's highest court ruled that the mayor acted in "good faith," and only with the intention of "protecting the immense majority of the population from the social evils and diseases" brought about by the illicit trade, it, nevertheless, ordered him to return the women to their homes. Additionally, the court found him guilty of contempt and slapped him with a "nominal fine" of 100 pesos for failing to comply with the writ of *habeas corpus* it earlier issued to have the women returned to Manila.[133]

Another Methodist to carry such moralizing impulse was Miguel Binag, the representative of Isabela Province in the fifth Philippine Legislature. In 1922, he introduced a bill that would abolish cockfighting in the country. Binag, who was also the brother of Pastor Ambrosio Binag and a member of Ilagan MEC, was presented by Bishop Locke and allowed to speak about his bill during the annual conference that same year. Prior to his presentation, the conference, upon motion by Cottingham, had already passed a resolution to give the junior lawmaker's bill its "heartiest support and approval."[134] It can be assumed that Congress did not pass the bill as cockfighting persists to this day. This, nevertheless, did not deter another prominent Methodist to launch a crusade against the sport and other forms of vice in his province. Pio Valenzuela, the governor of Bulacan, who Cottingham called the "anti-gambling, anti-vice, good roads governor" in 1924, was known for his "strong aversion" to gambling, including *jueteng*, a widely popular illegal numbers game in the Philippines. During his second term he waged a campaign to rid the province of vice by ordering the constabulary to conduct raids on gambling joints and the arrest of local *jueteng* operators.[135]

---

132. *PO*, January 1919, 2.

133. Ibid., 2–3; Laubach, *People of the Philippines*, 408–9; Zacarias Villavicencio et al. v. Justo Lukban et al., G. R. No. L-14639 (Republic of the Philippines Supreme Court 1919).

134. *PIAC* (1920), 47; *PIAC* (1922), 26, 30, 68.

135. *PIAC* (1924), 43; Crisostomo, *Dr. Pio Valenzuela*, 238.

Figure 4.1. Bishop William Perry Eveland, MEC missionary bishop of Southern Asia, 1912. Bishop Eveland was the first MEC bishop appointed to solely administer MEC work in the Philippines and reside in Manila. Source: Drew University Methodist Library, Madison, New Jersey.

Figure 4.2. Philippine Islands Annual Conference, First MEC, Vigan, Ilocos Sur, January 20–25, 1914: (first row seated, left to right) Benito Tovera, Ubaldo Nacpil, Roman Calica, Severino Cordero, Felipe Marquez, Estanislao Guerrero, Servillano Castro, Catalino Santos; (second row seated, left to right) Candido Magno, Filomeno Galang, Arthur Chenoweth, Harry Farmer, Bishop William Eveland, Oscar Huddleston, Alba Snyder, Daniel Klinefelter; (third row standing, left to right) Charles Bernhardt, Catalino Guansing, Gregorio Curament, Julian Santos, Edwin Lee, Marvin Rader, Berndt Peterson, Balbino Gatdula, Juan Macaspac; (fourth row standing, left to right) Cirilo Casiguran, Domingo Reyes, Charles Koehler, Pedro Cruz, Melecio de Armas, Santos Beley, Mauricio Loria, Felix Cruz, Pedro Sison, Arcadio de Ocera. Source: The United Methodist Church Archives—GCAH, Madison, New Jersey. Mission Photograph Albums—Philippines #2, 105.

Figure 4.3. District Superintendent Joshua F. Cottingham preaching before a gathering of Methodist workers from Central District, Malolos, Bulacan, c. 1916–17: (seated behind, left to right) Dionisio D. Alejandro, Victorino Jorda, unidentified. Source: The United Methodist Church Archives—GCAH, Madison, New Jersey. Mission Photograph Albums—Philippines #3, 39.

Figure 4.4. Arthur L. Beckendorf, missionary in charge of Nueva Ecija, with his wife, Maud, and their son Robert, 1917. Source: The United Methodist Church Archives—GCAH, Madison, New Jersey. Mission Photograph Albums—Philippines #3, 77.

Figure 4.5. Filipino Methodist Pentecostal meetings based from accounts described in this chapter. Illustrations by Pol Galvez.

Figure 4.6. Joseph Clemens is shown and his wife, Mary Knapp Strong Clemens, at the New York Botanical Garden, c. 1920s. A former United States Army Chaplain, Clemens was appointed conference evangelist in 1923. By the end of his evangelistic career in the Philippines in 1929, it was estimated that he had baptized more than 16,000 people. Source: Smithsonian Institution Archives. Image # SIA2008-0146.

Figure 4.7. Dionisio D. Alejandro, senior bachelor of philosophy student, Asbury College, Wilmore, Kentucky, 1914. Source: Archives and Special Collections, Asbury University, Wilmore, Kentucky.

Figure 4.8. The first Filipino graduates of Asbury College: (top, left to right) Cornelio D. Juan, and Dionisio D. Alejandro (class of 1915); (bottom) Nicolas C. Dizon (class of 1917). After Henry Clay Morrison's visit to Manila, Dionisio Alejandro and Cornelio Juan began their studies at Asbury in the fall of 1911. Two years later, Nicolas Dizon followed them. Source: Archives and Special Collections, Asbury University, Wilmore, Kentucky.

Figure 4.9. Wilhelmina Erbst, missionary in charge of WFMS work in Cagayan Province, on a Philippine pony. Erbst was one of the few WFMS missionaries who functioned as a revivalist, preaching without restrictions to both male and female audiences. Source: The United Methodist Church Archives—GCAH, Madison, New Jersey. Mission Photograph Albums—Philippines #3, 193.

Figure 4.10. Central District women workers, Central District Conference, Bulacan, Bulacan, 1915: (standing, left to right) Inez Godoy, Bertha Cottingham, Consuela (Garcia) Alejandro, Fidela (Gatdula) de Jesus; (seated, left to right) Flora Galang, Leona Marcelino, Vicenta Jorda. Source: The United Methodist Church Archives—GCAH, Madison, New Jersey. Mission Photograph Albums—Philippines #3, 111.

Figure 4.11. Epworth League Christmas Institute, Vigan, Ilocos Sur, December 26, 1927–January 1, 1928. Source: The United Methodist Church Archives—GCAH, Madison, New Jersey. Mission Photograph Albums—Philippines #4, 45.

Figure 4.12. Knox Memorial MEC prohibition sign, Manila, c. 1920s. It states: "Liquor wastes food, men, money. Liquor increases crime, poverty, sickness. The Philippine Islands need prohibition." Source: The United Methodist Church Archives—GCAH, Madison, New Jersey. Mission Photograph Albums—Philippines #3, 177.

5

Refinement, Moral Crusades, and Schism, 1925–1933

> What we are looking for are missionaries who are Spirit filled at all times, if a missionary cannot keep a lap ahead of us in Christian living there is no place for him in the Islands.
>
> —A Filipino pastor, quoted in *WCPIAC* (1931)

Period of Methodist Refinement

Pentecostal revivalism continued to remain a main feature of MEC life and culture in the Philippines in the years following its first twenty five years, even as the country's socio-economic landscape was rapidly evolving under American rule. The revivalism developed during Bishops William P. Eveland and Charles E. Locke's terms (1912–1924), as we have seen earlier, continued to enjoy similar status even during the tumultuous term of the controversial Bishop Charles Bayard Mitchell (1924–1928),[1] and under Bishop Edwin F. Lee's watch (1928–1941). While the beginning of the period saw MEC membership swell to about sixty-one thousand,[2] it also marked a decrease in the annual average number of missionaries as the Great Depression took its toll on the American economy—from thirteen in 1925 to a mere six in 1933. Of the twelve missionaries who worked among Filipinos and had significant presence during the period, there remained five veterans, Joshua F. Cottingham, Archie L. Ryan, Arthur L. Beckendorf, Berndt O. Peterson, and Rex R. Moe, who continued to support or promote,

---

1. See summary of Mitchell's speech during the 1926 Conference in *PIAC* (1926), 9. A similar tone from the bishop a year afterward was also hinted at in *PIAC* (1927), 65.

2. This is a fairly accurate estimate as substantiated in Bibay, "Membership and Statistical Records," 52–53.

to a lesser degree, *culto Pentecostal* culture within their charges.³ Moe left the field permanently in 1929. Beckendorf followed a year later, and Ryan, who became president of UTS, remained until his recall in 1932. For his part, Peterson, the second most senior MEC missionary, persistently promoted the same emphasis. In 1930, for instance, he reported that his district had a "unanimous desire to make the new Conference year Pentecostal in working and witnessing for Christ."⁴ That same year he underscored its importance by arguing in an article in the MEC monthly *Philippine Observer* that "sociologists state that the most important problem among all people is getting along with one another. Pentecostal baptism of the Holy Spirit solves that problem when that experience is maintained in the daily life."⁵

Cottingham, who arrived from furlough in 1925, was not in his usual revivalist mode, as he found much of his time consumed by other responsibilities during the first half of the period. Aside from serving as Superintendent of the Manila District from 1926 to 1929, he was also chair of the Tagalog Bible Revision Committee of the ABS and taught Greek at UTS.⁶ It was not until after he was appointed conference evangelist in 1930 that he began to resume *culto Pentecostal* duties, mostly headlining in special district workers's gatherings throughout the Conference. For example, in Tuguegarao, Filipino Superintendent Benito S. Tovera described the altar scene in a meeting led by the charismatic missionary: "We yearned for the rebaptism of our souls by His divine and majestic power . . . We are glad to report that the yearnings of our souls have been answered. The natural self was filled by the Spirit of God."⁷ Cottingham was back to his old self. It was also while serving in this capacity that he would influence the young Ruben Candelaria, of whom more will be said in the next chapter.

While Cottingham and other senior missionaries, continued to promote *culto Pentecostal* revivals, it was, however, different for the newly arrived missionaries. Despite their participation in the MEC's revivalistic assault on "sin," they seem to have departed from the Pentecost lingua franca

---

3. For an example of Ryan and Beckendorf's revivalism, see *PIAC* (1925), 37.

4. *PIAC* (1930), 63.

5. *PO*, June 1930, 5.

6. See Del Rosario, "Schism," 635–36.

7. *PIAC* (1932), 52. Other examples include, *PIAC* (1932), 54; *PIAC* (1932), 65. Cottingham also figured at a consecration service of the Manila District Christmas Institute in 1929. See *PO*, February 1930, 7.

of their predecessors, perhaps indicative of the changing face, or at least refinement, of Protestant mainline evangelical culture in the United States.

Samuel Stagg: A New Breed of Revivalist

Samuel Wells Stagg (1897–1956), Wesley Foundation (student work) director, clearly epitomized the shift after his arrival in 1923 as he began work as a youth evangelist by conducting mass meetings in Manila and in the provinces.[8] For instance, in a six-day campaign in Ilocos District in 1924, District Superintendent Joseph W. Moore wrote that his preaching "was winning, convincing and full of the power of the spirit of Christ, and hundreds of young people flocked into the open-air pavilion to hear him."[9] In another occasion, and this time preaching to a more mature audience at a revival meeting in Laoac, Pangasinan, on September 20, 1924, he recounted: "On the evening of the twentieth, the members presented themselves at the altar. They cried to God for victory and power, and God as he always does, heard their supplications and filled each and every one waiting heart. God laid a burden on every one for lost souls."[10]

While Stagg's revival work looks very similar to that of his senior colleagues, his brand of evangelism quickly took a different turn as his meteoric popularity catapulted him to the editorship of the *Philippine Observer* and to Central Student Church that same year. Central at that time had been home to a number of prominent professionals, academics, and students, or in the words of Otto Houser, his predecessor, "where Christian Senators and Representatives and perhaps future Presidents are being made."[11] Accordingly, Stagg did not disappoint with his thought-provoking "sermon for thinkers,"[12] winsome charisma, and unyielding evangelistic zeal. Hence, Central's membership quickly swelled to more than twelve hundred by 1929, thereby necessitating the construction of a twelve hundred-seat Gothic style cathedral. Designed by famous architect Juan M. Arellano, the

---

8. A brief biography of Stagg is found in Del Rosario, "Schism," 331–33. Certain elements in his life can be inferred from a "historical fiction" by his daughter, Mary R. Webb, *Not My Will*.

9. *PIAC* (1925), 43.

10. *PO*, November 1924, 27.

11. See Houser to Donohugh, 9 August 1920, Houser, Otto H. (Rev. & Mrs.), MFUMC.

12. See Central Student Church advertisement in *PO*, November 1924, 27.

building featured a proportionately long nave, a high-arched roof, and a choir gallery at the back of the chancel that can seat 108 choristers. It was dedicated on June 19, 1932.[13] Central Student's new building at the center of the nation's capital signaled, not only the birth of Main Street Methodism in the Philippines, but also Philippine Methodism's impressive rise from its working class roots to a church that caters to those in the upper echelons of society. Thus, given the type of audience he ministered to at Central, it is not hard to discern why Stagg's evangelical preaching was more respectable.

Despite the formative influence of YMCA revivalism, which led him to respond to the call to ministry while studying at the University of Southern California, and his involvement with the SVM,[14] Stagg's preaching did not carry the same Pentecostal motif that was promoted by his senior colleagues. A case in point was his sermon "The Rewards of Purity," where he counseled his young audience at Central:

> We keep in spiritual condition by a daily walk with Jesus Christ. He is the source of all our power. We can never be defeated when He is back of us.
>
> If you would claim the rewards of purity, cultivate Christ's presence. Practice the presence of God daily. When evil temptations sweep menacingly down upon you, flee from them and take refuge in the presence of Jesus. Evil dare not come nigh Him. Sin flees from the pure presence of Christ as darkness flees before the coming of dawn. "KEEP THYSELF PURE!"[15]

Stagg's view of holiness comes with a tinge of Keswick suppressionist view, but minus the assent to pneumatological language. Rather than advocating the indwelling presence of the Holy Spirit as an antidote to sin as we have seen in the *culto Pentecostal* revivals, Stagg proposed that the constant "presence of Jesus," or in other words, Jesus's spiritual presence, would enable one to live in purity. His articulation of holiness may not only be a reflection of the growing impact of a christocentric evangelical liberalism upon American Protestant culture, as seen, for example, in the Social Gospel movement,[16] but also the waning influence of Pentecost-themed

---

13. See *PIAC* (1929); *PO*, June 1932, 2; *PO*, July 1932, 10–11.

14. Stagg admitted to John Mott that he was "led into the ministry" through the YMCA. See Stagg to Mott, 10 June 1925, Stagg, Samuel Wells (Rev. & Mrs.), 1922–1933, Folder 1, MFUMC. He is also listed as a "sailed" volunteer in Stauffer, *Christian Students and World Problems*, 500.

15. Samuel W. Stagg, *Ideal Woman*, 62–63.

16. See Dorrien, *Making of American Liberal Theology*, 547–48.

spirituality in the American Methodist vernacular during the period. Nevertheless, in spite of the refinement of Stagg's holiness message, his social commentaries were still very much coherent with the moral crusade of the denomination. To illustrate, he clearly manifested this in the essay, "A Needed Moral Crusade: Shall Manila Have a Red Light District?," where he vehemently opposed the legalization of prostitution as well as the designation of a red light district in Manila. "I ask you a serious question—Can a city or a nation expect the continued blessings of Almighty God if it legally recognizes that which it knows to be sin? God's command is unmistakably clear. 'Thou shalt not commit adultery.' Can a people turn its back deliberately upon the commandments of God and escape suffering[?] O my friends, my Filipino friends!," Stagg reasoned.[17]

While it would be futile to fully present and assess Stagg's spiritual ideology here, other evidences further highlight his differences with the veteran missionaries. In 1928, for instance, Stagg protested when Ryan, who was UTS president, enforced a resolution requiring the faculty to sign a statement on orthodoxy, which was clearly an attempt to define the seminary's stand on the Fundamentalist-Modernist divide of the 1920s.[18] In another sermon, he argued that "a man can believe in evolution even of the Darwinian type and still be a devout Christian."[19] Likewise, in an article in the *Observer* in 1924, Stagg Christianized Charles Darwin's law of natural selection by arguing that Jesus taught of the spiritual life to be evolving or "growing and developing," and taking place "in response to new factors in [the] environment."[20] Surely, Stagg carried a more sophisticated, if not progressive, version of evangelicalism than that of his senior colleagues, which endeared him even more to the intellectual elites at Central Student Church. This context, as well as a complex web of other issues, would set the stage for the "Stagg Schism" in 1933, which we will outline in another section. While Stagg deviated from his older colleagues, female missionary evangelists and Filipino pastors, in addition to Cottingham, kept the *culto Pentecostal* flame alive during the same period.

---

17. *PO*, August 1924, 19.

18. See Del Rosario, "Schism," 347–55. For a study on the rise of American Fundamentalism and the resultant Fundamentalist-Modernist controversy, see, for example, Marsden, *Fundamentalism*, part 3.

19. Stagg, *Ideal Woman*, 117.

20. *PO*, December 1924, 18.

WFMS Revivalists and Filipino Preachers Keep the Fire Burning

The newly arrived WFMS evangelists, undeniably, breathed more life into *culto Pentecostal* culture than their male counterparts. The holiness thrust of the annual Junior League Institutes held for Filipino women workers seemed to best establish this point. Mary A. Klinefelter of the Central and Cabanatuan districts, for example, who attested to the "indwelling of the Spirit" as one of the "essential doctrines of the Christian Church,"[21] helped transform one Institute in Solano, Nueva Vizcaya, in 1925 as an occasion for holiness-themed revivalism. "Several addicted to chewing betel-nut and smoking had determined, God helping them, to quit these habits and requested our prayers," testified Klinefelter.[22] Leila V. Dingle (1897–1989), who prominently engaged in revival work among students in the Tarlac District,[23] also contributed to the Pentecost tone of the Institutes in her stations. For instance, after preaching on "how to live the Spirit-filled life" during a series of morning devotions at the Institute in 1930, an impromptu Pentecostal service culminated the event. She reported: "Many of the workers were hungry for more 'power,' more 'strength to overcome temptations' etc., and as we met about an improvised altar the Holy Spirit Himself talked to their hearts and satisfied their desires, and many of their letters since then have testified that the joy and the Presence 'lasts'!"[24] Incidentally, what Dingle helped inspire in the north, Hazel Davis also stirred in Central Luzon. Summarizing the two Institutes she helped organize in Bulacan and Nueva Ecija that same year, she recollected:

> Most of the attendants are nominal Christians but with little or no knowledge of the inward witness of the Spirit. The altar services that followed were times of earnest seeking for newness of life through faith in Christ. Some of the girls had many sins to be forgiven, some fewer sins, but all voluntarily came forward for spiritual help. One woman received new light on some little sins of which she had been guilty. She did not receive the Lord's blessing until she confessed her need and yielded herself completely to God. Their simple faith, their tears, their earnest pleading in prayer, shall always be sacred memories.[25]

21. Klinefelter to Johnson, 30 June 1922, Klinefelter, Mary Anna, MBUMC.
22. *WCPIAC* (1926), 22.
23. See, for example, *PIAC* (1932), 60.
24. *WCPIAC* (1931), 28.
25. Ibid., 30.

Besides the holiness revival emphasis of the newly arrived WFMS reinforcements, the nationals also stepped up to keep MEC *culto Pentecostal* culture alive. We should remember that even as male missionary contribution decreased, Filipinos, who had been influenced or exposed to Pentecost or holiness-themed revivalism years earlier, were already in leadership positions and, thereby, accounted for its continued existence during the period. This was best exemplified by the leadership provided by Filipino district superintendents who, like their American predecessors, kept the culture alive in a myriad ways in their respective fields. In 1927, for example, Superintendent Severino Cordero, after calling upon his pastors to begin the year with a "spiritual revival," facilitated "nine consecutive pentecostal meetings and through our going six times to pray in the secluded places of the hills." "I am confident in assuring you and in bearing witness that during those moments the anointing of the Spirit fell upon our souls, when we had acknowledged with abundant tears our many short-comings in the service entrusted to us," he added.[26] Esteban T. Cruz (1890–1975), who worked under Cottingham in the Central District, also did not waste a moment to promote "the great need for the baptism of the Holy Spirit" among his constituencies after assuming the highest post in his district in 1930.[27] The following year, the new superintendent did not detract from his original emphasis, and together with his co-workers "reached a conclusion that Central District needed the baptism of the Holy Spirit, which baptism ought to be full and dominant in the life and soul of every believer, most especially our workers."[28]

Correspondingly, this was also the disposition in nearby Pampanga Province where Arcadio de Ocera and his co-workers passed a resolution that "after the Annual Conference we would set aside 30 nights for revivals in the whole district just for church members." "In this revival, we will do our best to reach all the backsliders and unconverted members," explained Ocera. But such revivalism came with an added feature unlike anything seen before, mirroring the marriage between heart religion and church doctrine and polity when the esteemed leader added: "During this pentecostal service, we will teach the members the 25 articles of religion and the

---

26. *PIAC* (1927), 43.
27. *PIAC* (1931), 49.
28. *PIAC* (1932), 65.

polity of the church. Thus, they may have not only a genuine conversion to the Lord but also an intelligent understanding of our church discipline."[29]

Aside from the Filipino superintendents, the prevalence of Pentecost-themed revivalism would also find expression beyond the altar. One girl in Ilocos Sur in 1929, for instance, led four people to be "baptized with the Holy Spirit thru her definite work."[30] The culture also took a life of its own and sometimes expressed a degree of supernaturalism which competed with local folk religiosity. A case in point was that of a Vigan Junior League girl who embarrassed a so-called "witch doctor" who was trying to drive away "spirits" from an ill Methodist girl. She pressed her way through the crowd and "laid her hand on the almost-crazy girl," praying for her until she calmed down, but not without stirring resentment from the "old men."[31] Surely, it would not be far fetched to imagine that the prevalence of *culto Pentecostal* culture in the warp and woof of early Philippine MEC life helped create the seedbed for supernaturalistic tendencies or for beliefs in the miraculous like divine healing to emerge, even though not necessarily promoted, especially among those belonging to the grassroots level of the denomination.

Filipino pastors also persisted in the dissemination of holiness revival piety. In Pangasinan, veteran missionary Brendt Peterson's account of a revival initiated by an unnamed pastor in 1930 showed that nothing much has changed in terms of the shape and content of *culto Pentecostal* revivalism, which still produced results not dissimilar from the ones which we have already dissected in detail in the previous chapter:

> The pastor had preached night after night with great power. The call for prayer was made. The pastor urged definite appeals for personal repentance from all sin. Prayers of repentance with weeping and moaning everywhere. Gradually the subjective appeal was changed to that of intercession for others. The pastor went among the kneeling people urging definiteness in their search for an experience of God in their lives. And then something happened. I can not explain it. I was kneeling too with the rest. Another missionary was in another room. Many were praying and praising God. Now one sensed that realization and victory were everywhere. As we were coming away from the meeting I asked my fellow missionary if he had noted anything peculiar. "Did I, I should say I did.

29. *PIAC* (1933), 54.
30. *WCPIAC* (1930), 22–23.
31. Ibid., 21–22.

That was the genuine thing tonight." I think permanent records of that meeting were made in heaven. The practical results were seen in the lives of those people who had been in the meetings,—the putting away of bad habits and overcoming of harmful attitudes. There was a willingness to serve uncomplainingly in difficult situations and tasks.[32]

While the character and results of *culto* Pentecostalism, as illustrated in this example, have been very much unchanged after more than twenty years since it was introduced in the Philippines, what makes this account quite unique, however, is the reversal of roles in the revival narrative. The missionary, in this case, had become the recipient of revival instead of the one leading the revival. Unlike his colleague who was in another room, Peterson was so moved by the preaching of the Filipino preacher that he ended up kneeling at the altar along with the others. What happened to Peterson that evening shows how *culto Pentecostal* revivals not only have become venues showcasing this reversal of roles, but also the coming of age of Filipino preachers in their ability to lead revival meetings.

But it was not only the Filipino preacher that has vastly evolved during the period. The vision for society of Methodists like Mayor Lukban, Governor Valenzuela, and Congressman Binag, who we have mentioned in the previous chapter, have now been carried on by a new breed of Filipino Methodists in the public square. These new voices have not only exemplified the brand of morality that was pervasive in the fabric of Filipino Methodist culture, but also expanded their discourse and actions to include aspirations for the independence of the Philippines and deep concern for the welfare of the Filipino people. Most notable among them was Jorge Bocobo, the fifth president of the University of the Philippines (hereafter UP).

Jorge Bocobo: A Moral Voice for the Era

Jorge Cleofas Bocobo (1886-1965) was born on October 9, 1886, to a *principalía* family in Gerona, Tarlac, who joined the Aglipayan Movement when it broke out in that region.[33] He later converted to Methodism, under the ministry of Felipe Marquez, his "father in the faith," most likely in 1902 when the highly esteemed minister was stationed in Gerona.[34] We have ear-

32. *PO*, June 1930, 5.
33. Olivar, *Aristocracy of the Mind*, 37.
34. See *PDIC* (1900-1902), 57; *PDIC* (1903), 6; *PDIC* (1904), 35; *PO*, March 1934, 5.

lier noted in chapter 2 that many of those who joined Methodism in northern Tarlac came from this movement, and the young Bocobo was among them. A year later, Bocobo left with the first batch of one hundred bright young Filipino *pensionados* (government scholars) to the United States. He went on to study law at Indiana University in Bloomington, where he graduated in 1907. The same year, after returning to the Philippines, Bocobo became a member of the Central Student Church in Manila while working as a law clerk in the Executive Bureau and, three years later, as instructor at the UP College of Law, where he eventually became dean in 1917. Three of his students, José P. Laurel, Manuel A. Roxas, and Elpidio R. Quirino, later became presidents of the Republic of the Philippines. It was during his time as dean that he would gain national prominence for his many outstanding achievements as an educator and jurist, and as a highly respected Methodist layperson. Just months before Bocobo assumed the UP presidency in 1934, Bishop Edwin Lee, speaking before the annual conference, summed him up as an "outstanding Methodist layman who has won a place in the social and educational life of the country."[35]

In 1929, Bocobo compiled his collection of inspirational speeches, mostly among UP students and commencement addresses, in the book *Streams of Life*. One section titled "The Ascending Life" contained messages echoing not only Bocobo's campaign for "purity" or a "higher life" Christianity, but also his call for an uncompromising stance against any social manifestations of sin.[36] For example, in his address before the YMCA Institute commencement in 1927, Bocobo preached:

> Wrong is wrong, under whatever guise. It should be fought tooth and nail, at all times and in all places, whenever and wherever it may manifest itself. It should be fought, regardless of all considerations of tact, expediency or good policy. It should be fought, no matter what arguments of public good may be invoked. We should be warned that wrong in its naked and bold aspect rarely ever comes out, but is in most cases garbed in some form of alleged necessity or public policy. That is why, if our house of life is extremely low, we may be brought under the influence of these reasonings of alleged public welfare which are put forth in order to justify the continuation of wrong customs and practices, such as cockfighting and drinking.[37]

35. Paraphrased in *PIAC* (1934), 15.

36. See especially "Life's High Tide" where Bocobo spoke on the "higher life," and "The House of Life," which is about purity, in Bocobo, *Streams of Life*, 13–14.

37. Ibid., 13–14.

It is interesting to see how the holiness values perpetuated in MEC churches during the period was captured in this talk as well as in other speeches in the collection. However, we need to clarify that Bocobo's articulation of moral living was more christocentric, and did not carry with it the language of Pentecost promoted by *culto Pentecostal* revivalists. He instead taught the constant presence of the "light of Jesus" to counter sin, which was very much consistent with the teachings of Samuel Stagg, his pastor at the Central Student Church, as we have pointed out earlier. For instance, in the same message, he admonished: "Lastly, the illumination of our house shall be the life of Christ . . . What light so benign and yet so radiant as the inextinguishable light of Jesus? With it our house shall never be overtaken by darkness, but shall be in the perennial brilliancy of the law of God."[38]

Regardless of his christocentric take on holiness, his view of morality, without a doubt, defined his public persona and endeared him to his peers. For example, UP Regent and future United Nations General Secretary Carlos P. Romulo mentioned that one of the reasons why his colleagues chose Bocobo for the presidency was because he was a "moral crusader."[39] True to the moniker, Bocobo, while serving as dean of the UP College of Law, strongly advocated for the extension in the Philippines of two American laws dealing with what he felt were two social evils of his time: the Volstead Act, which prohibited the sale and manufacture of alcoholic beverage; and the Mann Act, which outlawed human trafficking involving prostitution and other sexual activities.[40] Bocobo also cracked down on what he felt were inappropriate expressions of art in the university. For example, he reportedly dismissed the student José Garcia Villa, a famous Filipino poet, in 1929 for his "Man Songs," a series of erotic poems published in one newspaper. Also in 1936, as UP president, Bocobo suggested to modify Guillermo Tolentino's masterpiece *The Oblation*, a nude statue of a young man with outstretched arm commissioned by the previous UP president Rafael Palma, by adding a leaf to cover his private parts.[41] While replicas of *The Oblation* continue to adorn UP campuses today, the leaf covering stands as a sober reminder of Bocobo's moral legacy.

38. Ibid., 16.
39. Olivar, *Aristocracy of the Mind*, 36.
40. See Cabildo, *Appraisals*, 47.
41. Balares and Co, "Oblation: The Truth Behind the Leaves," *Oble*, 2 March 2011, para. 4.

Whereas Bocobo was seen as a strict moralist, his crusade was far from simplistic. His morality was very much connected to his robust sense of justice and human rights. He was a well-known nationalist who advocated for the country's independence from the United States, dedicating two of his books, *For Freedom and Dignity* (1933) and *General Wood and the Law* (1923) for the cause. Bocobo also wrote the prayer for the National Day of Prayer on February 22, 1926, designated by the Philippine Congress for the purpose of praying for Philippine independence.[42] In the prayer, Bocobo beseeched God to compel the leaders of the United States to keep their promise: "We entreat Thee, O most gracious Father, stay Thou the hand that would smite our liberties. Send forth Thy spirit unto our rulers across the seas and so touch their hearts and quicken their sense of justice that they may in honor keep their plighted word to us. Let not the covetous designs of a few interests prevail in the councils of the sovereign nation nor sway its noble purposes toward our country."[43]

In addition to his aspirations for Philippine independence, Bocobo was one of the few Filipinos who did not turn a blind eye to distressing developments in Europe. As the Nazis began their campaign of violence against European Jews, Bocobo was one of the very few leading national figures to express outrage and, along with other like-minded individuals, formed the Committee for Racial and Religious Tolerance. On November 19, 1938, more than a week after the *Kristallnacht* (Crystal Night), a night when Nazi mobs destroyed synagogues and looted Jewish-owned businesses in Germany, the committee organized an indignation rally at the Ateneo de Manila campus in Intramuros. Bocobo was the main speaker at the historic event, which was attended by about a thousand people. Two months later, at a Jewish Junior League gathering in Manila, he called for a Jewish settlement to Mindanao. Bocobo's efforts, as well as that of other individuals, served as an impetus for President Manuel Quezon to allow the settlement of 1,200 German Jews in the Philippines in the months that followed, at a time when many countries, including the United States, refused them.[44]

Upon the end of his tenure at UP in 1939, Bocobo joined President Quezon's cabinet as Secretary of Public Instruction (now Department of

---

42. Apilado, *Revolutionary Spirituality*, 228–230.

43. *Dagiti Naimbag a Damag*, 6 March 1926, 13; cf. ibid., 228.

44. From an interview with Racelle Rosenblatt Weiman, director of the Dialogue Institute at Temple University. See Flores, "How President Quezon"; *Bocobo Papers*, 15.

Education). Two years later, he was appointed Supreme Court Justice, even serving during the Japanese occupation upon President Quezon's order, alongside fellow Methodist Chief Justice José Abad Santos who was executed by the Japanese in 1944.[45] After the war, Bocobo was incarcerated under the charge of collaborating with the Japanese but was released after his acquittal. In 1947, he led the commission that produced the New Civil Code of the Philippines, which included among its features the "supremacy of justice over legalism," the "liberalization of women's rights," and the implementation of social justice."[46] Philippine Congress enacted it and President Elpidio Quirino signed it into law through Republic Act No. 386 on June 18, 1949. For this achievement, one of Bocobo's biographers dubbed him as the "Father of the First Brown Race Civil Code." [47] Bocobo continued with his moral campaign for years and, for his many efforts, was honored with the "The Moral Leader of the Decade Award" during the Citizens for Moral Crusade Conference in 1961.[48]

The persona of Bocobo, as well as that of other prominent Filipino MEC laypersons, was very much consistent to his denominations's brand of morality. His public reputation helped reinforced not only non-Methodists's impression of his religion, but also Filipino Methodists's expectation of themselves. The high moral standard perpetuated by this public image was soon to backfire against them, however.

The Stagg Morality Play and Other Ironic Twists

But even while the period was undoubtedly a time of continued interest in Pentecost and holiness-themed revivalism, the straight-laced standards these ubiquitous revivals intended to achieve did not necessarily produce an unblemished Filipino clergy and missionary workforce. For example, one leading Filipino clergy poignantly pointed out to one WFMS missionary in 1930: "We do not want the missionaries here to run our church, we can do that, of course not as well, but we are learning. What we are looking for are missionaries who are Spirit filled at all times, if a missionary cannot keep a lap ahead of us in Christian living there is no place for him in the

---

45. Chief Justice Abad Santos served with the Mary Johnston Committee of the Philippine Annual Conference from 1925-1935. See, for example, *PAC* (1935), 8.
46. Rivera, *First Brown Civil Code*, 91.
47. Ibid., 1-2, 81-82.
48. Ibid., xxiv.

Island."⁴⁹ The clergypersons's forthright statement hinted of a shift in the dynamics of Filipino-missionary relationship. Clearly, there was already a more developed sense of self-agency among Filipinos by this time that led the unnamed pastor to assert independence from missionary administration. However, one exception remained, which definitely demonstrates the legacy of *culto Pentecostal* revivalism in the fabric Filipino Methodist culture. Only missionaries who were filled with the Holy Spirit "at all times" and, as a result, exude holiness were welcome. Looking deeper into the context of the pastor's statement, one cannot simply ignore its proximity to the tumultuous events surrounding the "de Armas case," which highlights the interplay between the moral impulse of Philippine Methodism and its aspiration for ecclesiastical independence.

In 1928 Melecio de Armas, minister for sixteen years and one of Cottingham's "lieutenants" in the Manila District was accused of attempting to force a teenage girl from the church in Orani, Bataan, into an adulterous affair with him. A committee of four senior Filipino ministers assembled by Cottingham on June 1929, after hearing de Armas and the girl's pastor and reviewing witnesses's accounts from an initial investigation, exonerated de Armas. The case lay dormant for two years, but, upon pressure, was revived by the Manila District. The ensuing investigation would pit Stagg, who became the counsel for the prosecution, against Cottingham, now conference evangelist, who upon testimony ended up libeling the minister who helped revive the case. Cottingham later recanted his testimony under threat of a legal action. After a frustrating setback, Stagg later resigned as counsel, dismissed the investigation as a "travesty," and proceeded to carry the fight in the court of MEC public opinion. He presented evidence and vilified "corrupt" missionaries and their Filipino allies through a series of mimeographed letters, but not without irritating others and raising doubts as to his intentions.⁵⁰ For example, one prominent lay person from another church in Manila asked: "Is Rev. Stagg really after justice as he claims? If so, I just wonder what brand?"⁵¹

---

49. Quoted in *WCPIAC* (1931), 37.

50. The sequence of events surrounding the de Armas case is summarized in Del Rosario, "Schism," 387–426. Among a number of documents from Stagg detailing the case, see, for example, Stagg to the Board of Foreign Missions, 2 February 1933, Stagg, Samuel Wells (Rev. & Mrs.), 1922–1933, Folder 5, MFUMC.

51. Benito Pañgindian "Stagg Staggers as Laymen Refused to be Bullied," mimeographed manuscript, Stagg, Samuel Wells (Rev. & Mrs.), 1922–1933, Folder 5, MFUMC.

Nonetheless, Stagg's mimeographed assaults did pay off. The case was elevated to the Annual Conference session in February 1932, which finally found de Armas guilty of adultery and expelled him from the ministry. But after the decision was appealed before the General Conference in Atlantic City three months later, its appellate court overturned the decision as counter arguments from the prosecution were lost, apparently during transmittal.[52] In the ensuing fallout following the reversal, Stagg positioned himself as a champion of morality, working to "clean up" the mission as he unleashed vitriol against the senior missionaries. For example, he credited himself for previously confronting one "leading older missionary" at UTS for maintaining a *querida* (mistress) in the absence of his wife, which ultimately led to the missionary's recall.[53] He also pursued to put to a stop Cottingham's alleged "corrupting influence" by demanding the board to recall him on grounds of his previous false testimony, and launched a petition to have him charged in the upcoming Annual Conference session.[54] Obviously, given Cottingham's already tarnished reputation, the board, upon Bishop Lee's request, issued a recall order for him, but not without issuing one for Stagg as well. Cottingham left prior to the 1933 Conference, never to return again. Notwithstanding, Stagg, with the support of his loyal members at Central Church, defied the order, calling it "illegal" and a way to silence "missionaries who stand for righteousness." He further widened his range of attacks by endeavoring to have Bishop Lee charged with "maladministration," and threatened to do the same against the mission board secretaries in New York if they will discontinue his salary without sufficient grounds.[55] He eventually managed to remain in the country until the next Annual Conference, where he took a prominent role in the events that were about to unfold.

The full ramifications of the General Conference decision did not become apparent until the first day of the Conference session on March 22, 1933, in San Nicolas, Pangasinan, when de Armas's name was restored

---

52. See Del Rosario, "Schism," 405–16.

53. See Stagg to the Board of Foreign Missions, 2 February 1933, Stagg, Samuel Wells (Rev. & Mrs.), 1922–1933, Folder 5, MFUMC. Stagg did not name the missionary.

54. See Stagg to Tuck, 16 September 1932; "To the President and Secretary of the Annual Conference," TDS; Stagg Samuel Wells (Rev. & Mrs.), 1922–1933, Folder 5, MFUMC.

55. See Stagg to Edwards, 5 January 1933; Stagg to the Board of Foreign Missions, 2 February 1933; Stagg, Samuel Wells (Rev. & Mrs.), 1922–1933, Folder 5, MFUMC. For details, see Del Rosario, "Schism," 426–51.

to its rolls by order of Bishop Herbert Welch, who presided in the absence of Bishop Lee. Subsequent motions and appeals made by Stagg and Cipriano Navarro, a well respected Filipino clergy and one of Stagg's associates in the Wesley Foundation, and others set in motion a report by the prosecuting counsel. A series of discussions by Navarro ensued, which, however, produced little results that day. By the fourth day, after further hearing closing arguments on the matter, the die was cast when the bishop, after "renewed and serious consideration," reiterated that he was in no position to ignore the General Conference's decision. This, therefore, led Navarro to announce his withdrawal and move "that we here and now declare ourselves independent from the American General Conference." Navarro and Stagg left, along with forty-three other ministers (from a total of 106 present), seventeen deaconesses and Bible women, four WFMS missionaries, and a number of laypersons.[56] This was the beginning of what would later become the "Philippine Methodist Church." A year later, only nineteen clergy remained with the "New Movement," while the rest returned to the MEC. It was also estimated that the MEC lost more than 1,600 members to the schism.[57]

The first Sunday after the Pangasinan fallout, some members of the official board of the Central Student Church, along with Stagg and Navarro, initiated a walkout, although a peaceful one due to the acquiescence of MEC authorities during the morning service at the newly completed sanctuary. Melquiades J. Gamboa, vice chair of the official board and prominent law professor at the nearby UP, captured the main pretext of the new movement when he announced at the beginning of the service: "We cannot surrender the moral issue for the finest church building in the Philippines. We cannot continue to support a church that protects a corrupt ministry." A significant number of the congregants, under the leadership of Stagg, Navarro, and Gamboa, left and boarded designated buses that took them to the nearby Plaridel Masonic temple where they launched what would later become the "Cosmopolitan Church."[58] Romeo Del Rosario, in his dissertation on the schism (1982), confirms that the "moral issue" was a major reason, notwithstanding some qualifications and nuances, behind

---

56. *PIAC* (1933), 10–28. Cf. Del Rosario, "Schism," 460–74. We can infer from Del Rosario that thirty-four Filipino clergy (including Navarro) left with Stagg. We, instead, count forty-four based on a comparison between the Conference rolls prior to the walkout and the one made shortly after that.

57. See Del Rosario, "Schism," 510–13.

58. Ibid., 475–85.

the secession.⁵⁹ Thus, it would not be hard to comprehend why just after de Armas irrevocably resigned shortly after the Conference, Pampango minister Eusebio M. Manuel, who was one of the seceders, rejoined the MEC. "Really, I don't know of any more reason now to split the Church, because the original cause, namely, the moral issue, is already settled," he reasoned.⁶⁰ Despite the development, not all followed suit, because the longstanding "background causes," which had simply coalesced around the morality issue, were still left unsettled. These causes included antagonism between seceding and loyalist missionaries, resentment of seceding nationals against certain missionaries, infighting among nationals, and varied attitudes about autonomy, among others. The de Armas case was a perfect storm waiting to happen.⁶¹

Given the MEC mission's commitment to the message of holiness, it is not unimaginable that a breakdown of morality within their ranks could provoke furor and embolden schismatic tendencies. As we have demonstrated in the previous chapter, the denomination's perception of the state of morality from within and without was integral to its practice of holiness revivalism. The impeccable persistence of *culto Pentecostal* rituals in the warp and woof of Philippine MEC life throughout the years, without a doubt, helped fashion a high standard of discipline among Philippine Methodists—at least, as far as their self-concept, how they viewed missionaries, and how the public perceived them were concerned. Thus, to fall short would mean far-reaching consequences. This perhaps explains why the case was initially swept under the rug by Cottingham and dragged until 1933 by individuals who were probably in denial. Even the Orani MEC, which filed the original complaint against de Armas, protested upon Stagg's relentless tinkering and his purportedly "very false" claim about a recent development, because it placed them in a negative light among Roman Catholics and IEMELIF members in their town.⁶² The very image and reputation, which the Methodists had carefully crafted and which had helped gain for them some measure of respect in the public sphere, had indeed become both a blessing and a curse.

59. Ibid., 640–50.
60. *PO*, June 1933, 5.
61. The "background causes" are summarized in Del Rosario, "Schism," 640–50.
62. See Orani MEC Officers to Cruz, 8 February 1932, Stagg, Samuel Wells (Rev. & Mrs.), 1922–1933, Folder 5, MFUMC.

Sometime after 1934, and in another ironic twist, Stagg also yielded to the very temptation he had championed against when he indulged in extramarital affairs as confirmed by his daughter in 1996.[63] Given his struggles with guilt and increasing disillusionment with the ministry, Stagg later resigned from Cosmopolitan in 1939. Leaving his family and losing his faith, he engaged in espionage work for the United States Naval Intelligence as war loomed over the horizon. Mary Boyd, Stagg's wife, was ordained by Bishop Cipriano Navarro shortly thereafter, thus making her the first female to be ordained in the autonomous Methodist denomination.[64] When Japanese forces occupied Manila on January 1942, she was permitted to continue her work with Cosmopolitan until the Japanese military police arrested her for aiding the guerilla movement. Along with Hawthorne Darby and Helen Wilk, two former WFMS missionaries who joined the Filipino Methodist secession in 1933, Mary had to endure torture in the hands of her captors at Fort Santiago. After more than eight months in captivity, the three, along with twenty-seven detainees, were eventually beheaded on August 30, 1944 at the Manila North Cemetery.[65] Samuel, on the other hand, survived the war, relocated and remarried in Palawan, and held the pseudonym "Jungle Philosopher" for a column he wrote for the *Philippine Free Press*. He later succumbed to a heart attack in 1956.

---

63. Stagg's indiscretions went relatively unnoticed, but not until his daughter confirmed them during a reunion at Cosmopolitan Church in 1996, and substantiated in a foreword by Senator Jovito V. Salonga in Webb, *Not My Will*, v–x. Details of events, although partly fictionalized, can be found in pages 192–207, 215–16, 237.

64. Ibid., 231–34.

65. Ibid., 245–87; Go, *The Hour Had Come*, 147–54, 163–65.

Figure 5.1. Filipino District superintendents, 1932: (top, left to right) Benito S. Tovera (North Cagayan), Alejandro Vidal (Pangasinan), Esteban T. Cruz (Central), Arcadio de Ocera (Pampanga); (bottom, left to right) Severino Cordero (Ilocos Sur), Ciriaco Inis (South Cagayan), Lorenzo T. Tamayo (Tarlac), Pedro B. Cruz (Manila, Bataan, and Zambales). This was the same year that all the districts had been placed under Filipino leadership. Source: The United Methodist Church Archives—GCAH, Madison, New Jersey. Mission Photograph Albums—Philippines #4, 111.

Figure 5.2. Jorge C. Bocobo, dean of the College of Law, University of the Philippines, chairman of the board of trustees, Central Student Church, Manila, 1931. He later assumed the presidency of the university in 1934. Source: The United Methodist Church Archives—GCAH, Madison, New Jersey. Mission Photograph Albums—Philippines #4, 113.

Figure 5.3. Samuel W. Stagg, Central Student Church pastor, and his wife, Mary Boyd Stagg, with the dormitory basketball team, Methodist Boys' Dormitory, Manila, 1925. The couple was also in charge of the dormitory that year. Source: The United Methodist Church Archives—GCAH, Madison, New Jersey. Mission Photograph Albums—Philippines #3, 214.

Figure 5.4. Samuel W. Stagg (first person on the right) with the Central Student Church evangelistic teams starting out to keep Sunday afternoon teaching and preaching appointments in villages around Manila, c. 1925–1929. Source: The United Methodist Church Archives—GCAH, Madison, New Jersey. Mission Photograph Albums—Philippines #3, 214.

Figure 5.5. Cipriano Navarro, pastor of Lingayen MEC, Lingayen, Pangasinan, 1928. He was clergy delegate of the Philippine Islands Annual Conference at the General Conference of 1928. Along with Samuel Stagg and others, he founded the Philippine Methodist Church in 1933. Source: The United Methodist Church Archives—GCAH, Madison, New Jersey. Mission Photograph Albums—Portraits #4, 133.

Figure 5.6. Interior view of Central Student Church showing part of the auditorium, the choir, its new organ, and its affluent attendees, August 20, 1933. Source: *PO*, August 1933.

Figure 5.7. Philippine Islands Annual Conference, Central Student Church, Manila, February 20–26, 1935. See Gothic style exterior of Central Student Church. Source: The United Methodist Church Archives—GCAH, Madison, New Jersey. Mission Photograph Albums—Philippines #4, 132.

6

The Methodist Healing Revival, and Its Consequences, 1934–1965

> My difficulties began when I went with the Pentecostal missionaries and I invited them to preach in the Methodist Churches.
>
> —Ruben Candelaria, *When a Methodist Minister Receives Christ's Promise and Power!*

The Aftermath, the War Years, and Another Twist

While Cottingham, the linchpin of *culto* Pentecostalism for the era, limped his way back to Indiana nursing a stained reputation, the brand of revivalism he had helped propagate persisted. Even as the church reeled from the effects of the schism, Superintendent Esteban T. Cruz, one of Cottingham's closest allies, admonished his co-workers shortly after returning from the Conference to see that "each church in the district seek a special baptism of the Holy Spirit."[1] In Zambales, Arcadio de Ocera reported that the consecration service at a lyceum held in Olongapo in 1934 "made us feel the real baptism of the Holy Spirit and the presence of the Divine Power."[2] In 1936, as the nation entered a new era with the inauguration of the Philippine Commonwealth Government three months earlier, the all-Filipino State of the Church Committee acknowledged that a "deepening sense of purity and righteous living is being felt." The same Committee also admonished the church to support President Manuel L. Quezon, the nation's newly elected president, in his "moral crusade" platform through

---

1. *PIAC* (1934), 59.
2. *PIAC* (1935), 56.

"evangelization and revivals."[3] Philippine Methodists still believed that revivalism, in addition to evangelism, was integral to the spread of holiness or their particular brand of morality throughout the land.

Even after the Conference was divided to become the Philippine Annual Conference (hereafter Southern Conference) and the Philippine North Annual Conference (hereafter Northern Conference) in 1936, *culto Pentecostal* culture still remained evident on both fronts. For example, Berndt Peterson, who by this time was the oldest of the five remaining male missionaries, held "Pentecostal services" in the northernmost district of the Southern Conference a year later.[4] Superintendent Benito M. Reyes also asserted that many "testified to the fullness in their lives of the Holy Spirit" during a lyceum in Zambales in 1938.[5] Correspondingly, in the Northern Conference, Leila Dingle continued to wave the holiness banner in Pangasinan by "bringing sinners to repentance and for rededication of many members."[6] Revival efforts were also supplemented by outside help with the arrival of visiting MEC Holiness evangelist Willa Daisy Caffray, who engaged in a two-month campaign in early 1939 in which about seven hundred people sought "pardon or reclamation or for a personal Pentecost." "Many workers and pastors as well as lay members acknowledged their hunger for the outpouring of the Holy Spirit upon their work, and God did not disappoint them, all praise to His Name," Caffray wrote.[7] A year later, and as if unaware of the looming conflict in the Pacific, the Northern Conference's Committee on Evangelism urged the churches to "endeavor to revive the old members who are sleeping and that a baptism of the Holy Spirit shall be sought."[8] Incidentally, the Philippines Central Conference was established that same year.[9]

The arrival of Japanese forces at the end of 1941 and the surrender of Filipino and American forces months later, nonetheless, signaled the beginning of the demise of *culto Pentecostal* practice as the country braced

3. PIAC (1936), 104–5. For membership statistics, see Bibay, "Membership and Statistical Records," 144.

4. *PAC* (1938), 51.

5. *PAC* (1939), 44.

6. *NPAC* (1940), 47.

7. From Caffray's letter on April 1939 from Peking, as quoted in Robinson, *From Brass to Gold*, 266. See also *NPAC* (1939), 14. From more on Caffray, see Pope-Levison, *Building the Old Time Religion*, 133–34.

8. *NPAC* (1940), 57.

9. Alejandro, *From Darkness to Light*, 172–76.

itself for a grueling conflict and the harsh realities to come under Japanese rule. Dionisio Alejandro, who had been readmitted to the ministry in 1939, maintained that Pentecostal meetings "became impossible to hold" during the war years,[10] probably due to restrictions imposed by the occupying government against public assemblies. Evidence, nonetheless, suggests that some limited degree of revival activity did persist.[11] Even the Annual Conference session in Atlag, Malolos, in 1944, the only one to take place during the war, was an occasion for the "outpouring of the Spirit of God," notwithstanding the presence of Japanese observers, as Alejandro acknowledged.[12] It was under the same persistent pressure that Filipino Methodists elected him their first bishop during the adjourned session of the Central Conference that same year.[13]

Japan's intrusion into Methodist life, however, quickly dissipated after the decisive American victory at the Battle of Leyte, which opened the way for a series of campaigns that finally routed the Japanese. Overall, the war left scores of Methodist Church (MEC adopted the name after the Uniting Conference of 1939) sanctuaries around the country in ruins and hundreds of Methodist Church members and workers dead.[14] Consequently, with "liberation" also came the task of rebuilding, which resulted in a reorientation of priorities. Cunningham posits that it was during this period that Philippine Methodists, akin "to their American counterparts, began to give up on the revival methods."[15] A survey of post-war Conference reports reveals that this was indeed the case as the myriad manifestations of the once ubiquitous Pentecost and holiness-themed revivalism exponentially decreased, if not faded into memory. Even returned women missionaries and Filipino clergy who figured prominently in the promotion of this revivalism in the pre-war years seemed to have capitulated to newer preoccupations, perhaps reflecting changes in American Methodist evangelical culture after the war.[16] Ruben V. Candelaria, Superintendent of the Manila

10. Ibid., 107.
11. See, for instance, *PAC* (1944), 33–34; *PAC* (1946), 71; *PCC* (1948), 49–50.
12. Alejandro, "Episcopal Address," *PCC* (1948), 35.
13. Alejandro, *From Darkness to Light*, 191–99; *PCC* (1948), 48–49.
14. Alejandro, *From Darkness to Light*, 200–206.
15. Cunningham, "Diversities," 75.
16. See reports by district superintendents, missionaries, State of the Church Committee and Committee on Evangelism during the period in *PAC* (1946–1951) and *NPAC* (1946–1951).

District, captured the spirit of the period when he complained, albeit with some solutions to offer, at the 1951 Conference that the "lack of passion to propagate the gospel is generally characteristic among our churches and workers alike. There is a need in regaining this passion. We are praying for a revival of religion in our churches and among our workers, and we know that that that [sic] revival will come."[17]

But as Candelaria led his district into a renewed revivalistic thrust, the denomination's shift away from holiness-Pentecostal revivalism seemed to have taken its course. Indicative of this shift was Alejandro's gripe that same year against Pentecostals and their visiting evangelists, who, according to him, only knew how to "shout and rent [sic]." "Praying at the top of one's voice and shouting hysterically all the time does not necessarily indicate the coming down of the Third Person of the Trinity in all His power and glory. And why speak of Pentecostal experience when what most of the people needed was not sanctifying but regenerating grace?" the former bishop protested.[18] In another odd twist, Alejandro, the Asbury student who had been "sanctified" thirty five years earlier, seemed to have set the stage not only for official Methodist attitude towards Pentecostals, but also for the betrayal of his own holiness past by preferring "regenerating" grace over "sanctifying" grace. His position marked a watershed between a sober Methodist evangelicalism, where conversionism was the motif; and the noisy *culto Pentecostal* of old, where Spirit baptism was the vernacular.

Accordingly, the shape of Methodist revivalism was now reduced to a faint image of its *culto Pentecostal* past both in content and intensity. When Cagayan Valley missionary Curran L. Spottswood led a "great evangelistic campaign" at the Knox Memorial Methodist Church on the third week of November 1953 it was reported that every night "the altar was filled to capacity by those who surrendered or reconsecrated themselves to Jesus Christ." In other words, Spottswood's altar calls, as if following Alejandro's cue, focused more on justifying grace as he called people to surrender or re-surrender their lives to Jesus. Nothing in the report pertaining to the event indicated any reference to the Holy Spirit or any pneumatological motif that was typical with the revivals of the previous generations. Also, gone were the shouts of hallelujahs and amens. Perhaps, the closest thing that came close to these exuberant expressions of worship was the spontaneous

---

17. *PAC* (1951), 62.
18. Quoted in Cunningham, "Diversities," 76.

shout, "Hip, hip, hurrah!" from the choir at the close of the final service.[19] As Filipino Methodists turned to a more conversionist and restrained form of revivalism, they would never have guessed that the Pentecostal AG Church would soon profit from the very culture their predecessors helped propagate three decades earlier.

The Assemblies of God in Manila and the Deliverance of Clarita Villanueva

Though the beginnings of the AG in the Philippines is usually traced from the work of a missionary who arrived in Manila in 1926, historians give more credence to the role of *balikbayans* (returned Filipino immigrants), who had encountered Pentecostalism in the United States. Among them was Rodrigo Esperanza, a former MEC exhorter from Pozorrubio, Pangasinan, who went to California in 1928 and later became the denomination's first Filipino General Superintendent. The successful work begun by these indigenous pioneers, particularly in a number of towns in the provinces through the 1930s, resulted in the official establishment of the AG in the country in 1940, and consequently in the influx of American AG missionaries in the years that followed.[20] The denomination experienced phenomenal growth in the 1950s, as suggested by Eleazar E. Javier, as it began shifting its sights to Main Street Manila and other urban centers throughout the country.[21]

At the forefront of this shift was Lester Frank Sumrall (1913–1996), who had left a large pastorate in South Bend, Indiana. He initially took over the work at Glad Tidings Revival Center in a rented marketplace in Maypajo, Caloocan, soon after arriving with his family in July 1952.[22] Three months later, Sumrall audaciously launched an aggressive campaign in Manila by organizing the "salvation and divine healing" crusade of healing evangelist Adolpho C. Valdez Jr. at the San Lazaro race track from Novem-

---

19. See *PAC* (1954), 52; *Philippine Christian Advance*, December 1953, 10–11. See also Cunningham, "Diversities," 75.

20. See Esperanza, "Assemblies of God," 17–51; Seleky, "Six Filipinos"; Javier, "Pentecostal Legacy," in Kwantes, *Supplement*, 63–73.

21. Javier, "Personal Memoir," 299; Javier, "Pentecostal Legacy," 71. See also Kim, "Filipino Pentecostalism," 237.

22. For Sumrall's call and arrival in Manila, see Sumrall, *Modern Manila Miracles*, 146–48; Sumrall, *Real Manila Story*, 6–8.

ber 23 to December 7. Called "the first largest protracted meeting" in the Philippines, the event gathered an estimated crowd of twenty thousand.[23] The success of the Valdez salvation-healing revival not only helped increase the membership at the Maypajo Revival Center, but also generated a much-needed support base for the establishment of the Manila Bethel Temple, Sumrall's project in the city, which he hoped would be a "great evangelistic center."[24] By January 1953, Sumrall had been able to secure $20,000 from the AG Missionary Department to purchase a jungle lot on Taft Avenue, just a few yards from Central Methodist Church. Sumrall also bought an old B-17 hangar in the city to reuse its steel.[25]

It was during the preparation phase for Bethel that an immense opportunity presented itself to Sumrall when he figured prominently in the deliverance of Clarita Villanueva, a seventeen-year-old girl who was detained at the Bilibid Prison in Manila for vagrancy. Villanueva made national headlines throughout May that year due to extensive radio and print media coverage of her struggles with two invisible beings collectively called "The Thing," which purportedly left her with human-like bite marks on various parts of her body, including the neck, arms, forearms, fingers, and hands.[26] Embarrassed by the negative press the city was getting, Mayor Arsenio Lacson sought the help of professionals and religious practitioners, including doctors, priests, spiritualists, psychologists, and university professors to address the phenomena. Their efforts, nevertheless, did very little to relieve the girl from her predicament.[27] Villanueva's ordeal was even featured in a forty-five minute evening segment on radio station DZFM, which included interviews of her and that of eyewitnesses and experts, while interspersed with audio recordings of her convulsions and "piercing screams followed by pandemonium." Deeply bothered by Villanueva's agony as he listened to the broadcast, Sumrall decided to act the next morning after much prayer. With the help of friends, he was able to secure permission from the mayor and the Manila Police Department's chief medical examiner, who enabled him to see the girl at the prison chapel. Upon seeing the American for the

23. Sumrall, *Modern Manila Miracles*, 25; *PE*, 15 February 1953, 6.
24. Sumrall, *Modern Manila Miracles*, 29.
25. Ibid., 22–30; Sumrall and Dudley, *Life Story*, 153; Javier, "Personal Memoir," 301.
26. For newspaper coverage and witness accounts detailing Clarita Villanueva's ordeal and encounter with Sumrall, see Sumrall, *Clarita Villanueva*, 7–108; Sumrall and Dudley, *Life Story*, 161–73.
27. Sumrall, *Clarita Villanueva*, 8–20.

first time, Villanueva, who was under the control of the "devil," as Sumrall maintained, started cursing him in English even though it was known that she could not converse in English and needed an interpreter.[28] Sumrall recalled the ensuing struggle:

> After she spoke, I had her sit on a wooden bench and I drew a chair up in front of her and began saying, "Clarita I have come to deliver you from the devils, in the name of Jesus Christ, the Son of God." Suddenly the girl went to a fit of rage. She screamed, "No! No! They will kill me!" Her body became rigid and she became unconscious. This had baffled the doctors when they tried to analyze her case, but I had dealt with devils before and understood some of their antics. So taking hold of her head with both hands I cried, "Come out of her you evil and wicked spirit of hell. Come out of her in Jesus name!"[29]

The next day, after three similar tussles with the Pentecostal missionary, the "two devils" left Villanueva. Although, they would attack her once more a few days later, she ultimately drove them away by uttering a prayer that Sumrall taught her. According to Sumrall, this was Villanueva's last encounter with the two, as well as the beginning of her recovery and return to normalcy. The Court of First Instance eventually released her into Sumrall's custody a few weeks later. News of the girl's deliverance by Sumrall instantly made him a "household name." Furthermore, it won a great degree of favor for the work of the AG in the city as a grateful Mayor Lacson passed a special ordinance granting them a free building permit for the construction of Bethel Temple—the first Protestant church to be given such.[30] Accordingly, it also laid the groundwork for a much bigger salvation-healing revival led by visiting evangelist Clifton Erickson, a rising figure in the healing revival movement.[31] The meeting was held at the Roxas Park, right across City Hall, with a permit granted gratis by the revered mayor.[32]

---

28. Ibid., 84–92.
29. Ibid., 92.
30. *PE*, 1 November 1953, 6; Sumrall, *Clarita Villanueva*, 109–10.
31. Clifton Erickson was among the "rising revivalists" who attended the first healing convention organized on December 1949 by Gordon Lindsay of the *Voice of Healing*. See Harrell, *All Things Are Possible*, 18–19.
32. Sumrall, *Modern Manila Miracles*, 110; Sumrall, *Real Manila Story*, 21–22; Sumrall, *Clarita Villanueva*, 110.

Beginning on the third week of January 1954, the "great revival of Roxas Park," as Sumrall later termed it, attracted nightly crowds estimated at between thirty and fifty thousand throughout the six-week gathering. Sumrall also reported that nearly ten thousand came forward "for a prayer of salvation," and thousands crowded around the platform to get healed each night. Sumrall documented sixty-one cases in his *Modern Manila Miracles*.[33] Preparatory afternoon services were also held by Erickson, first in Maypajo and then, beginning January 25, in Bethel. Thus, when it opened for its first Sunday service a few days later, Manila Bethel Temple, more popularly known as the "Christ is the Answer Church," was poised not only to be the largest Protestant Church, but also to be the fastest growing church in the country. On its fourth Sunday, on the closing Sunday of the Erickson campaign, 2,396 individuals reported for Sunday School.[34] The church also took the unusual step of initially conducting services in four different languages, Tagalog, Ilocano, English, and Chinese—a setup similar to its more established Protestant neighbors.[35]

Upon his return to Indiana, Sumrall was replaced in Manila by Ernest Reb of the Oriental Missionary Crusade. In January 1955, evangelist Ralph Byrd of Atlanta, Georgia, began a three-month healing revival campaign in ten cities throughout the country. Byrd is credited with introducing the "baptism of the Holy Spirit" as evidenced by *glossolalia* (speaking in tongues) into the work of the AG in the country.[36] In 1956, Sumrall returned with Oral Roberts, who conducted meetings, again held at Roxas Park. Other famous healing evangelists who conducted similar campaigns in Manila during the period included Rudy Cerullo, and Tommy L. Osborn.[37]

We should note, however, that the Manila healing revival was part of a much bigger movement, which David Harrell identifies as the "Healing Revival" movement which lasted from 1947 to 1958 and brought worldwide prominence to a number of independent healing evangelists, such as William Branham, Oral Roberts, and others.[38] The series of salvation-healing

---

33. Sumrall, *Real Manila Story*, 20. See documented healings in Sumrall, *Modern Manila Miracles*, 65–100. See *PAC* (1954), 53.

34. Sumrall, *Real Manila Story*, 23; Sumrall, *Modern Manila Miracles*, 46; *PE*, 21 March 1954, 8.

35. Sumrall, *Modern Manila Miracles*, 42–43.

36. See *PE*, 27 March 1955, 7; *PE*, 31 July 1955, 6; Javier, "A Personal Memoir," 292; Esperanza, "Assemblies of God," 49.

37. Esperanza, "Assemblies of God," 49; Javier, "A Personal Memoir," 298.

38. Harrell, *All Things Are Possible*, 5–6. It is understood that the healing movement

revivals held in Manila during this period was the most ambitious form of open-air meetings ever attempted on Philippine shores. They represented a huge leap from the more localized evangelistic meetings held by other Protestant churches at that time. Furthermore, they also launched, on a much larger scale, a new form of revivalism in the country by infusing the standard revival themes of salvation and holiness in Christ with the message of divine healing. Thus, we can assert with confidence that these meetings were the progenitors of the mass healing movement in the Philippines, which now find preeminence mostly among Catholic Charismatic groups and indigenous Pentecostal churches in the country.[39] In as much as the Manila healing revival provided a significant turning point for the AG, it also provided the premise for the defection of Manila District Superintendent Ruben Candelaria and other Methodists to Pentecostalism.

The Dove, the Eagle, and Methodists Caught Up in the New Revival

In his published accounts of the Manila healing revival, Sumrall consistently recognized the significant contributions of Ruben V. Candelaria (1909–1989). For example, in his *The True Story of Clarita Villanueva* (1955), Sumrall acknowledged that "one of the greatest blessings" that came to him as a result of the deliverance of Clarita Villanueva was the friendship of Ruben.[40] Sumrall also released *A Methodist Minister Receives Christ's Promise and Power* (1956), Ruben's personal testimony and retelling of the events leading up to his "Pentecost."[41] In *The Dove and the Eagle* (1962), Sumrall detailed the lives and roles of Ruben the "Dove" and his cousin David the "Eagle" in the Manila healing revival. The book's title was a reiteration of Oral Roberts's declaration at the Roxas Park healing revival in 1956. Recounting Roberts's prayer, Sumrall wrote:

> "Ruben, you are a *Dove*." Then with his hand upon David's head he said, "David you are an *Eagle*; you have within you the spirit of an

---

is different from the Latter Rain movement, a parallel movement during the same period. Both movements were rejected by most Pentecostal denominations. See Riss, "The Latter Rain Movement," 33; Dayton, "Evangelical Healing Movement," 2.

39. One of the largest of these groups is the Roman Catholic El Shaddai movement. An excellent in-depth study is found in Wiegele, *Investing in Miracles*.

40. Sumrall, *Real Manila Story*, 18; Sumrall, *Clarita Villanueva*, 111.

41. Candelaria, *A Methodist Minister*.

Eagle. As Ruben, with his Dove-spirit, longs for companionship, so you with your Eagle-spirit, long for the solitude of high places. You are both blessed of God and anointed of God to perform your different tasks."[42]

Ruben held undeniable status in Philippine Methodism. Born April 27, 1909, in Nueva Ecija, he left his career as a public school teacher to become a Methodist preacher in 1931. After an impressive stint in a number of congregations like Jaen, Cabanatuan, Taytay, Iba, Tuguegarao, and Tondo, he quickly rose within the ranks of the denomination. In 1950, Bishop José L. Valencia (1898–1995) appointed him superintendent of the Manila District, an area covering twenty-seven churches mostly in Manila, Quezon City, and Rizal. Ruben also chaired the Philippine Annual Conference's committee on worship, and taught worship in the denomination's School of Ministerial Training. In 1952 he held the distinction of being elected by his colleagues to the General Conference in Seattle.[43]

Despite Ruben's seemingly secure and rising reputation in Methodism, the nascent Manila healing revival would eventually propel him towards Pentecostalism. Two events led to this: first, when he saw Dr. Mercedez Diaz, a longtime acquaintance from Knox Methodist Church, and a cripple now walking without her crutches after attending the Valdez revivals; and second, when the reputed daily *Manila Times* reported Clarita Villanueva's deliverance through Sumrall, who the paper also erroneously referred to as a "Methodist missionary."[44] Though initially critical of the Valdez meetings, the two events led the Superintendent to yearn for Pentecostal power in his ministry, and to personally seek out Sumrall, partially to verify whether the renowned missionary was indeed Methodist. That same day, his desire to meet him quickly came to fruition when another Methodist clergy asked his assistance to borrow from Sumrall Oral Roberts's healing film *Venture into Faith* (1952). The two wasted no time, and that same afternoon met

---

42. As quoted in Sumrall, *Dove and the Eagle*, 8–9. Special thanks to Rev. Jesse Candelaria, son of David Candelaria, for pointing out the book to me. Jesse Candelaria, e-mail, 24 February 2005.

43. Sumrall, *Dove and the Eagle*, 13–14; Valencia, *Under God's Umbrella*, 70–71. See *PAC* (1950), 37; *PAC* (1952), 13–14; *PAC* (1953), 118; *Philippine Christian Advance*, March 1952, 9.

44. Sumrall, *Clarita Villanueva*, 98–99; Sumrall, *The Real Manila Story*, 15; Candelaria, *Methodist Minister*, 9–12. The fact that Sumrall was mistaken for a "Methodist missionary" perhaps highlighted a public perception that Methodists were more likely to engage in such activities than other Protestants.

the missionary in his office in Polo, Bulacan. Just before they left, Ruben professed his desire for power or "blessing," inciting Sumrall to pray for him and lay his hand upon him. Though it was Ruben's first exposure to what he called "Pentecostal prayer," an enduring friendship was forged; or, as Ruben aptly described, they "became brothers."[45]

The same friendship paved the way for the official entry of the healing revival among Methodists in the Manila District and, to some degree, in other Protestant churches under the Philippine Federation of Christian Churches (hereafter PFCC). After launching the campaign by previewing Roberts's film at Knox Methodist Church, Sumrall and Ruben soon found themselves booked to speak in fifty-one churches, mostly Methodist, in Manila, Rizal, Bulacan, Nueva Ecija, Bataan, and Mountain Province. Usually spending three nights in each church, they showed Roberts's film, "preached deliverance, and prayed for the sick." They also distributed back issues of Gordon Lindsey's magazine *Voice of Healing*, the "primary voice" of the worldwide healing revival movement. Ruben reported that no church was large enough to accommodate the crowds that flocked to the meetings, and that "hundreds and thousands of people were saved and healed."[46] The campaign culminated during the Manila District Conference held at the Taytay Methodist Church from January 7–9, 1954, where, in the evenings at the town plaza, Sumrall preached to a crowd of about three thousand and prayed for the sick.[47] These initial efforts, as both Sumrall and Ruben opined, had "in a large measure, prepared the way" for the success of the Erickson revivals, where Ruben alternated as interpreter with his cousin David, another central figure in the revival.[48]

David M. Candelaria, Ruben's first cousin and pastor of the Taytay Methodist Church, also had a remarkable career in the denomination. David was born on April 12, 1912, to a devout Methodist family who attended the church in San Leonardo, Nueva Ecija, where the "Gracious

---

45. Candelaria, *Methodist Minister*, 12–15; Sumrall, *Clarita Villanueva*, 116; Sumrall, *Dove and the Eagle*, 4; Javier, "Personal Memoir," 91. For more on *Venture into Faith*, see Harrell, *Oral Roberts*, 124–25.

46. *PAC* (1954), 53; Sumrall, *Clarita Villanueva*, 117; Sumrall, *Real Manila Story*, 19–20; Sumrall, *Dove and the Eagle*, 16; Sumrall and Dudley, *Life Story*, 175; Candelaria, *Methodist Minister*, 16. For more on the *Voice of Healing*, see Hewett, "Voice of Healing," 1178–79.

47. *PAC* (1954), 53.

48. Ibid.; Sumrall and Dudley, *Life Story*, 175; Sumrall, *Real Manila Story*, 19; Sumrall, *Clarita Villanueva*, 117; Sumrall, *Modern Manila Miracles*, 2.

Filipino Revival" we described in chapter 4 took place in 1916. Dedicated to the ministry in his infancy by his parents after experiencing what he claimed was miraculous healing, David later fulfilled their prayers when he finally decided to enter the ministry. This took place at the CI in Magalang, Pampanga, in 1931 during the consecration service where Cottingham was the guest preacher. "*Yung lahat ng sermon tila ako lang ang sinesermonan* . . . [all of the sermons seem to be specifically directed at me . . .]," he recalled. On the final night, as Cottingham finished preaching on the gospel text, "the harvest is plentiful, but the workers are few," he appealed to those who were "able and willing" to come to the front. Candelaria described: "*Parang bang mayroong nagtindig sa akin na ako ang unang nagpunta sa unahan* [As if somebody pulled me up that I was the first one to go to the front]."[49] He soon left his government clerk position in Cabanatuan and began studies at UTS. After graduating at the top of his class, he served congregations in Hagonoy and Taytay, which both grew in "leaps and bounds." For twelve consecutive years, he was secretary of the powerful Committee on Conference Relations in the Conference. He was also dean of the Pastor's School for five years.[50]

Early on in the campaign in 1953 when Sumrall preached at the Manila District workers meeting at Knox Methodist Church, David had what he called his "first experience with Pentecost." He soon opened the Taytay Church for a healing revival one Sunday evening in August. It was while the Roberts film was being shown that David was "healed" from a lingering illness. Also, among those who testified to their healing were his wife Felicisima and their eldest son Jesse.[51] That meeting thrust the Taytay church not only to the forefront of the Manila healing revival, but also on a trajectory towards Pentecostalism. At a time when the AG did not yet have a significant presence in the Tagalog area, Taytay Methodist Church acted as a quasi-AG church as it actively supported the nascent healing revival. For example, Taytay Methodists "occasionally" attended special meetings at Glad Tidings Revival Center in Maypajo. When Sumrall started "The Healing Hour," a fifteen-minute radio program at the height of the Erickson campaign, the generous Methodist congregation

49. David M. Candelaria, interview, 19 May 2005. It appears that this CI took place in the CI of 1932 and not 1931 as Candelaria claimed. For details about the Magalang CI, see *PO*, January 1932, 2.

50. *PAC* (1952), 16; *PAC* 1953, 116–17; Sumrall, *Dove and the Eagle*, 25–26. See also David M. Candelaria, interview, 19 May 2005.

51. *World Harvest*, February 1963, 6–7; Sumrall, *Dove and the Eagle*, 26–28.

helped foot the bill. It also filled "coconut banks" to help raise funds for the construction of the Bethel facility.[52]

The salvation-healing revival among Methodists and their participation in the Erickson campaign should be seen as part of the broader revival movement, as we have indicated earlier, within the denomination at that time. What eventually drew Ruben to Sumrall was his yearning for a recovery of what he termed "lost power," a sense of empowerment he had initially experienced at a retreat in Guiguinto, Bulacan in November 1931 under Cottingham's preaching:

> I shall never forget that gathering as long as I live. Dr. J. F. Cottingham, a missionary in the Philippines for almost forty years [sic], spoke on the Power of the Holy Spirit. At about the close of his message, the Holy Spirit fell upon the expectant congregation of about sixty pastors and women workers. The women started crying and wailing as that minister, full of the Holy Spirit, shouted, "Hallelujah!" And "Glory to God!" encouraging us to shout and praise the Lord. And so even the ministers were gripped by the power of the Holy Spirit; and everyone of us were crying and praying under the spell of God's mighty power. All of us went forward to the altar, and for over two hours, knelt in prayer and consecration. From that moment on I decided I would stick to the ministry of the Lord Jesus Christ and praise His Name.[53]

Ruben, who was assistant pastor in Cabanatuan at that time, also attributed to this experience an impetus to audaciously engage in street preaching and conduct a successful evangelistic meeting afterwards.[54] The fact that he allowed Sumrall to include this account in *The True Story of Clarita Villanueva*, published a year after he left Methodism, suggests that Ruben wanted to clarify that his role in the healing revivals did not emerge from a vacuum, but instead harkened back to Methodism's *culto Pentecostal* past. However, by using the phrase "lost power," he also assumed that the same practice, along with the culture and values it had helped perpetuate, had long since become muted, if not vanished, and therefore needed to be revived. By explicitly citing a past glory, he saw his actions, along with other Methodists, as more faithful to Methodism than what his detractors would allow. Incidentally, Ruben's flight to Pentecostalism was also reminiscent

---

52. Sumrall and Dudley, *Life Story*, 176; Sumrall, *Modern Manila Miracles*, 60–63; Sumrall, *Dove and the Eagle*, 31; Javier, "Personal Memoir," 290–92.

53. See Sumrall, *Clarita Villanueva*, 112–13.

54. Ibid.

of the tendency among holiness people who had adopted "the doctrine of Pentecostal baptism in the Spirit," to eventually embrace divine healing.[55]

Pentecostal Defections and Consequences

Despite the positive results of the salvation-healing campaign in Methodist churches, the Methodist leadership was, however, unhappy with the collaboration between Sumrall and the Candelarias. An anticipatory clash would occur at the Conference in Cabanatuan City on February, 1954, just days after the Erickson campaign. At one point during the Conference, Ruben was put through what he described as a "friendly 'inquisition'" by Bishop Valencia, some American missionaries, and church dignitaries. They questioned, among other things, his friendship and cooperation with Sumrall, and Sumrall's free access to Methodist pulpits. Accused of violating the *Book of Discipline*, Ruben countered, "if there should be a conflict between my Bible and my discipline, I would have no difficulty in deciding which one will prevail." Thus, for his refusal to acquiesce to their demands, the bishop "fired" him. Ruben filed for a sabbatical leave a few days later.[56]

Though his fate had been decided, Ruben still made a last ditch effort to promote divine healing at that same Conference. In his report before the assembly, he not only reiterated the work of revival in the district and his participation in the Erickson campaign, but also insisted on the need for the church to incorporate divine healing in its evangelistic efforts to successfully "beat Roman Catholic propaganda and power so deeply entrenched in the country." He also reminded them of the episcopal address at the General Conference two years earlier, which had admonished the denomination to learn from the Pentecostals. Ruben's recommendations, however, provoked a two-hour heated debate that eventually led to the formation of a special committee of five to study the question of divine healing. The debate, nevertheless, failed to silence Ruben and his supporters. At the evening service, he preached on the subject using texts from the Book of Hebrews and was supported by a number of lay delegates who rose to testify to their own healing. When the committee reported on the last day, it recommended eight Bible texts affirming divine healing. Though the committee clearly affirmed the practice in principle, it failed, however, to

---

55. Dayton, *Theological Roots of Pentecostalism*, 136; Dayton, "Evangelical Healing Movement," 7–18.

56. Candelaria, *Methodist Minister*, 16–22; Sumrall, *Dove and the Eagle*, 16–21.

explicitly address Ruben's recommendations. The church was simply unwilling to imitate what the Pentecostals were doing.[57]

Thus, Ruben's stellar career in Methodism basically ended at the close of the conference. Left without an appointment and a parsonage, he eventually accepted Sumrall's offer to take the Tagalog pastorate of the thriving Bethel Temple. He filed for "voluntary withdrawal" at the Conference a year later.[58] In January 1955, with the encouragement of visiting evangelist Ralph Byrd and Ernest Reb, the new senior pastor of Bethel, Ruben claimed to have experienced the baptism of the Holy Spirit "according to the Bible pattern" after being prayed for by the two in his office.[59] Ruben recalled: "I had gone the four days without a drop of water or any kind of food . . . I was so weak. I could hardly raise my hands, but as I did I felt something coming. All of a sudden I was I realized I was speaking in other tongues. I had been baptized with the Holy Spirit just like the disciples in the upper room in Jerusalem 2,000 years ago. Hallelujah!"[60] Four days later David, who was still connected with the Methodist Church, also experienced his "Pentecostal infilling" at Reb's home in Bethel Temple. The congregation in Taytay would soon follow suit.[61]

About a week after his Pentecost, David invited Reb, who was joined by some deacons and members from Bethel, to conduct a weeklong revival meeting in his church. On February 11, the first evening, an outpouring of the Holy Spirit came to the church, which, according to Javier, who was a member of the church at that time, was "similar to Acts 2."[62] In the article, "When God Baptized a Methodist Church" in Sumrall's *World Harvest* magazine in 1963, David vividly recollected the supernatural aspects of this event:

> About one week after I received my baptism in the Spirit there was a Holy Ghost revival in my church and, on the first night, there was a great outpouring and anointing. About 80 people received the Baptism that first night in a most unique way, unique because

57. PAC (1954), 26, 34; PAC (1954), 52–53; PAC (1954), 70–71.
58. PAC (1955), 36; Candelaria, *Methodist Minister*, 22–24; Sumrall, *Dove and the Eagle*, 21–22.
59. Candelaria, *Methodist Minister*, 24–32; Sumrall, *Dove and the Eagle*, 22–24; PE, 27 March 1955, 7.
60. Candelaria, "God Spoke to Me," 4.
61. *World Harvest*, February 1963, 7; PE, 27 March 1955, 7.
62. Jesse Candelaria, e-mail, 24 February 2005; Javier, "Personal Memoir," 292; PE, 27 March 1955, 7.

not one of those 80 people had ever seen anyone receive the Baptism before. Neither had any one of those 80 heard any person speak in tongues before.

Secondly, it was unique because about 200 people around the community came running toward the church that evening. *They came carrying buckets of water to help us extinguish the fire—because they thought our church was burning.* On the top of our building they saw a great cloud of smoke and they thought the church was afire but, when they came, they found out that they were wrong. *It was not an earthly fire—it was the fire of the Holy Spirit from on high*, burning and melting the hearts of men and women to become worthy witnesses of Jesus Christ our Lord and Saviour. Truly has God done much for us all, for which I am so grateful and thankful to Him. Hallelujah![63]

The Taytay Revival of 1955 marked another distinctive turn for Methodist *culto Pentecostal* revivalism. It highlighted what appears to be the first-ever recorded occurrence of *glossolalia* among Methodists in a Methodist Church building courtesy of Reb and other visitors from Bethel who led the meeting. But the account about the "great cloud of smoke" that billowed from the church and was mistaken as "earthly fire" by the surrounding community, as maintained by David, added a supernatural twist to the occasion. As people rushed to the church to douse the fire, they instead witnessed a congregation of worshippers in a heightened state of spiritual bliss, speaking in tongues while most of them laid "slain" on the floor, according to David in a separate account.[64] Hence, what simply started as the congregation's interest in divine healing revivalism, eventually led them to experience *glossolalia*, a phenomena that was so central to Pentecostal thought and practice. The breach that separated them from other traditional Methodists had further widened, and ultimately ended their relationship with the Methodist Church.

At the Conference in March, a complaint was filed against David under Paragraph 921 of the *Doctrines and Discipline* (1952) by one of his members who was probably reacting to the previous Pentecostal incident at Taytay Church. Though David was cleared by the investigating committee, tensions were, however, far from over.[65] A year later, when Bishop Valencia decreed to transfer him to another church, he finally decided to secede and,

---

63. *World Harvest*, February 1963, 7.
64. David M. Candelaria, interview, 19 May 2005.
65. *PAC* (1955), 33–34.

along with most of the members of his congregation, formed the Taytay Methodist Community Church (hereafter TMCC). The subsequent trial organized by the Conference ultimately "expelled" David. After the defection, less than half of the 460-member congregation rejoined the Methodist Church under the new pastor, Eladio Reyes. Finding themselves evicted from their place of worship, the original Methodist congregation eventually worshipped in several locations until opening a new church building in Barangay San Isidro, which is less than a kilometer away from the original one. The bitter separation between the two congregations also resulted in an acrimonious legal standoff over church property that reached the Court of First Instance of the Rizal Province, which in turn decided in favor of the Methodist Church. Further appeals by David's group on the provincial court's ruling also reached the Philippine Supreme Court and the Court of Appeals in 1963. Ultimately, they relinquished the original building and opened a new one on April 9, 1972, also in Barangay San Isidro in Taytay.[66]

Though it never joined the AG, the TMCC continued to maintain friendly relations with the Pentecostal denomination. For example, young people from the church and its daughter churches studied at Bethel Bible Institute, some of whom eventually served in the AG with distinction. Prominent among them was Eleazar Javier (1938–1912), Ruben's son-in-law, who became one of the pastors at Bethel Temple after being granted release by TMCC in 1961. He later rose within the ranks to serve as General Superintendent of the Philippine General Council of the AG from 1977–1997.[67] After his stint with the AG national leadership, he became senior pastor of TMCC. During his pastorate, the church was renamed, "The Messiah Community Church" in 2002, as if to signal a break from its Methodist roots.[68] For the Taytay Methodists who stayed with the Methodist Church, its Pentecostal impulse never completely evaporated as it experienced resurgence in the 1980s and in the early 1990s with the ascent of the Charismatic movement in the country.[69] The church, which remains

---

66. David M. Candelaria, interview, 19 May 2005; *World Harvest*, February 1963, 7; *PAC* (1957), 39; *PAC* (1959), 26; *PAC* (1963), 117–18; *PAC* (1964), 79. See also Taytay Methodist Community Church v. Eladio M. Reyes, G. R. No. L-15731 (Republic of the Philippines Supreme Court 1963), http://www.lawphil.net/judjuris/juri1963/apr1963/gr_l-15731_1963.html (accessed October 9, 2016).

67. Javier, "Personal Memoir," 293, 298; Javier, "Pentecostal Legacy," 57–82.

68. See David M. Candelaria, interview.

69. Although the Catholic Charismatic renewal movement reached the Philippines in the early 1970s, the movement exploded in the late 1970s and early 1980s. See Kessler and Rüland, "Responses to Rapid Social Change," 78.

Charismatic in orientation to this day, emerged as the fastest growing UMC congregation in the Philippines during that period.[70] Prominent Taytay Methodists were also instrumental in the forming of Aldersgate United Methodist Renewal Fellowship, a Charismatic renewal group operating within the UMC in the Philippines in 1992.[71]

While David and the TMCC continued to battle with the Methodist Church for ownership of the Taytay property in the 1960s, Ruben also had a fair share of legal entanglements at Bethel Temple that ironically pitted him against the AG leaders in the United States or the "A. G. 'fathers' in Springfield" over what he felt was their unwillingness to hand over leadership to Filipinos at Bethel—a sentiment reminiscent of early Philippine Methodist struggle for autonomy.[72] On November 1963, barely two weeks after Ruben had been elected to head Bethel as its first Filipino administrator, the Philippines General Council of the AG acted to wrest control of the church by sending two armed guards to prevent the congregation from gathering for services; but this, however, proved futile. Four months later, two criminal cases were filed against Ruben in the Court of First Instance of Manila.[73]

Bethel's tenuous relationship with its parent denomination ultimately came to a head on May 1965 when the General Council, which had met for its convention, dissolved the Manila-based Central District which Bethel was under, thereby depriving its workers of their licenses to preach. In response to this, Ruben and the other ministers, as well as their supporters, resolved to separate and form the Philippine Assemblies of God, Inc. (hereafter PAG), a "self propagating, self-governing, and self-supporting" church, which also elected Ruben as its first General Superintendent.[74] Internal disagreements among the nationals at Bethel, mainly involving the status of its missionary pastor, however, eventually forced three groups to leave, including that of Ruben's, which began holding its own services in a rented building close to Bethel. Even after Ruben's death in 1989, the PAG continued to maintain a network of about forty churches in the Southern

---

70. Taytay UMC experienced phenomenal growth from 1982–1994. See Amable, "Intensive Study of Church Growth," 58. For Taytay UMC's history, see "The History of the Taytay UMC."

71. See Padang, *Primer for United Methodists*, 79–81.

72. Candelaria, "The A. G. Show," 8–9; Esther C. Javier, e-mail, 10 February 2006.

73. Candelaria, "The A. G. Show," 7–9.

74. Tupas, "Philippine Assemblies of God," 10.

Tagalog region.[75] Manila Bethel Temple, on the other hand, ceased to be connected with the AG, but continued to prosper under its American pastor and his successor. Now called Cathedral of Praise, the six-thousand-seat megachurch has been under the helm of Lester Sumrall's great-nephew, David E. Sumrall, since 1980.[76]

As for the Methodist Church, the defections took a significant toll on its membership. This was substantiated by Dwight E. Stevenson, a Disciple of Christ educator who visited the Philippines in 1955, when he wrote that the AG "proselytized heavily" from the Methodist Church in Manila.[77] A perusal of the statistics in the Philippines Annual Conference journals from 1955 to 1960 indicates that the Manila District lost 430 members from a number of churches, excluding Taytay, by "transfer to other denominations." Interestingly, the statistics never showed any decrease in the Taytay membership even after the break in 1956 except for its Sunday School attendance, which was cut to half in the 1957 record. Since we know that more than 230 members left Taytay, it is safe to say that about six hundred members left the Methodist Church. Aside from the Taytay Methodist Church, the hardest hit included: Kamuning Methodist Church in Quezon City; Central Methodist Church in Manila; and Martyr's Methodist Church in Paranaque.[78]

These losses, however, were overshadowed by gains posted by the district under the leadership of Cottingham's apostle, and the now veteran Esteban T. Cruz, who quickly replaced Candelaria. As the AG increasingly advanced in Manila and other urban centers around the country, the Methodists turned much of their attention to rural frontiers south of Manila. After launching an "unprecedented evangelistic program and missionary enterprise" in 1956 in southern Luzon and the Visayan islands, the district planted thirty-six new churches in what was later to become the Southern Luzon Visayas District.[79] Also in 1956, Manila Methodists, along with

75. Esther C. Javier, e-mail, 10 February 2006.

76. Sumrall and Dudley, *Life Story*, 177–78. The Cathedral of Praise is cited as one of the ten largest independent Pentecostal churches in the country in Suico, "Pentecostalism in the Philippines," in Anderson and Tang, *Asian and Pentecostal*, 355. Strang, on the other hand, claims that it is the "largest church in the Philippines with more than 24,000 members" in "Sumrall, Lester Frank," 1110.

77. Stevenson, *Christianity in the Philippines*, 20.

78. See *PAC* (1955), 100–1; *PAC* (1956), 118–19; *PAC* (1957), 104–5; *PAC* (1958), 122–23; *PAC* (1959), 160–61; *PAC* (1960), 164–65.

79. *PAC* (1965), 77.

member churches of the PFCC, as if to show the AG that they, too, can muster mammoth crowds, welcomed Billy Graham at the Rizal Stadium for what the PFCC monthly newsletter described as a "reverent and orderly" evangelistic "crusade."[80]

Since Graham, at that time, began to emerge as the symbol of popular American evangelical culture,[81] the support Philippine Methodists gave to his campaign can be interpreted as part of their increasing realignment with a new form of Protestant evangelicalism. This form carried with it a revivalism that was more acceptable to mainstream Protestants, "reverent and orderly," and conversionist-oriented. Thus, it was no accident that Methodists similarly launched an unprecedented "Philippines Evangelistic Crusade" in 1964 to win new Roman Catholic converts to Methodism. These resulted in a series of "crusades" beginning at Manila's downtown Plaza Miranda, a busy thoroughfare in Quiapo, featuring the future bishop Paul Locke Granadosin as evangelist. These crusades were continued in a number of towns and cities in southern Luzon and in the Visayas.[82]

With the last vestiges of *culto Pentecostal* culture snuffed out, Filipino Methodists increasingly assumed an antithetical stance to the very things the Pentecostals represented. Perhaps, wary of being identified with the "hysterically shouting" Pentecostals, they instead opted for a more respectable form of revivalism. Hence, developments in popular evangelical culture in the 1960s as represented by Graham facilitated Philippine Methodism's shift to outdoor mass evangelistic crusades for years to come.

---

80. *Philippine Christian Advance*, March 1956, 24; Cunningham, "Diversities," 79.

81. We should note that Graham's collaboration with the so-called "liberal" Federal Council of Churches, PFCC's counterpart in the United States, would eventually split Graham's "neo evangelicals" from hardcore fundamentalists in 1957. See Marsden, "Fundamentalism," 28–30; Rosell, *Surprising Work of God*, 157–59.

82. See *PAC* (1964), 96; *PAC* (1965), 123–26.

THE METHODIST HEALING REVIVAL, AND ITS CONSEQUENCES, 1934–1965

Figure 6.1. Cagayan Valley missionary Curran L. Spottswood preaching at the "great evangelistic campaign" at Knox Memorial Methodist Church on the third week of November 1953. Source: *Philippine Christian Advance*, December 1953.

Figure 6.2. Philippines Central Conference, Central Methodist Church, Manila, November 11, 1948: (left to right) Bishop J. Waskom Pickett, Ruth R. Pickett, Bishop Dionisio D. Alejandro, Consuela G. Alejandro. Source: Archives and Special Collections, Asbury University, Wilmore, Kentucky.

Figure 6.3. Lester F. Sumrall, AG missionary to Manila, c. 1950s. Source: Sumrall, *Modern Manila Miracles* (1954).

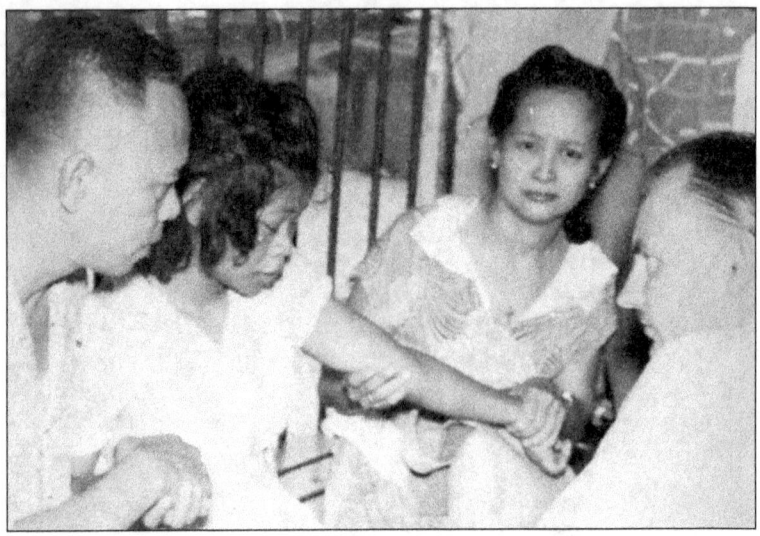

Figure 6.4. Lester Sumrall observes Clarita Villanueva in her cell before praying for her healing and deliverance, Bilibid Prison, Manila, May 1953. Source: Sumrall, *Clarita Villanueva* (1955).

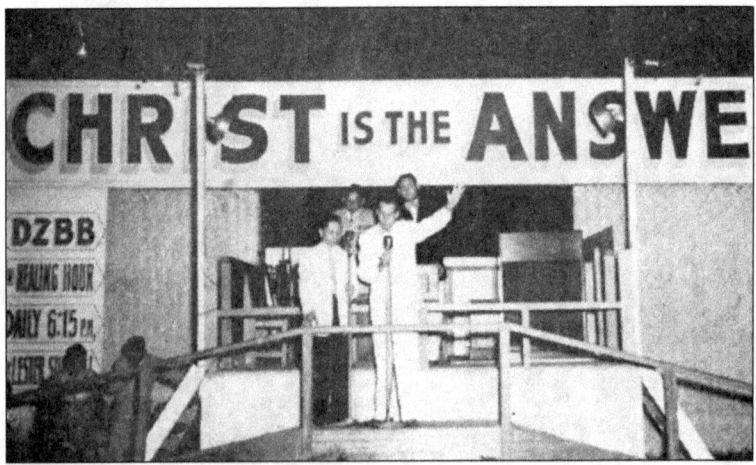

Figure 6.5. Clifton Erickson's six-week Salvation-Healing Revival, Roxas Park, Manila, January–March, 1954. District Superintendent Ruben Candelaria translating for healing evangelist Clifton Erickson. Methodist minister David Candelaria, pastor of Taytay Methodist Church, and AG missionary Lester Sumrall are seated behind them. Source: Sumrall, *Modern Manila Miracles* (1954).

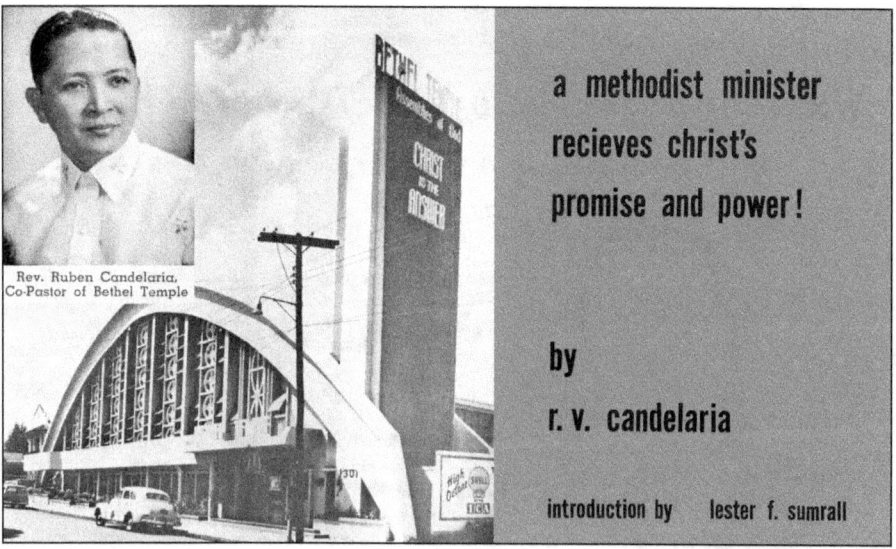

Figure 6.6. Former District Superintendent Ruben V. Candelaria (inset), co-pastor of Bethel Temple, and his book, *A Methodist Minister Receives Christ's Promise and Power* (1956). Sources: Sumrall, *The Dove and the Eagle* (1962); Candelaria, *A Methodist Minister* (1956).

Supernatural Smoke Appeared on Top of Church

WHEN GOD BAPTIZED A METHODIST CHURCH

With the Holy Ghost — "THE DAVID CANDELARIA STORY"

into my pulpit but, when I invited Rev. Sumrall to preach for me the following Sunday, I was surprised to hear him say that he would not come. I did not know that Ruben (my cousin) had told him so many things about me that, although they were true, were quite unfavorable to me. However, I insisted with all sincerity until he promised that he would come Sunday evening with my cousin, Rev. Ruben Candelaria, who was also my District Superintendent. They brought with them a film of Oral Roberts titled "Venture Into Faith."

Before this time I was operated on in the Mary Johnston Hospital for Hemorrhoids and, after having been released from the hospital for exactly ten and one-half months, I was bleeding every day—sometimes profusely — and the medical doctors were unable to do anything to help me, much less to stop my bleeding. I thought I was dying. While this film was being shown, I became so over-

Figure 6.7. David Candelaria, former pastor of Taytay Methodist Church and founding pastor of Taytay Methodist Community Church, and an article he wrote in 1963 narrating his conversion to Pentecostalism and the Pentecostal revival at Taytay Methodist Church in 1955. Source: *World Harvest*, February 1963.

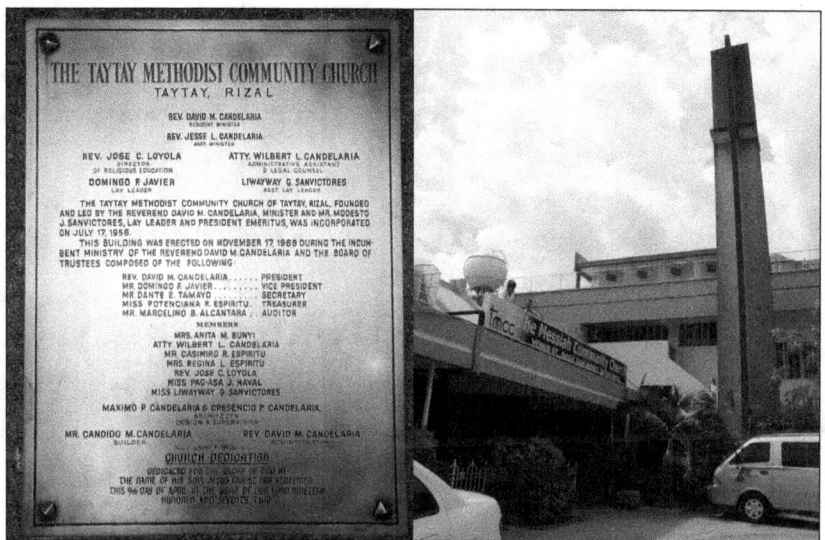

Figure 6.8. Taytay Methodist Community Church marker and The Messiah Community Church building, Barangay San Isidro, Taytay, Rizal, May 19, 2005. This was the church built by David Candelaria and his supporters after they ceded the old Methodist Church building in Taytay to the Methodist Church after a prolonged legal battle. Source: Photograph by author.

Conclusion

The story of *culto Pentecostal* revivalism reveals to us many things regarding the development and contours of Pentecostal revivalism in the Methodist Church in the Philippines. One of the things that the narrative helps unearth is the theological location of the missionaries who, together with the contributions of pioneer indigenous workers, helped lay the foundations of Methodism in the Philippines. We have established that these missionaries were mostly cast from the molds of the American evangelical revivalist tradition—meaning, they often heeded the call to overseas mission volunteerism through some ritualized form of post-conversion consecration, where they realized a sense of empowerment and purpose higher than themselves. We have noticeably seen this with the bishops and the mission recruits who later made their mark in the country, as is evident in their testimonies of post-conversion experiences in Holiness movement-inspired events and, in the case of many missionaries, with their connections with the SVM. Thus, even though not all of them functioned as revivalists *per se*, and did not share homogenous views on other issues, there appeared to be a general acceptance of revival methods among them. Accordingly, missionary theological location also points to the theological sources of *culto Pentecostal* revivalism. Furthermore, as we have established, the sources point to both formal and informal denominational channels, which defied geographical borders while tapping into a larger web of transatlantic and transpacific holiness revival spiritual culture.

The audience is also an important factor not to be left out of the equation. Despite the emotionalism involved in the *culto Pentecostal* revivals, this should never distract us from seeing that their doctrinal content, although mostly rooted in the American evangelical experience, obviously made sense to Filipino Methodists who rushed to, if not lingered at, the altar to respond to calls for Spirit baptism or holy living. We need to consider seriously that their act of response involved some degree of rationality and was not merely a spur-of-the-moment reaction to emotional appeals.

This runs counter to recent socio-scientific analyses which explain the success of the Pentecostal movement in the Philippines on the basis that Filipinos, along with other Asian cultures, are "right brained dominant" or emotional, in effect unwittingly suggesting that Western cultures are less emotional. But what is really at stake here is the notion that those who turn to ecstatic forms of Christianity, or any ecstatic forms of religion for that matter, do not make any rational decisions at all. For so long as theology or belief is taken out of the equation and all that is talked about are the other products that missionaries brought with them, we are missing the bigger picture. Since missionary revivalists were talking in theological terms, we need to acknowledge that their audiences, including the indigenous workers, who later retransmitted these terms more effectively in the vernacular, found something valuable in them. Their life's questions, perhaps, were being answered by the ideas the revival messages conveyed.[1]

Additionally, we should remember that the same ideas were not entirely foreign to the people who accepted them, and appropriated them later; that they were not merely received in a vacuum, but had been filtered through a pre-existent culture, which already contained its own language, memories, experiences, images, and concepts. Hence, it was perhaps Philippine cultural precedents and not Filipino neurological physiology which accounts more for the appeal of Pentecost revivalism. As we have pointed out, the revivals drew parallels, although inadvertently, from different elements already present in Philippine culture, such as indigenous musical culture, folk mysticism and, to some degree, supernaturalism. Nevertheless, Pentecostal services also underwent a process of translation (either through missionaries or through national workers) in the Philippines. But something also happened in the translation process: the original meanings, to some degree, were modified and indigenized.[2] As we have suggested in the previous chapters, the American Methodist-imported practice found new forms of reception, application, configuration, and meaning in the Philippine Methodist context. While the extent of modification requires further research, we have established that by the time Pentecostal services reached Philippine Methodism, they were openly allowed to flourish within the denomination's official structures and encouraged to take center stage in

---

1. A similar argument is found in Porter, "Cultural Imperialism," 384; Robert, "Shifting Southward," 53.

2. This reflection is based from a discussion by Andrew Walls on the "translation principle," in Walls, *Missionary Movement*, 26–42.

the activities of the church, perhaps at a time when they were already being relegated to the fringes of American Methodist life. Pentecostal meetings also found unique application, for example, when they were intensified to counteract the 1909 Zamora schism. We have also demonstrated that there was greater receptivity to women as preachers or revival ritual practitioners by Filipino mixed audiences—a configuration not typically found in other Asian cultures at that time.

In addition to its intersection with Philippine culture, the socio-religious context also provided essential ground for *culto Pentecostal*'s success. It is worth noting that the American-imported revival meetings, unintentionally, became venues of empowerment for their Filipino participants as they allowed for a different expression of worship where usual conventions of religious hierarchy and social order of class, gender, and even color were broken, albeit temporarily. They also implicitly illuminated Methodism's opposition to the intricacies of Roman Catholic mass and the hierarchical structures they represented, while providing ritualized expressions for religious freedom. While the rituals themselves disrupted the social order, and thereby provided fodder for virulent attacks against MEC churches, they also, paradoxically, helped win some degree of respect for the denomination for publicly demonstrating Methodism's ability to reorder and discipline the lives of its adherents. Consequently, the persistent ritualizing of morality in the ubiquitous Pentecostal meetings, without a doubt, also helped shape Philippine Methodist self-identity and behavior in the society. This was made apparent, for example, by a long line of Filipino Methodists in prominent positions in the government who unabashedly championed moral causes in the public square, just like the ones addressed in the *culto Pentecostal* revivals—a legacy not lost even today.[3]

Nevertheless, the same high standards of discipline that Pentecostal meetings helped fashion proved to be a bane for Philippine Methodists as they placed enormous pressures upon them. This was precisely what happened in the morality plays that would finally instigate the Stagg schism. It seems ironic to note that *culto Pentecostal*, which was once used to cushion and counter the toll of the Zamora secession in 1909 by emphasizing membership quality over quantity, also contributed to the disappointments surrounding the de Armas fiasco two decades later. The ensuing debacle

---

3. See Deats, *Story of Methodism*, 52–58. This same moral impulse is not lost on former Supreme Court Chief Justice Reynato Puno, a United Methodist lay preacher who claimed that the "justice system is based on our morality which is based on our spirituality." See "Puno Calls for Moral Force."

showed that the same missionaries and nationals whom we have identified as vanguards of holiness, or at least of moralizing piety, were also susceptible to inconsistencies and moral ambiguities. This, however, demonstrates that the *culto Pentecostal* story is not only a recognition of what Methodists may have done right in the Philippines, but also of their limitations, despite their lofty moral ideals. It also reminds us that the pervasive *culto Pentecostal* culture reflected more what Filipino Methodists aspired to be rather than what they really were. Perhaps Christian history must always be prepared to allow its "heroes" some humanity and contradictions in order to tell their stories more accurately.

The potential for denominational rifts occasioned through the holiness motif of *culto Pentecostal* was just one side of the coin, however. The other side, which involved pneumatology, along with its inherent allusion to supernaturalism or the miraculous, also later proved its volatile potential once it came into contact with modern Pentecostalism in the 1950s. Thus, it is not an overstatement to say that it was not an accident that the Manila Healing Revival found greater appeal among Methodists over all other Protestants in the city at that time. Although the majority of those who participated, of course, were Roman Catholics, it was former Methodists, not newly converted Catholics, who quickly helped supply the immediate leadership needs of the AG in Manila. The morphing of some Philippine Methodist elements to Pentecostalism was reminiscent to that of a much more significant number of holiness people in the United States who eventually became Pentecostals at the onset of the modern Pentecostal revival beginning in 1906. Although the Philippine branch of the Methodist Church was, of course, not a holiness denomination strictly speaking, it had enough holiness elements to serve as fertile ground for AG proselytizing. This, then, reminds us that Pentecostal missions or the spread of worldwide Pentecostalism cannot be simply explained by Pentecostal missionaries; their numbers were too small to account for that growth in the first place.[4] The AG healing revivals' intersection with Philippine Methodism showed that Pentecostal missions in one particular field could profoundly benefit from an existing Protestant presence heavily influenced by the Holiness movement.

We should also remember that Methodist attraction to the healing revivals can be best understood if seen as a radicalization of *culto Pentecostal* revivalism while most of the older holiness-influenced Methodist guards who

---

4. See list of Pentecostal missionaries in Anderson, *Spreading Fires*, 288.

stayed with the denomination, on the other hand, represented its mellowing. Alejandro's complaints against a newly emerging Philippine Pentecostalism marked a watershed moment between a mainstream-oriented Methodist revivalism and the old Methodist *culto Pentecostal* revivalism. Those who were in power did not oppose the doctrine of divine healing itself but, perhaps wary of being identified with the "hysterically shouting" Pentecostals, they increasingly assumed an antithetical stance to the very things the Pentecostals represented. Thus, they opted for a mainstream form of revivalism as epitomized in their collaboration with the PFCC to bring about Billy Graham's 1956 "crusade" in Manila (the Pentecostals countered by bringing in Oral Roberts a few months later). This was indicative of their rising realignment with a newly emerging form of evangelicalism, which carried with it a revivalism that was more acceptable to mainstream Protestantism, "reverent and orderly," and conversionist-oriented. It was this type of revivalism that would define their revival campaigns for years to come.

However, it would be inaccurate to interpret Philippine Methodism's trajectory at this juncture as a sign of *embourgeoisement*. We should note that Methodists had begun to be much more self-aware of the need for upward mobility as early as the 1930s as underscored, for example, in the construction of their Central Student Church cathedral. Furthermore, it appears, though, that it was the AG that had become more socially-aspirant at this point on account of their aggressive campaigns in Manila and other urban centers in the country. The social status of the Methodists who participated in the AG revivals, at least the ones we have mentioned in chapter 6, also shows that Pentecostalism does not only attract the socially deprived or the "disinherited," to borrow the word Robert Mapes Anderson famously attached to American Pentecostals.[5] Hence, to analyze the differences between the two camps simply along social lines would seem to be problematic.

Thus, given the implications we have already outlined, no historical presentation of the Methodist Church in the Philippines would be accurate without recognizing the role played by holiness-Pentecost-themed revivalism in shaping the denomination to what it is today. We must understand not only how *culto Pentecostal* practice, together with the culture it inspired, helped set John Wesley's Philippine progeny apart from their Protestant neighbors during the first half of the twentieth century, but also why Pentecostal impulses continue to manifest themselves within the denomination

5. See Anderson, *Vision of the Disinherited*.

in a myriad of ways even to this day. In hindsight, it may also help illuminate why, even after the emergence of liberation theology in the intellectual culture of Philippine Christianity during the social-political upheavals of the Marcos dictatorship era of the 1970s and 1980s, Filipino Methodists remain generally evangelistic. Furthermore, even their most progressive theological thinkers, as demonstrated in a recent study, still hold on to a "holistic view of social transformation," where "personal" dimensions of spirituality are still recognized as essential.[6]

---

6. A recent study has investigated the theologies of three prominent Philippine Methodist thinkers, namely: Bishop Emerito P. Nacpil, Bishop Daniel C. Arichea Jr., and Elizabeth S. Tapia. See Tangunan, "Social Transformation in the Philippines," 184–205.

Bibliography

Primary Sources

Alejandro, Dionisio D. *From Darkness to Light: A Brief Chronicle of the Beginnings and Spread of Methodism in the Philippines.* Quezon City, Philippines: United Methodist Church Philippines Central Conference Board of Communications and Publications, 1974.

———. "From Roman Catholicism to the Protestant Faith." In *Voices from Many Lands*, edited by Gilbert C. Nee, 27–40. Louisville: Pentecostal, 1936.

———. "The Holy Spirit in Christian Experience." In *Selected Philippine Sermons*, edited by Gerald H. Anderson and others, 68–82. Manila: Union Theological Seminary, 1967.

———. "My Impressions." *PO*, September 1924.

Alejandro, Dionisio D., and José L. Valencia. *The Episcopal Address of the Bishops of the Methodist Church of the Philippines Central Conference, Central Church, Manila, October 28th, 1964.* Manila: n.p., 1964.

Badley, Brenton T. *Warne of India: The Life-Story of Bishop Francis Wesley Warne.* Madras: Madras, 1932.

"Baquit Aco Protestante?" *PCA*, 1 February 1902.

Bowie, Mary E. *Alabaster and Spikenard: The Life of Iva Durham Vennard, D.D., Founder of Chicago Evangelistic Institute.* Chicago: Chicago Evangelistic Institute, 1947.

Brown, William A. "A Little Old Woman." *The Epworth Herald*, April 4, 1903.

Cabildo, Arcadio G. "Maikling Talambuhay Ni Obispo Nicolas Zamora." *Ang Ilaw*, January–September 1975.

Calkins, Harvey R. "A Paramount and Present Duty." *IW*, 7 October 1909.

Candelaria, David M. "When God Baptized a Methodist Church with the Holy Ghost: The David Candelaria Story." *World Harvest*, February 1963.

Candelaria, Ruben V. "The A.G. Show in the Philippines Is On." In *Bethel Temple 12th Anniversary*, 7–9. Manila: Bethel Temple 12th Anniversary Committee, 1966.

———. "God Spoke to Me . . . 12 Years Ago." In *Bethel Temple 12th Anniversary*, 4. Manila: Bethel Temple 12th Anniversary Committee, 1966.

———. *A Methodist Minister Receives Christ's Promise and Power.* Southbend, IN: Calvary, 1956.

Castells, Francisco P. "A Story of the Philippines." *The Christian and Missionary Alliance*, 12 May 1900.

Central Student Church: Manila, Philippine Islands. New York: Board of Foreign Missions, Methodist Episcopal Church, 1930.
Chenoweth, Arthur E. "Philippine Sketches." *WWM*, January 1904.
Crabtree, Mary M. "Life at the Harris Memorial Bible School," *WMF*, June 1919.
———. "One of Our Filipina Deaconesses." *WMF*, July 1912.
Davidson, Leonard P. "The Province of Luzon." *The Assembly Herald*, July 1901.
Dean, John Marvin. *The Cross of Christ in Bolo-Land*. Chicago: Revell, 1902.
De Gamoneda, Francisco J. *Plano de Manila y sus de Arrabales* [map], 1898, 1:10,000. "Philippines Maps." University of Texas Libraries Perry-Castañeda Library Map Collection. http://www.lib.utexas.edu/maps/historical/manila_and_suburbs_1898.jpg.
"Death and Burial of Bishop Eveland." *CA*, 3 August 1916.
Devins, John B. *An Observer in the Philippines: Or Life in Our New Possessions*. Boston: American Tract Society, 1905.
Diffendorfer, Ralph E., ed. *The World Service of the Methodist Episcopal Church*. Chicago: Methodist Episcopal Church Council of Boards of Benevolence, Committee on Conservation and Advance, 1923.
Dizon, Nicolas C. "Notes around the Circles." *PO*, February 1921.
Dunn, Glenn, et al. "Revival in Manila." *PE*, 21 March 1954.
Erbst, Wilhelmina. "Through Pampanga Province," *PCA*, August 1910.
———. "Travel and Teaching in the Mountains of Luzon," *WMF*, November 1918.
Ernsberger, David O. "Story of the South Indian Conference." In *India Mission Jubilee of the Methodist Episcopal Church in Southern Asia: Story of the Celebration Held at Bareilly, India, from December 28th, 1906, to January 1st, 1907, Inclusive*, edited by Frederick B. Price, 168–88. Calcutta: Methodist, 1907.
Eveland, William P. "Concerning the Philippines." *CA*, 24 April 1913.
———. "A Message from Bishop Eveland." *PO*, August 1912.
———. "A Translated Worker." *WMF*, September 1914.
Farmer, Harry E. *The Philippine Mission of the Methodist Episcopal Church*. New York: Board of Foreign Missions of the Methodist Episcopal Church, 1910.
———. "Street Preaching." *PCA*, October 1905.
Fernandez, Eugenio. "On a Stormy Sea." In *Voices from Many Lands*, edited by Gilbert C. Nee, 57–69. Louisville: Pentecostal, 1936.
The Florence B Nicholson Bible Seminary of the Methodist Episcopal Mission, Manila, P. I. Manila: Methodist, 1907.
Fox, John. "New Bible Agent Named." *The New York Observer*, 6 September 1906.
Fritz, William G. "Evangelistic Work in Manila." *GIAL*, September 1901.
"From Foreign Fields." *The Institute Tie*, January 1902.
Galvez, Francisco S. "A Great Religious Leader Dies." *PO*, January 1934.
Goodell, Willard A. "From the Provinces." *PCA*, 20 December 1902.
Goodrich, Jay C. *Bible Work in the Philippine Islands*. New York: American Bible Society, 1906.
"The Growth of a Circuit." *PCA*, October 1904.
Harper, Isaac B. "The Annual Conference." *PCA*, March–April 1910.
———. "The Zamora Defection." *PCA*, March 1909.
———. "Will Zamora's Church Succeed?" *PCA*, April–May 1909.
Hearne, Edward W. "College Men in the Philippines." *The Intercollegian*, April 1900.

Hibbard, David S. *Making a Nation: The Changing Philippines*. New York: Board of Foreign Missions of the Presbyterian Church in the U.S.A., 1926.
"The History of the Taytay United Methodist Church." Computer printout. Taytay United Methodist Church, Taytay, Rizal.
Horst, Floyd M. "Hundreds Saved in Manila." *PE*, 15 February 1953.
Horst, Glenn M. "I Saw Revival in the Philippines." *PE*, 31 July 1955.
Huddleston, Oscar H. "The Filipino a Good Subject for Evangelization." *PCA*, January 1908.
"Instituto Biblico." *PCA*, 1 September 1903.
"Interview with Bishop Oldham." *PCA*, July 1906, 4.
Javier, Eleazer E. "The Pentecostal Legacy." In *Supplement to Chapters in Philippine Church History*, edited by Anne C. Kwantes, 57–82. Manila: OMF, 2002.
———. "The Pentecostal Legacy: A Personal Memoir." *Asian Journal of Pentecostal Studies* 8, no. 2 (2005) 289–310.
Klinefelter, Daniel H. *Adventures with God: A Personal Testimony of Divine Guidance and Special Help*. Glendale, CA: Church, 1934.
Koehler, Charles W. "Evangelistic Outlook." *PCA*, July 1910.
"Koehler Oratorical Contest." *PO*, November 1911.
Knox, Martin Van Buren. *A Winter in India and Malaysia among the Methodist Missions*. New York: Hunt & Eaton, 1892.
Locke, Charles E. "Message from Bishop Locke." *PO*, December 1920.
Mansell, William A. "Normal Revivals." *IW*, 19 August 1909.
Manuel, Eusebio M. "Why I Stay in the 'Mother Church.'" *PO*, June 1933.
Martin, Thomas H. "Dagupan as a Missionary Center." *GIAL*, February 1901.
———. "My Work in the Philippines." *GIAL*, February 1901.
McLaughlin, Jesse L. "Converting Power in Manila." *GIAL*, February 1901.
———. "Gospel Power in the Philippines." *GIAL*, October 1901.
———. "Methodism vs. Roman Catholicism." *PCA*, June 1907.
———. "Philippine Island District." *GIAL*, February 1901.
Merritt, Timothy. *The Christian's Manual, a Treatise on Christian Perfection: with Directions for Obtaining That State*. New York: Carlton & Porter, 1824.
"Mexico Methodist Church." *PCA*, 1 August 1903.
"Missionary Society of the Methodist Episcopal Church: Meeting of the Board of Managers." *GIAL*, December 1899.
Moore, Joseph W. "Central Student Church Dedicates New House of Worship." *PO*, July 1932.
Moots, Cornelia C. *Pioneer "Americanas" or First Methodist Missionaries in the Philippines*. Bay City, MI: Moots, 1903.
———. "Our World Tour of Evangelism Chapter XXX: In the Philippines." *PH*, 4 May 1910.
———. "Our World Tour of Evangelism Chapter XXI: Manila." *PH*, 11 May 1910.
———. "Our World Tour of Evangelism Chapter XXXII: Upon the Stormy Deep." *PH*, 18 May 1910.
———. *Some Chapters of My Life Story*. Louisville: Pentecostal, 1941.
———. *World Tour of Evangelism*. Louisville: Pentecostal, 1911.
Mudge, James. "Long Ago in Lucknow V." *IW*, 15 February 1910.
"Narcissa." *WMF*, January 1909.
"New Central Church Dedication Set for June 19." *PO*, June 1932.

Oldham, William F. "Bishop Oldham's Testimony." *PO*, April 1932.

———. *Christian Motive Power for Missions*. Chicago: Chicago Evangelistic Institute, n.d.

———. "'God Keeps': A Personal Testimony of Spiritual Experience, IV." *CA*, 29 November 1917.

———. *India, Malaysia, and the Philippines: A Practical Study in Missions*. New York: Eaton & Mains, 1914.

———. *Thoburn: Called of God*. New York: Methodist Book Concern, 1918.

Owens, Charles A. "From Manila." *WWM*, September 1899.

Pangilinan, Hiram G. *What if God Comes? A Story of Revival*. Quezon City, Philippines: Revival, 2011.

Peterson, Berndt O. "Pentecost and the Philippines." *PO*, June 1930.

———. "A Zealous Worker." *PCA*, April 1906.

"Philippine Islands." *The Sailors' Magazine and Seamen's Friend*, November 1902.

"Philippine Islands Annual Conference." *PCA*, March 1908.

Prautch, Arthur W. "Beginning of Methodism in Manila." *GIAL*, February 1901.

———. "The Beginning of Methodist Work in Manila." In *The Methodist Quarter-Centennial Celebration 1899–1924: Knox Memorial Church Souvenir*, 38–39. Manila: Knox MEC, 1924.

———. "Methodist Mission." *GIAL*, May 1901.

———. "Reminiscences." *PCA*, 20 December 1902.

———. "Report of the Soldier's Institute in Manila." *GIAL*, September 1901.

Rader, Marvin A. "Why the Bible Institute?" *PCA*, October 1905.

Reyes, Simon D., ed. *Ang Imnaryong Ebangheliko*. Manila: Methodist Cooperative Association, 1946.

Roberts, Walter N. *The Filipino Church: The Story of the Development of an Indigenous Evangelical Church in the Philippine Islands as Revealed in the Work of the Church of the United Brethren in Christ*. Dayton, OH: Foreign Missionary Society and Women's Missionary Association United Brethren in Christ, 1936.

Robinson, John E. "Notes by the Way." *IW*, 16 April 1908.

Ryan, Archie L. "A Good Testimony." *PO*, September 1918.

———. "A Gracious Filipino Revival." *PO*, April 1916.

———. *Religious Education in the Philippines: A Study of the Organization and Activities of the Philippine Islands Sunday School Union, Now the Philippine Council of Religious Education*. Manila: Methodist, 1930.

Go, Puan Seng. *The Hour Had Come: How Faith Brought Us Through Peril*. Grand Rapids: Douma, 1958.

Smith, Amanda Berry. *An Autobiography: The Story of the Lord's Dealings with Mrs. Amanda Smith, the Colored Evangelist*, with an Introduction by James M. Thoburn. Chicago: Meyer & Brother, 1893.

A Spiritual Awakening among India's Students: Addresses of Six Student Conferences of the Student Volunteer Movement Held at Jaffna, Lahore, Calcutta, and Madras. Madras: Addison, 1896.

Stagg, Samuel W. "A Christian View of Evolution." *PO*, December 1924.

———. "A Needed Moral Crusade: Shall Manila Have a Red Light District?" *PO*, December 1924.

———. *The Ideal Woman and Other Themes*. Manila: Methodist, 1928.

Stauffer, Milton T., ed. *Christian Students and World Problems: Report of the Ninth International Convention of the Student Volunteer Movement for Foreign Missions,*

Indianapolis, Indiana, December 28, 1923, to January 1, 1924. New York: Student Volunteer Movement for Foreign Missions, 1924.

Steward, Theophilus G. *Fifty Years in the Gospel Ministry*. Philadelphia: AME Book Concern, 1915.

Stuntz, Homer C. "The Influence of Protestantism." *PCA*, February 1905.

———. "The Missionary Outlook in the Philippines." *GIAL*, October 1901.

———. "The Philippines." *PCA*, February 1906.

———. *The Philippines and the Far East*. Cincinnati: Jennings and Pye, 1904.

———. "Philippine Islands District—Malaysia Mission Conference." *GIAL*, August 1901.

———. *The Philippine Mission of the Methodist Episcopal Church*. New York: Missionary Society of the Methodist Episcopal Church, 1905.

Sumrall, Lester F. *The Dove and the Eagle: A Story of the Great Philippine Revival*. South Bend, IN: World Temples, 1962.

———. "Manila Calls for Help!" *PE*, 1 November 1953.

———. *Modern Manila Miracles*. Springfield, MO: Erickson, 1954.

———. *The Real Manila Story*. South Bend, IN: Lester Sumrall Evangelistic Association, 1964.

———. *The True Story of Clarita Villanueva: A Seventeen-Year Old Girl Bitten by Devils in Bilibid Prison, Manila, Philippines*. Manila: Sumrall, 1955.

Sumrall, Lester F., and Tim Dudley. *The Life Story of Lester Sumrall: The Man, the Ministry, the Vision*. Green Forest, AR: New Leaf, 2003.

Taylor, William. *Four Years' Campaign in India*. New York: Phillips & Hunt, 1875.

———. *Ten Years of Self-Supporting Missions in India*. New York: Phillips & Hunt, 1882.

Thoburn, James M. "Bishop Thoburn's Report." *WWM*, June 1899.

———. *The Church of Pentecost*. Rev. ed. Cincinnati: Jennings & Pye, 1901.

———. *My Missionary Apprenticeship*. New York: Philips & Hunt, 1884.

———. "News from Manila." *WWM*, December 1899.

———. "Notes from Manila." *IW*, 7 April 1899.

———. "Notes from Manila." *IW*, 31 March 1899.

———. "Wayside Notes: An Autobiography, Chapter XXXIV." *Western Christian Advocate*, 23 August 1911.

"Training School for Methodist Preachers." *PCA*, November.

Turner, Fennell P., ed. *Students and the Present Missionary Crisis: Addresses Delivered before the Sixth International Convention of the Student Volunteer Movement for Foreign Missions, Rochester, New York, December 29, 1909, to January 2, 1910*. New York: Student Volunteer Movement for Foreign Missions, 1910.

———. *Students and the World-Wide Expansion of Christianity: Addresses Delivered before the Seventh International Convention of the Student Volunteer Movement for Foreign Missions, Kansas City, Missouri, December 31, 1913 to January 4, 1914*. New York: Student Volunteer Movement for Foreign Missions, 1914.

Tupas, Ramon. "Philippine Assemblies of God, Inc." In *Bethel Temple 12th Anniversary*, 10. Manila: Bethel Temple 12th Anniversary Committee, 1966.

Valencia, José L. *Under God's Umbrella*. Quezon City, Philippines: New Day, 1976.

Warne, Francis W. *Bishop Frank W. Warne of India: His Conversion, Call to the Ministry, and Other Spiritual Experiences*. New York: Board of Foreign Missions Methodist Episcopal Church, 1915.

———. *A Covenant-Keeping God: A Narrative of Personal Experiences*. New York: Methodist Book Concern, 1925.

———. "Dedication of the First Protestant Church on the Philippine Islands." *CA*, 11 October 1900.

———. *A Filipino Evangelist*. New York: Missionary Society of the Methodist Episcopal Church, 1903.

———. *From Baluchistan to the Philippines: Four Years of Methodist Episcopal Mission Work in Southern Asia*. New York: Missionary Society, Methodist Episcopal Church, 1904.

———. *Ideals That Have Helped Me*. New York: Methodist Book Concern, 1928.

———. "Jottings from Manila." *IW*, 27 April 1900.

———. "Jottings from Manila II." *IW*, 4 May 1900.

———. "Methodism and Religion in the Philippines." *GIAL*, July 1900.

———. "Third Visit to Manila." *GIAL*, August 1901.

Wesley, John. *The Nature, Design, and General Rules of the United Societies in London, Bristol, Kingswood, and Newcastle Upon Tyne* (1743). In *The Methodist Societies—History, Nature, and Design*, edited by Rupert E. Davies. *Works*, 9:67–75.

Yap, Jose A. "After Billy Graham What." *Philippine Christian Advance*, March 1956.

Zamora, Nicolas V. "Our Gospel Crusade in the Philippines." *Christian Herald*, 22 July 1903.

———. "Solo á Jesus." *PCA*, 1 July 1904.

Secondary Sources

Abinales, Patricio N., and Donna J. Amoroso. *State and Society in the Philippines*. Lanham, MD: Rowman & Littlefield, 2005.

Anderson, Allan. *Spreading Fires: The Missionary Nature of Early Pentecostalism*. Maryknoll, NY: Orbis, 2007.

Anderson, Benedict R. "Cacique Democracy in the Philippines: Origins and Dreams." *New Left Review* 169 (1988) 3–33.

Anderson, Gerald H., ed. *Studies in Philippine Church History*. Ithaca, NY: Cornell University Press, 1969.

Apilado, Mariano C. *Revolutionary Spirituality: A Study of the Protestant Role in the American Colonial Rule of the Philippines, 1898–1928*. Quezon City, Philippines: New Day, 1999.

Arcilla, José S. *An Introduction to Philippine History*. 4th ed. Quezon City, Philippines: Ateneo de Manila University Press, 1998.

Balares, Her L., and Jian M. Co. "Oblation: The Truth Behind the Leaves." *Oble*, 2 March 2011. Accessed 9 January 2012. http://www.oblenews.org/2011/03/oblation-the-truth-beneath-the-leaves/.

Bebbington, David W. *Holiness in Nineteenth-Century England: The 1998 Didsbury Lectures*. Carlisle: Paternoster, 2000.

Bibay, Bienvenido A. "Membership and Statistical Records of the Methodist Church in the Philippines, 1913–1963." BD thesis, Union Theological Seminary, Manila, 1965.

Brasher, John Lawrence. "The North in the South: The Holiness Methodism of John Lakin Brasher." *Methodist History* 27, no. 1 (1988) 36–47.

———. *The Sanctified South: John Lakin Brasher and the Holiness Movement*. Urbana: University of Illinois Press, 1994.

Brown, Kenneth O. *Holy Ground, Too: The Camp Meeting Family Tree.* Hazleton, PA: Holiness Archives, 1997.
———. "Stokes, Elwood Haines." In *HDHM*, 285.
Bundy, David T. "Bishop William Taylor and Methodist Mission: A Study in Nineteenth Century Social History, Part II." *Methodist History* 28, no. 1 (1989) 3–21.
———. "Keswick and the Experience of Evangelical Piety." In *Modern Christian Revivals*, edited by Edith W. Blumhofer and Randall H. Balmer, 118–44. Urbana: University of Illinois Press, 1993.
———. "Keswick Higher Life Movement." In *NIDPCM*, 820–21.
———. "The Legacy of William Taylor." *International Bulletin of Missionary Research* 18 (1994) 172–76.
Carwardine, Richard. *Transatlantic Revivalism: Popular Evangelicalism in Britain and America, 1790–1865.* Contributions in American History 75. Westport, CT: Greenwood, 1978.
Case, Jay R. "And Ever the Twain Shall Meet: The Holiness Missionary Movement and the Birth of World Pentecostalism, 1870–1920." *Religion and American Culture: A Journal of Interpretation* 16, no. 2 (2006) 125–59.
Chambers, John Whiteclay, II. *The Tyranny of Change: America in the Progressive Era.* New Brunswick, NJ: Rutgers University Press, 2000.
Chiles, Robert E. *Theological Transition in American Methodism, 1790–1935.* New York: Abingdon, 1965.
Clymer, Kenton J. "Methodist Missionaries and Roman Catholicism in the Philippines, 1899–1916." *Methodist History* 18, no. 3 (1980) 171–78.
———. "Methodist Response to Philippine Nationalism, 1899–1916." *Church History* 47 (1978) 421–33.
———. *Protestant Missionaries in the Philippines, 1898–1916: An Inquiry into the American Colonial Mentality.* Urbana: University of Illinois Press, 1986.
Collins, Kenneth J. *The Theology of John Wesley: Holy Love and the Shape of Grace.* Nashville: Abingdon, 2007.
———. *A Real Christian: The Life of John Wesley.* Nashville: Abingdon, 1999.
Constantino, Renato. *The Philippines: A Past Revisited.* Quezon City, Philippines: Renato Constantino, 1975.
Coppedge, Allan. "Entire Sanctification in Early American Methodism: 1812–1835." *Wesleyan Theological Journal* 13 (1978) 34–50.
Copplestone, J. Tremayne. *Twentieth-Century Perspectives, the Methodist Episcopal Church, 1896–1939.* History of Methodist Missions 4. New York: United Methodist Church, 1973.
Cunningham, Floyd T. "Diversities within Post-War Philippine Protestantism." *Mediator* 5, no. 1 (2003) 42–144.
———. *Holiness abroad: Nazarene Missions in Asia.* Pietist and Wesleyan Studies 16. Lanham, MD: Scarecrow, 2003.
Dayton, Donald W. "From Christian Perfection to the 'Baptism of the Holy Ghost.'" In *Aspects of Pentecostal-Charismatic Origins*, edited by Vinson Synan, 39–54. Plainfield, NJ: Logos, 1975.
———. "'Good News to the Poor': The Methodist Experience after Wesley." In *The Portion of the Poor: Good News to the Poor in the Wesleyan Tradition*, edited by Douglas M. Meeks, 65–96. Nashville: Kingswood, 1995.

BIBLIOGRAPHY

———. "Holiness Churches: A Significant Ethical Tradition." *Christian Century* 92, no. 7 (1975) 197–201.

———. "James Dean, Popular Culture and Popular Religion." In *From the Margins: A Celebration of the Theological Work of Donald W. Dayton*, edited by Christian T. Collins Winn, 227–42. Princeton Theological Monograph Series 75. Eugene, OR: Pickwick, 2007.

———. "Pneumatological Issues in the Holiness Movement." In *From the Margins: A Celebration of the Theological Work of Donald W. Dayton*, edited by Christian T. Collins Winn, 111–35. Princeton Theological Monograph Series 75. Eugene, OR: Pickwick, 2007.

———. "The Rise of the Evangelical Healing Movement in Nineteenth Century America." *Pneuma* 4, no. 1 (1982) 1–18.

———. *Theological Roots of Pentecostalism*. Grand Rapids: Baker, 1987.

Dayton, Donald, and Robert K. Johnston, eds. *The Variety of American Evangelicalism*. Downers Grove, IL: InterVarsity, 1991.

Crisostomo, Isabelo T. *Dr. Pio Valenzuela: Misunderstood Patriot*. Quezon City, Philippines: Kriz, 2001.

Deats, Richard L. *Nationalism and Christianity in the Philippines*. Dallas: Southern Methodist University Press, 1968.

———. "Nicolas Zamora: Religious Nationalist." In *Studies in Philippine Church History*, edited by Gerald H. Anderson, 325–36. Ithaca, NY: Cornell University Press, 1969.

———. *The Story of Methodism in the Philippines*. Manila: National Council of Churches in the Philippines for Union Theological Seminary, 1964.

Del Rosario, Romeo L. "The Schism in the Methodist Episcopal Church in the Philippines in 1933." PhD diss., Boston University, 1982.

Dieter, Melvin E. "The Wesleyan Perspective." In *Five Views on Sanctification*, edited by Stanley N. Gundry, 11–46. Grand Rapids: Zondervan, 1987.

———. *The Holiness Revival of the Nineteenth Century*. 2nd ed. Studies in Evangelicalism 1. Metuchen, NJ: Scarecrow, 1996.

Doeppers, Daniel F. "The Philippine Revolution and the Geography of Schism." *Geographical Review* 66 (1976) 158–77.

Doraisamy, Theodore R. *Oldham, Called of God: Profile of a Pioneer, Bishop William Fitzjames Oldham*. Singapore: Methodist Book Room, 1979.

Dorrien, Gary. *The Making of American Liberal Theology: Imagining Progressive Religion, 1805–1900*. Louisville: Westminster John Knox, 2001.

Espinosa, Gastón. "Borderland Religion: Los Angeles and the Origins of the Latino Pentecostal Movement in the U.S., Mexico, and Puerto Rico, 1900–1945." PhD diss., University of California, 1999.

———. "Francisco Olazábal and Latino Pentecostal Revivalism in the North American Borderlands." In *Embodying the Spirit: New Perspectives on North American Revivalism*, edited by Michael J. McClymond, 125–46. Baltimore: John Hopkins University Press, 2004.

Everhart, Janet S. "Maggie Newton Van Cott." In *Women in New Worlds: Historical Perspectives on the Wesleyan Tradition*, edited by Rosemary S. Keller et al., 300–317. Nashville: Abingdon, 1982.

Fegan, Brian. "The Social History of a Central Luzon Barrio." In *Philippine Social History: Global Trade and Local Transformations*, edited by Alfred W. McCoy and Ed C. de Jesus, 91–129. Quezon City, Philippines: Ateneo de Manila University Press, 1982.

BIBLIOGRAPHY

Flores, Wilson L. "How President Quezon and Five Cigarmakers in Manila Rescued 1,200 Holocaust Jews." *Philippine Star*, 6 January 2013. Accessed 22 May 2013. http://www.philstar.com/Sunday-life/2013/01/06/893625/how-president-quezon-and-five-cigarmakers-manila-rescued-1200.

Garrett, Guy D. "The Missionary Career of James Mills Thoburn." PhD diss., Boston University, 1968.

Goh, Robbie B. H. *Sparks of Grace: The Story of Methodism in Asia*. Singapore: Methodist Church in Singapore, 2003.

Hanners, Amy, and Gregory Webb. "Joseph Clemens: Soldier, Scientist and Missionary." Accessed 10 January 2009. http://chronicles.dickinson.edu/studentwork/engage/clemens/#9.

Harrell, David E. Jr. *All Things Are Possible: The Healing and Charismatic Revivals in Modern America*. Bloomington: Indiana University Press, 1975.

Hatch, Nathan O., and John H. Wigger, eds. *Methodism and the Shaping of American Culture*. Nashville: Kingswood, 2001.

———. "The Puzzle of American Methodism." In *Methodism and the Shaping of American Culture*, edited by Nathan O. Hatch and John H. Wigger, 23–40. Nashville: Kingswood, 2001.

Heitzenrater, Richard P. *Wesley and the People Called Methodists*, 2nd ed. Nashville: Abingdon, 2013.

Hempton, David. *Methodism: Empire of the Spirit*. New Haven: Yale University Press, 2005.

———. "Methodist Growth in Transatlantic Perspective." In *Methodism and the Shaping of American Culture*, edited by Nathan O. Hatch and John H. Wigger, 41–85. Nashville: Kingswood, 2001.

Hewett, James A. "Voice of Healing." In *NIDPCM*, 1178–79.

Hollister, John N. *The Centenary of the Methodist Church in Southern Asia*. Lucknow: Methodist Church in Southern Asia, 1956.

Hutchison, William R. *Errand to the World: American Protestant Thought and Foreign Missions*. Chicago: University of Chicago Press, 1987.

Jenkins, Philip. *The Next Christendom: The Coming of Global Christianity*. New York: Oxford University Press, 2002.

Jones, Charles E. *Perfectionist Persuasion: The Holiness Movement and American Methodism, 1867–1936*. Lanham, MD: Scarecrow, 2002.

Kent, John. *Holding the Fort: Studies in Victorian Revivalism*. London: Epworth, 1978.

Kessler, Christl, and Jürgen Rüland. "Responses to Rapid Social Change: Populist Religion in the Philippines." *Pacific Affairs* 79, no. 1 (2006) 73–96.

Kim, Elijah Jong Fil. "Filipino Pentecostalism in a Global Context." *Asian Journal of Pentecostal Studies* 8, no. 2 (2005) 235–54.

Kostlevy, William C. *Holiness Manuscripts: A Guide to Sources Documenting the Wesleyan Holiness Movement in the United States and Canada*. Philadelphia: Scarecrow, 1994.

———. "Morrison, Henry Clay." In *HDHM*, 207–8.

———. "Mudge, James." In *HDHM*, 209–10.

———. "Taylor University." In *HDHM*, 291.

Kwantes, Anne C. *Presbyterian Missionaries in the Philippines: Conduits of Social Change (1899–1910)*. Quezon City, Philippines: New Day, 1989.

Langford, Thomas A. *Practical Divinity*. Vol. 1. Nashville: Abingdon, 1998.

Laubach, Frank C. *The People of the Philippines: Their Religious Progress and Preparation for Spiritual Leadership in the Far East*. New York: Doran, 1925.

Lindström, Harald. *Wesley and Sanctification: A Study in the Doctrine of Salvation*. Wilmore, KY: Asbury, 1981.

Long, Kathryn T. "Consecrated Respectability: Phoebe Palmer and the Refinement of American Methodism." In *Methodism and the Shaping of American Culture*, edited by Nathan O. Hatch and John H. Wigger, 281–307. Nashville: Kingswood, 2001.

———. "Palmer, Phoebe Worrall." In *HDHM*, 226–27.

Maddox, Randy L. *Responsible Grace: John Wesley's Practical Theology*. Nashville: Kingswood, 1994.

———. "Holiness of Heart and Life: Lessons from North American Methodism." *Asbury Theological Journal* 51, no. 1 (1996) 151–72.

Maggay, Melba P. "Early Protestant Missionary Efforts in the Philippines: Some Intercultural Issues." In *Asian Church and God's Mission: Studies Presented in the International Symposium on Asian Mission in Manila, January 2002*, edited by Wonsuk Ma and Julie C. Ma, 29–41. Manila: OMF, 2003.

———. *The Gospel in Filipino Context*. Manila: OMF, 1987.

Marsden, George M. *Fundamentalism and American Culture: The Shaping of Twentieth Century Evangelicalism, 1870–1925*. New York: Oxford University Press, 1980.

———. "Fundamentalism and American Evangelism." In *The Variety of American Evangelicalism*, edited by Donald W. Dayton and Robert K. Johnston, 22–35. Downers Grove, IL: InterVarsity, 1991.

McClymond, Michael J. "Issues and Explanations in the Study of North American Revivalism." In *Embodying the Spirit: New Perspectives on North American Revivalism*, edited by Michael J. McClymond, 1–46. Baltimore: John Hopkins University Press, 2004.

McDonald, William, and John E. Searles. *The Life of Rev. John S. Inskip: President of the National Association for the Promotion of Holiness*. Boston: McDonald & Gill, 1885.

McGee, Gary B. "'Baptism of the Holy Ghost & Fire!' the Mission Legacy of Minnie F. Abrams." *Missiology* 27, no. 4 (1999) 515–22.

———. "The Calcutta Revival of 1907 and the Reformulation of Charles F. Parham's 'Bible Evidence' Doctrine." *Asian Journal of Pentecostal Studies* 6, no. 1 (2003) 123–43.

———. "'Latter Rain' Falling in the East: Early-Twentieth-Century Pentecostalism in India and the Debate over Speaking in Tongues." *Church History* 68, no. 3 (1999) 648–65.

———. "Pentecostal Phenomena and Revivals in India: Implications for Indigenous Church Leadership." *International Bulletin of Missionary Research* 20, no. 3 (1996) 112–17.

Mackenzie, Kenneth M. *The Robe and the Sword: The Methodist Church and the Rise of American Imperialism*. Washington, DC: Public Affairs, 1961.

McLoughlin, William G. *Revivals, Awakenings, and Reform: An Essay on Religion and Social Change in America, 1607–1977*. Chicago: University of Chicago Press, 1978.

McQuilkin, J. Robertson. "The Keswick Perspective." In *Five Views on Sanctification*, edited by Stanley N. Gundry, 151–83. Grand Rapids: Zondervan, 1987.

Messenger, Troy. *Holy Leisure: Recreation and Religion in God's Square Mile*. Philadelphia: Temple University Press, 2000.

Míguez Bonino, José. "Wesley in Latin America: A Theological and Historical Reflection." In *Rethinking Wesley's Theology for Contemporary Methodism*, edited by Randy L. Maddox, 169–82. Nashville: Kingswood, 1998.

BIBLIOGRAPHY

Oconer, Luther J. "The *Culto Pentecostal* Story: Holiness Revivalism and the Making of Philippine Methodist Identity, 1899-1965." PhD diss., Drew University, 2009.

———. "Holiness Revivalism in Early Philippine Methodism." *Methodist History* 44, no. 2 (2006) 80–93.

———. "'Keswickfied' Methodism: Holiness Revivalism and the Methodist Episcopal Church in India, 1870-1910." *Wesleyan Theological Journal* 49 (2014) 122–43.

———. "The Manila Healing Revival and the First Pentecostal Defections in the Methodist Church in the Philippines." *Pneuma* 31, no. 1 (2009) 66–84.

———. "Methodism in Asia and the Pacific: Origins and Development." In *The T&T Clark Companion to Methodism*, edited by Charles Yrigoyen Jr., 152–65. New York: T. & T. Clark, 2010.

Padang, Jose L. *Primer for United Methodists*. 2006 ed. Tarlac City, Philippines: Marion Walker Scholarship Foundation, 2006.

Palugod, Sylvia. "Filipino Religious Consciousness." Unpublished Manuscript, Kultura at Pananampalataya Program, Institute for Studies in Asian Church and Culture, Quezon City.

Parker, Michael. *The Kingdom of Character: The Student Volunteer Movement for Foreign Missions (1886–1926)*. Lanham, MD: American Society of Missiology and University Press of America, 1998.

Peters, John L. *Christian Perfection and American Methodism*. Grand Rapids: Zondervan, 1985.

Poloma, Margaret M. *The Assemblies of God at the Crossroads: Charisma and Institutional Dilemmas*. Knoxville: University of Tennessee Press, 1989.

Pope-Levison, Priscilla. *Building the Old Time Religion: Women Evangelists in the Progressive Era*. New York: New York University Press, 2014.

———. "Vennard, Iva May Durham." In *HDHM*, 302–3.

Porter, Andrew. "'Cultural Imperialism' and Protestant Missionary Enterprise, 1780-1914." *Journal of Imperial and Commonwealth History* 25, no. 3 (1997) 367–91.

Price, Charles W., and Ian M. Randall. *Transforming Keswick*. Carlisle, Cumbria: OM, 2000.

Rafael, Vicente L. *Contracting Colonialism: Translation and Christian Conversion in Tagalog Society under Early Spanish Rule*. Ithaca: Cornell University Press, 1988.

———. *White Love: and Other Events in Filipino History*. American Encounters / Global Interactions. Durham, NC: Duke University Press, 2000.

Randall, Ian M. "Old Time Power: Relationships between Pentecostalism and Evangelical Spirituality in England." *Pneuma* 19 (1997) 53–80.

Richey, Russell E. "Organizing for Missions: A Methodist Case Study." In *Foreign Missionary Enterprise at Home*, edited by Daniel H. Bays and Grant Wacker, 75–89. Tuscaloosa: University of Alabama Press, 2003.

———. "Revivalism: In Search of a Definition." *Wesleyan Theological Journal* 28 (1993) 165–75.

Rieser, Andrew Chamberlin. *The Chautauqua Moment: Protestants, Progressives, and the Culture of Modern Liberalism*. New York: Columbia University Press, 2003.

Riss, Richard. "The Latter Rain Movement of 1948." *Pneuma* 4, no. 1 (1982) 32–45.

Robeck, Cecil M. *The Azusa Street Mission and Revival: The Birth of the Global Pentecostal Movement*. Nashville: Nelson Reference & Electronic, 2006.

Robert, Dana L. *American Women in Mission: A Social History of Their Thought and Practice*. Modern Mission Era, 1792–1992. Macon, GA: Mercer University Press, 1996.

———. "Holiness and the Missionary Vision of the Woman's Foreign Missionary Society of the Methodist Episcopal Church, 1869-1894." *Methodist History* 39, no. 1 (2000) 15-27.

———. "Shifting Southward: Global Christianity since 1945." *International Bulletin of Missionary Research* 24 (2000) 50-58.

Robert, Dana L., ed. *Converting Colonialism: Visions and Realities in Mission History, 1706-1914.* Studies in the History of Christian Missions. Grand Rapids: Eerdmans, 2008.

Robinson, Kenneth L. *From Brass to Gold: The Life and Ministry of Dr. D. Willia Caffray.* University Park, IA: Vennard College, 1971.

Robledo, Liwliwa T. "Gender, Religion and Social Change: A Study of Philippine Methodist Deaconesses, 1903-1978." PhD diss., University of Denver, 1996.

Rodgers, James B. *Forty Years in the Philippines: A History of the Philippine Mission of the Presbyterian Church in the United States of America, 1899-1939.* New York: The Board of Foreign Missions of the Presbyterian Church in the United States of America, 1940.

Rose, Delbert R. *Vital Holiness: A Theology of Christian Experience: Interpreting the Historic Wesleyan Message.* Salem, OH: Schmul, 2000.

Rosell, Garth M. *The Surprising Work of God: Harold Ockenga, Billy Graham, and the Rebirth of Evangelicalism.* Grand Rapids: Baker, 2008.

Russell, Andrew C. "Counteracting Classifications: Keswick Holiness Reconsidered." *Wesleyan Theological Journal* 49 (2014) 86-121.

Ryu, Dae Young. "The Origin and Characteristics of Evangelical Protestantism in Korea at the Turn of the Century." *Church History* 77, no. 2 (2008) 371-98.

Sanneh, Lamin. "Introduction: The Changing Face of Christianity: The Cultural Impetus of a World Religion." In *The Changing Face of Christianity: Africa, the West, and the World,* edited by Lamin Sanneh and Joel A. Carpenter, 3-17. New York: Oxford University Press, 2005.

Schlesinger, Arthur Jr. "The Missionary Enterprise and Theories of Imperialism." In *Missionary Enterprise in China and America,* edited by John K. Fairbank, 336-73. Cambridge, MA: Harvard University Press, 1974.

Schmidt, Jean Miller. *Grace Sufficient: A History of Women in American Methodism, 1760-1939.* Nashville: Abingdon, 1999.

Schneider, A. Gregory. "Heart Religion on the Divide." In *"Heart Religion" in the Methodist Tradition and Related Movements,* edited by Richard B. Steele, 127-74. Pietist and Wesleyan Studies 12. Lanham, MD: Scarecrow, 2001.

Schultze, Andrea. "Writing of Past Times: An Interdisciplinary Approach to Mission History." In *European Traditions in the Study of Religion in Africa,* edited by Frieder Ludwig and Afe Adogame, 323-28. Wiesbaden: Harrassowitz, 2004.

Schumacher, John N. *The Propaganda Movement: 1880-1895: The Creators of a Filipino Consciousness, the Makers of the Revolution.* Manila: Solidaridad, 1973.

———. *Revolutionary Clergy: The Filipino Clergy and the Nationalist Movement, 1850-1903.* Quezon City, Philippines: Ateneo de Manila University Press, 1981.

Seleky, Trinidad E. "Six Filipinos and One American: Pioneers of the Assemblies of God in the Philippines." *Asian Journal of Pentecostal Studies* 4, no. 1 (2001) 119-29.

———. "The Assemblies of God in the Philippines." MA thesis, Fuller Theological Seminary, 1965.

BIBLIOGRAPHY

Shiels, Richard D. "The Methodist Invasion of Congregational England." In *Methodism and the Shaping of American Culture*, edited by Nathan O. Hatch and John H. Wigger, 257–80. Nashville: Kingswood, 2001.

Sitoy, T. Valentino. *Several Springs, One Stream: The United Church of Christ in the Philippines*. Heritage and Origins (1898–1948) 1. Quezon City, Philippines: United Church of Christ in the Philippines, 1992.

Smith, Ted A. *The New Measures: A Theological History of Democratic Practice*. New York: Cambridge University Press, 2007.

Smith, Timothy L. *Called unto Holiness: The Story of the Nazarenes: The Formative Years*. Kansas City, MO: Nazarene, 1962.

———. "The Holiness Crusade." In *The History of American Methodism*, edited by Emory S. Bucke, 2:613–27. Nashville: Abingdon, 1964.

———. *Revivalism and Social Reform: American Protestantism on the Eve of the Civil War*. Baltimore: John Hopkins University Press, 1980.

Stevenson, Dwight E. *Christianity in the Philippines: A Report on the Only Christian Nation in the Orient*. Lexington, KY: College of the Bible, 1955.

Strang, Stephen. "Sumrall, Lester Frank." In *NIDPCM*, 1110.

Suico, Joseph L. "Pentecostalism in the Philippines." In *Asian and Pentecostal: The Charismatic Face of Christianity in Asia*, edited by Allan Anderson and Edmond Tang, 345–62. Oxford: Regnum, 2005.

Sweet, William Warren. *Revivalism in America: Its Origin, Growth and Decline*. New York: Abingdon, 1944.

Synan, Vinson. *The Holiness-Pentecostal Tradition: Charismatic Movements in the Twentieth Century*. 2nd ed. Grand Rapids: Eerdmans, 1997.

Taneti, James E. "Dalit Conversions to the Methodist Episcopal Church in Karnataka." *Methodist History* 45, no. 4 (2007) 204–13.

Taves, Ann. *Fits, Trances, & Visions: Experiencing Religion and Explaining Experience from Wesley to James*. Princeton, NJ: Princeton University Press, 1999.

Tucker, Karen B. Westerfield. *American Methodist Worship*. New York: Oxford University Press, 2001.

Trinidad, Ruben F. *A Monument to Religious Nationalism: History and Polity of the IEMELIF Church*. Quezon City, Philippines: Evangelical Methodist Church in the Philippines, 1999.

Tyson, John R. *Charles Wesley and Sanctification: A Biographical and Theological Study*. Grand Rapids: Francis Asbury, 1986.

Walker, Marion. "Methodist Supervision of Christian Education in the Philippines." MA thesis, Northwestern University, 1937.

Walls, Andrew F. *The Missionary Movement in Christian History: Studies in the Transmission of Faith*. New York: Orbis, 1996.

Warner, Laceye C. *Saving Women: Retrieving Evangelistic Theology and Practice*. Waco, TX: Baylor University Press, 2007.

White, James F. *Protestant Worship: Traditions in Transition*. Louisville: Westminster John Knox, 1989.

Webb, Mary R. *Not My Will: A Christian Martyr in the Philippines*. Pasig City, Philippines: Anvil, 1997.

Wigger, John H. *Taking Heaven by Storm: Methodism and the Rise of Popular Christianity in America*. New York: Oxford University Press, 1998.

Yrigoyen, Charles Jr., ed. *The Global Impact of the Wesleyan Traditions and Their Related Movements*. Pietist and Wesleyan Studies 14. Lanham, MD: Scarecrow, 2002.

Index

Ablaze Conference, 3
adultery, allegations/cases of, 143, 152–53, 156
Aetas, 121
Aglipayan movement, 52, 53, 109, 112, 147
Aguinaldo, Emilio P., 31
Alabado, Mercedes, 118
Alabado, Victoriano, 118
alcohol. *See* liquor, crusade against
Aldersgate Renewal Ministries Philippines, xvii, 2, 180
Alejandro, Consuela G., 137, 184
Alejandro, Dionisio D., 5–6, 36, 56, 87, 115–17, 115n87, 131, 135–36, 165–66, 184, 195
altar calls, 13, 33–34, 45–46, 72–73, 78–79, 83, 85–86, 92, 94–95, 97–101, 104–11, 120–21, 125, 140–41, 144, 146–47, 166, 175, 191
American Bible Society (ABS), 37, 55, 140
American Bible Society colporteurs, 46, 55
American colonial rule, 8–9, 19, 30, 32, 48–49, 53, 59, 126–27
Anderson, Benedict, 48
Anderson, Robet Mapes, 195
Angeles, Pampanga, 103
Anti-Nazi rally, 150. *See also* Bocobo, Jorge C.
Aparri Province, 56, 59, 101, 122
Arayat, Pampanga, 118
Arellano, Juan M., 141
Arichea, Daniel C., xvii, 196n6

Armand, Samuel H., 101–2, 102n39
Arthur, William, xiii, 15, 76
Asbury College, Wilmore, Kentucky, 18, 85, 115, 135–36
Assemblies of God, 2–3, 6, 9–10, 167–71, 174–75, 179–82, 185–87, 194–95
assurance, doctrine of, 94, 107. *See also* witness of the Spirit
Atlag, Malolos, Bulacan, 54, 65, 165
Atlag MEC, 54
Azusa Street Revival, 4, 107

Badley, Brenton T., 23
Bagumbayan MEC, Navotas, Rizal, 97
balikbayans, 117, 167
Bancal, Guagua, Pampanga, 55
Bancal MEC, 55
Bancusay, Tondo, Manila, 47, 54, 64
Baptists, 13–15, 24
baptism of the Holy Spirit, xii, 4, 8, 15, 75, 86, 93–95, 100–1, 106–7, 115–16, 140, 145, 163–64, 166, 170, 177–78, 191. *See also* Pentecostal baptism
baptisms, 35, 37, 39, 53–54, 103–5, 113, 134
Baron, Inocencia, 118
Basconcillo, Teodoro, 67
Bautista, José, 39, 47, 61
Bebbington, David, 5, 51, 101
Beckendorf, Arthur L., 102, 125, 132, 139–40
Beckendorf, Maud, 132
Beckendorf, Robert, 132
Beley, Santos, 130

INDEX

benevolent assimilation, 30. *See also* manifest destiny; white man's burden
Bernhardt, Charles, 130
betel leaf/betel nut chewing, 75, 95, 112, 144. *See also* tobacco use
Bethel Temple, Manila, 2, 168–70, 177–81, 187. *See also* Cathedral of Praise
Bible institutes, 57, 69, 75, 80, 98, 104–6
Bible Woman's Training School, 58, 90
Bible women, 58, 121, 154
Bilibid Prison, 168, 186
Binag, Ambrosio, 128
Binag, Miguel, 128, 147
Blakely, Mildred M., 90
Blas, Simeon, 74, 75
Board of Foreign Missions, New York, 79, 81, 93, 101. *See also* Missionary Society of the Methodist Episcopal Church
Boardman, William, xiii, 14
Bocobo, Jorge C., 9, 147–51, 158
Bonino, José M., 7
Book of Acts, xii, 177
Boxing, 126
Branham, William, 170
Britenburgh, Lewis, 43
British and Foreign Bible Society (BFBS), 51–52
Brown, William A., 55
Bulacan, Bulacan, 137
Bundy, David, xi–xiii, xvi, 17
Bunting, Jabez, xii
Butler, William, 21
Byrd, Ralph, 170, 177

Cabanatuan, Nueva Ecija, xi, 115, 117, 144, 172, 174–76
Caffray, Willa D., 164
Cagayan District, 98, 103, 120
Cagayan Valley, 95–96, 113, 166, 183
Calica, Roman, 114, 130
Caloocan, Rizal, 73
Camp meetings, 11, 19, 22
Canda, Gonzalo, 69
Candaba, Pampanga, 118

Candelaria, David M., xvii, 2, 6, 9, 171–80, 186, 188–89
Candelaria, Jesse, xvii, 172, 177
Candelaria, Ruben V., xvii, 2, 6, 9, 140, 165, 171–80, 186–87
Candelarias, 6, 9, 176
Captain Plummer, 32
Casiguran, Cirilo, 130
Castells, Francisco, 51, 51n91
Castro, Servillano, 130
Cathedral of Praise, Manila, 181, 181n76
Central Church/MEC/Student Church/Methodist Church, Manila, 36–37, 64, 67–68, 102, 141–43, 148–49, 153–54, 158–59, 161–62, 168, 181, 184, 195
Central District, 69, 97–98, 100, 102, 116, 119–20, 123n116, 125, 131, 137, 145
Central District Conference, 137
Cerullo, Rudy, 170
Chambers, John W. II, 29
Champness, Thomas, xiii
Charismatic movement, 2–3, 171, 179–80
Chautauqua, 123–25, 124n119
Chenoweth, Arthur E., 67, 130
Chicago Evangelistic Institute, 77, 79
Chitambar, Jashwant R., 23
Christian and Missionary Alliance, 14, 41, 45, 51
Christian Holiness Partnership, 15
Christian perfection, 12, 15. *See also* entire sanctification; full salvation; sanctification; sanctification experiences; second blessing
Christmas Institute (CI), 101, 122–25, 138, 140n7, 174
Church of God (Anderson, Indiana), 15
Church of the Nazarene, xiii, xvi, 5, 15
Church So Blessed, Quezon City, 3, 3n5
Clemens, Joseph, 103–4, 109–10, 134
Clemens, Mary Knapp Strong, 103, 134
cockfighting, 53, 55, 74–75, 95, 105, 109, 114, 126–28, 148. *See also* gambling; *jueteng*
Cody, Mary A., 40, 61

INDEX

colonialism, mission as agent of, 7, 29
Congregationalists, 4, 13–14
Cordero, Severino, 130, 145, 157
Corporal Wright, 55
Cortez, Enrique, 48
Cosmopolitan Church, Manila, 154–56
Cottingham, Bertha, 99, 119, 124, 137
Cottingham, Joshua F., 95, 99–104, 106–7, 112–13, 115–17, 119, 122–24, 128, 131, 139, 140, 143, 145, 152–53, 155, 163, 174–75, 181
Crosby, Fanny, 47
crucicentrism, 50–51
Cruz, Esteban T., 113, 145, 157, 163, 181
Cruz, Felix, 130
Cruz, Pedro B., 112, 117, 130, 157
culto Pentecostal/Pentecostalism, xv, 3–5, 8–10, 12, 24, 80, 87, 96–115, 117–22, 126, 133, 139–47, 149, 152, 155, 163–66, 175, 178, 182, 191–95. *See also* Pentecostal meetings/services
Cunanan, Mariano, 54
Cunanan, Vicente, 54
Cunningham, Floyd T., xvi, 5–6, 165
Curament, Gregorio, 130
Cutler, Genevieve, 43–45, 46n72, 62

dance halls/dancing, 113, 126–27
Dagupan, Pangasinan, 59
Darby, Hawthorne, 156
Darwin, Charles, 143
dasehra meetings, 22–23, 22n51
David, Pablo Angeles, 109n63
Davidson, Leonard P., 39, 55
Davis, Hazel, 144
Dayao, Benigno, 55
Dayton, Donald W., xvi, 15
De Armas, Melecio, 130, 152–55, 152n50, 193
De Jesus, Fidela, 119–20, 122, 137
De Ocera, Arcadio, 93, 100, 109–10, 113, 118, 130, 145–46, 157, 163
De Pano, Ulpiano, 112
Deats, Richard L., 5
Decker, Marguerite, 68

deeper life, 17, 86, 115–16. *See also* higher life; Keswick movement; victorious life
Del Rosario, Romeo, 154, 154n56
Dewey, George, 30
Diaz, Mercedez, 172
Dimagiba, Narcisa, 54, 65, 121
Dingle, Leila V., 144, 164
Discipline/Book of Discipline, 1, 44, 56, 114, 146, 176, 178
dispensationalism, xii
Dizon, Nicolas C., 117, 136
dormitories, 59, 159
Dreisbach, Gertrude, 68
Drew Theological Seminary, 37, 78, 102

Earl, A. B., 14
Ellinwood Seminary, 58
embourgeoisment, xii, 14, 18, 139–43, 195
entire sanctification, xii, 4, 11–13, 15, 18, 78. *See also* Christian perfection, sanctification; sanctification experiences
Epworth League, 40, 101–2, 122–25, 138
Epworth League Institute (ELI), 123–25, 123n117. *See also* Christmas Institute
eradication of sin, 16
Erbst, Wilhelmina, 119–21, 121n109, 137
Erickson, Clifton O., 169–70, 169n31, 173–76, 186
Esperanza, Rodrigo, 167
Eveland, William P., 80, 93–96, 95n4, 100, 106–7, 109, 118, 129–30, 139
evangelistic crusades, 182, 195
evil spirits, deliverance from, 146, 168–69. *See also* Villanueva, Clarita

family altars, 127, 127n130
Farmer, Harry E., 67, 72, 81, 96–97, 97n10, 99, 101, 130
Farmer, Olive, 68
Feliciano, Honorio, 47
Ferguson, Manie Payne, 45
Ferguson, Theodore P., 43n60
Fernandez, Eugenio, 117–18
Filipinization, 127, 127n129, 157

INDEX

Filipino Asburians, 115–17, 136
Finney, Charles G., xiii, 14
Fletcher, John, 13, 15
Florence Nicholson Seminary, 58, 81
Floridablanca, Pampanga, 109–10
folk religion/religiosity, 111, 111n68, 121, 146, 192. *See also* spiritism
Fox, Daniel O., 76
Freemasons, 37, 51–52, 52n93
Fritz, William G., 41, 48, 72–73
full salvation, 11, 75, 79, 84, 85, 92. *See also* also see Christian perfection; entire sanctification; sanctification; second blessing
fullness of the Spirit, 16–17, 77–78, 164. *See also* indwelling Spirit; Spirit-filled
Fundamentalist-Modernist Controversy, 143, 143n18

Galang, Filomeno, 130
Galang, Flora, 137
gambling, 43, 75, 95, 109, 126, 128. *See also* cockfighting; *jueteng*
Gamboa, Melquiades J., 154
Gapan, Nueva Ecija, 112
Garvin, William P., 46
Gatdula, Balbino, 130
Gemeinschaftsbewegung, xiii
General Conferences
    1832, 13
    1884, 21, 25
    1904, 18, 56, 76, 84
    1908, 18, 79, 84
    1912, 93
    1924, 116
    1928, 160
    1932, 153, 154
    1940, 115n85
    1952, 172, 176
Gerona, Tarlac, 147
Glad Tidings Revival Center, Maypajo, Caloocan, 167–68, 170, 174
glossolalia. *See* tongues, speaking in.
God's Bible School, xii
Godoy, Inez, 137
Goodell, Willard A., 41, 54, 65, 67

Goodrich, Jay C., 37, 52, 61
Gordon, Adoniram J., 17
Goucher, John F., 20
Graham, Billy, 182, 195
Granadosin, Paul L., 182
Great Depression, The, 139
Guansing, Catalino, 130
Guerrero, Estanislao, 130
Gugin, William T., 46

Hagonoy, Bulacan, 55, 174
Hallelujah, shouts of, 104–6, 114, 175
Harford-Battersby, Thomas, 16
Harrell, David E. Jr., 170
Harris Memorial Deaconess Training School, 58–59, 64, 121
Harris, Richard R., xii
healing, testimonies of, 170, 173–74, 176
healing revival, 9–10, 168–71, 173–75. *See also* salvation-healing revivals
Healing Revival movement, 170–71, 170n38
Hearne, Edward W., 37, 61
heart religion, 6, 51, 70, 108, 124, 145
higher life, 16–17, 78, 116, 148. *See also* deeper life; Keswick movement; victorious life
Holiness movement, xii, xv, 5, 6, 7, 12–15, 20, 23, 34, 84, 94, 191, 194
Holy Spirit, 3, 12, 15, 18, 20, 29, 32, 40, 43–44, 51, 76, 80, 87, 94, 107, 111–12, 114, 117, 120, 122, 126, 142, 144, 146, 152, 164, 166, 175, 177–78
Holy Week, 50, 72
Houser, Otto, 102, 141
Housley, Edwin L., 69, 97–98, 98n18, 104, 106, 113, 118
Housley, Pearl S., 69
Huddleston, Leona, 68
Huddleston, Oscar A., 51, 83, 98, 130
Hugh Wilson Hall, 59
Hunt, John, xiii
Hutchison, William, 29, 29n2
hymn singing, 37, 47, 108–9
hymnbooks, 37, 107–8
IEMELIF, 82, 84, 155

INDEX

Ilagan MEC, Isabela, 128
Ilagan, Isabela, 59
Ilocos District, 103, 141
ilustrados, 51
Indian Revival, 24, 76
Indiana University Bloomington, 148
indwelling of the Spirit, 16, 80, 142, 144.
　　See also fullness of the Spirit;
　　Spirit-filled
inerrancy, doctrine of, xii, 143
Inis, Ciriaco, 157
Inskip, John, 14
Interchurch Holiness Convention, 15

Jaeger, Harvey A., 43, 43n59
Jaen, Nueva Ecija, 172
Japanese occupation, 116, 151, 156, 164–
　　65. See also World War II
Javier, Eleazar E., xvii, 6, 167, 177, 179
Jesus Christ, 13, 14, 48–50, 55, 72–73, 76,
　　85–87, 94, 98, 104–5, 107, 111,
　　113, 122–25, 140–44, 149, 166,
　　169–71, 175, 178, 187
Jones Law, 127, 127n129
Jones, Alto V., 45–46
Jones, Charles E., 13, 15
Jones, E. Stanley, 23, 79
Jorda, Vicenta, 137
Jorda, Victorino, 105, 112, 131
jueteng, 128. See also cockfighting;
　　gambling
Julian, Cornelio D., 115, 115n85, 136
justification, doctrine of, 11, 72, 94

Kamuning Methodist Church, Quezon
　　City, 181
Katotohanan Society, 52, 82
Keen, Samuel A., xii, 18
Keswick movement, xiii, 8, 14–17, 19,
　　23–24, 101, 142
Klinefelter, Blanche, 68
Klinefelter, Daniel H., 51, 97, 97n15, 114,
　　130
Klinefelter, Mary A., 68, 144
Knapp, Martin W., xii
Knox Memorial MEC/Methodist Church,
　　37–38, 38n37, 64, 85–86, 92,
　　94–95, 116–17, 138, 166, 172–74,
　　183
Koehler, Charles W., 8, 80–84, 80n36,
　　90–91, 96–100, 107–8, 112, 130
Koehler, Ida, 90
Kristallnacht, 150

Lacson, Arsenio, 168–69
Lake Geneva, Wisconsin, 123–24,
　　124n119
Lakeside, Ohio, 123–24, 124n119
Lallave, Nicolas, 51, 51n91
Lankford, Sarah W., 13
Laoac, Pangasinan, 141
Lapitan, Victorino, 113
Latter Rain movement, 170n38
Laubach, Frank C., vi, 5
Laurel, José P., 148
Lazatin, Tomas, 54
Lee, Edwin F., 130, 139, 148, 153–54
Leonard, Adna B., 40
liberalism, 18, 142. See also
　　Fundamentalist-Modernist
　　Controversy
liberation theology, 196
Lindsey, Gordon, 173. See also *Voice of
　　Healing*
Lingayen MEC, Pangasinan, 160
Lingayen, Pangasinan, 58–59, 90, 125,
　　160
liquor, crusade against, 37, 42–44, 126–
　　27, 138, 148–49. See also Woman's
　　Christian Temperance Union
Locke, Charles E., 96, 124, 128, 139
Long, Kathryn, 14
Loria, Mauricio, 130
Lubao, Pampanga, 55
Lukban, Justo, 127–28, 147
lyceums, 98, 100, 163–64

Macaspac, Juan, 69, 130
Mackenzie, Kenneth, 30, 30n6
MacNeil, John, 44, 61
Maggay, Melba P., 6, 72n5
Magalang, Pampanga, 118, 174
Magno, Candido, 112, 130
Mahan, Asa, xiii, 14, 16

INDEX

Malabon, Rizal, 49, 74–75
Malaysia Annual Conference, 40, 53, 56, 95
Malibay, Pasay, 39, 53–54, 73
manifest destiny, 30. *See also* benevolent assimilation; white man's burden
Manila District, 2, 56, 82, 97, 101–2, 114, 117, 119, 122–23, 123n116, 127, 140, 152, 166, 171–74, 181
Manila District Conference
    1908, 80
    1954, 173
Manila healing revival, 170–72, 174
Manila-Dagupan Railway, 50
Mann Act, 149
Manuel, Eusebio M., 155
Marcelino, Leona, 137
Marcos dictatorship, 196
Marquez, Felipe, 47, 63, 67, 113, 130, 147
Marshall, Raymond E., 102
Martin, Thomas H., 41, 72
Martyr's Methodist Church, Parañaque, 181
Mary Johnston Hospital, 58, 64, 127, 151n45
mass movements, 53, 53n99
Matthews, Ed A., 55
McCabe, Charles, 35
McDonald, William, 14
Mckinley, William, 30–31
McLaughlin, Jesse L., 41, 47, 53, 61
McLaughlin, Myrtle W., 41, 61, 68
Merritt, Timothy, 12–13, 13n8
mestizos, 51, 53
Methodist Girls School, Manila, 40
Mexico MEC, 54–55, 66, 79, 88
Mexico, Pampanga, 54–55, 66, 79, 88
Miller, George A., 67
Missionary Society of the Methodist Episcopal Church (MSMEC), 31, 35, 40–41, 57
Mitchell, Charles B., 116, 139, 139n1
Moe, Rex R., 83, 98, 139–40
Moody Bible Institute, 17, 41, 97
Moody, Dwight L., 17, 17n28, 21, 36
Moody, Nellie, 44–46, 44n64, 46n72
Moore, Joseph W., 103, 141

Moores Hill College, 99, 101
Moots, Cornelia C., 8, 40–47, 43n59, 44n64, 46n72, 61–62
moral crusades, 9, 127–28, 143, 148–49, 163
Morrison, Henry Clay, 8–9, 18–19, 18n34, 23, 70, 79, 84–87, 92–93, 96–98, 103, 108, 112, 115–16, 118, 126, 136
Mott, John R., 142n14
movie theaters, 126
Mudge, James, 23

Nacpil, Emerito P., 2, 196n6
Nacpil, Ubaldo, 130
Narvacan, Ilocos Sur, 113
National Holiness Association (NHA), 14–15, 18–19, 22
National Holiness Missionary Society, 77
Navarro, Cipriano, 154, 154n56, 156, 160
Navotas, Rizal, 49
nominal Christianity/Christians, xii, 4, 11, 20–21, 144
new birth, doctrine of, 98. *See also* regeneration
North, Frank Mason, 101
Northern District, 56, 98
Northfield Conference, Moody's, 17, 19
Norton, Anna J., 40, 61

Oberlin perfectionism, xiii
Oblation, The, 149
Ocampo, Luis, 48, 54
Ocampo, Nicolasa, 48, 54
Oldham, William F., 8, 21, 23–24, 28, 56, 67, 70, 76–87, 77n27, 79n35, 91, 93–94, 97, 99, 112, 115
Olongapo MEC, Zambales, 163
Orani MEC, Bataan, 155, 155n62
Orani, Bataan, 117, 152
Osborn, Tommy L., 170
Owens, Charles A., 35, 36

Pachuca, Mexico, 101
Palma, Rafael, 149
Palmer, Phoebe W., 13–15
Pampanga District, 98, 100, 104, 123

INDEX

Pampanga District Conference 1919, 100
Pandacan MEC, 64, 70–71
Pandacan, Manila, 39, 64, 70–71, 88
Pangasinan District, 98
Pangasinan District Conference 1911, 114
Pangilinan, Hiram, 2–3
Panipuan, Mexico, Pampanga, 54
Paniqui District, 114
Panlilio, José, 54
Panlilio, Pacifico, 54
Parker, Edwin W., 23, 23n54, 36
Parrish, Rebecca, 58, 68
Pascual, Agaton, 114
Peñaranda, Nueva Ecija, 95, 106–7, 109
Peniel mission, 43–46, 43n60, 44n64, 46n72, 62
pensionados, 148
Pentecostal baptism, 80, 107, 140, 176. See also baptism of the Holy Spirit
Pentecostal meetings/services, xv, 3, 8–9, 12, 18–19, 57, 79–80, 82, 84–85, 87, 90–93, 96–114, 117–22, 133, 144–47, 164–65, 192–93. See also *culto Pentecostal*/Pentecostalism
Pentecostal movement/Pentecostalism, modern, xiii, xv–xvi, 3–4, 4n7, 6, 10, 20, 167, 171–72, 174, 188, 194–95
Pentecostal processions, 89
Peterson, Alice, 68
Peterson, Berndt O., 67, 98, 98n23, 114, 130, 139–40, 146–47, 164
Philippine-American War, 30–32, 31n10, 35, 53
Philippine Annual Conference
  1944, 165
  1954, 176–77
Philippine Assemblies of God, Inc. (PAG), 180–81
Philippine Federation of Christian Churches (PFCC), 173, 182, 182n81, 195
Philippine Islands Annual Conference
  1908, 56, 78
  1909, 81
  1910, 84–87, 85n58, 92, 119
  1913, 94, 95, 95n4
  1914, 130
  1922, 124, 128
  1923, 103
  1932, 153
  1933, 153–54
  1934, 148
  1935, 162
  1936, 164
Philippine Islands District, 21, 56
Philippine Islands District Conference
  1900, 41, 61
  1901, 44
  1903, 75
Philippine Islands Mission Conference
  1905, 56, 67
  1907, 68
  1908, 56
Philippine Methodist Church, 154, 160. See also Stagg, Samuel W.; Navarro, Cipriano
Pickett, J. Waskom, 184
Pickett, Ruth R., 184
Pierson, Arthur T., 17
Pilgrim Holiness Church, 5, 15
Plaza Miranda, 182
pneumatology, 4, 32, 142, 166, 194
Poblete, Pascual H., 34n22
Prautch, Arthur W., 36–39, 36n31, 38n37, 42, 47–48, 52, 61
Prautch, Elisa A., 36
premillennialism, xii
Presbyterian mission, 4, 39, 55, 55n104, 58
Presbyterians, 13–15, 24, 32–33, 34n22, 39, 51n91, 113–14,
principalía, 33, 49, 53–55, 147
procession preaching, 88
Progressive Era, 19, 19n35, 29, 30
prostitution, 126–27, 143, 149
Puno, Reynato, 3, 193n3

Quezon, Manuel L., 150–51, 163
Quirino, Elpidio R., 148, 151
Rader Hall, 59
Rader, Jean, 68

217

INDEX

Rader, Marvin A., 67, 82–83, 86, 97, 102, 127–28, 130
Radical Holiness, xi–xiii, 14
Rafael, Vicente L., 48
Rayner, Ernest A., 82
Rayner, Karla, 68
Reb, Ernest, 170, 177–78
Reformed holiness, 14. *See also* Keswick movement
regeneration, 12, 85, 166
repentance, 86–87, 104, 146, 164
revival spirit, 81, 83, 85, 114, 121
Revive Conference, 3
Reyes, Benito M., 164
Reyes, Domingo, 130
Reyes, Eladio M., 179
Robert, Dana L., 6, 19–21
Roberts, Oral, 170–74, 195
Robinson, John E., 21, 23, 78, 78n31, 164
Rodgers, James B., 4, 33, 39, 55
Roman Catholicism
    adherents, 35, 74, 88, 109–10, 155, 194
    conversion from, 48–49, 74–75, 115
    crusade against, 8, 52, 54, 70–74, 106, 193
    folk Catholicism, 111, 121 (*see also* folk religion/religiosity)
    mass, 33, 48–49, 73, 106, 193
    positive views, 50–51
    priests, 51–53, 73, 81, 87, 168
    veneration of images, 71–73, 88
Roque, Pablo, 112
Rosales, Pangasinan, 114
Roxas Park, 169–71, 186
Roxas, Manuel A., 148
Ryan, Archie L., 102, 102n40, 104–7, 109, 139–40, 143

Salamanca, José, 48
salvation-healing revivals, 168–70, 175–76, 186
Samson, Gerardo, 125
San Fernando, Pampanga, 55, 69, 89
San Isidro, Nueva Ecija, 45–46
San Leonardo, Nueva Ecija, 104, 107–9, 173
San Nicolas, Pangasinan, 153
San Vicente, Mexico, Pampanga, 54, 113, 118
sanctification, xii–xiii, xv, 4, 11, 13, 15, 17, 77, 79, 86, 92, 94, 99, 107, 115, 117. *See also* Christian perfection; entire sanctification; full salvation; second blessing; sanctification experiences
sanctification experiences, 20, 75, 78, 86, 115, 117, 166
second blessing, 12–13, 19, 86. *See also* Christian perfection; entire sanctification, full salvation; sanctification; sanctification experiences
Sanidad, Calixto C., 113
Santos, Catalino, 130
Santos, José Abad, 151
Santos, Julian, 130
Santos, Victoria T., 118
Sather, Carl S., 44
Schultze, Andrea, 7
Seamen's Bethel, 44–49, 64, 108, 113
Sempio, Segundo, 39
Seymour, William, 4
Sibul Springs, San Miguel, Bulacan, 101, 122–25
Simpson, Albert B., 14, 17
sin, 8, 16, 43, 74–76, 78, 83, 85–86, 94, 97, 105, 109, 127, 140, 142, 146, 148–49
Sison, Pedro, 69, 118, 130
slain in the Spirit, 78, 178
smoking. *See* tobacco use
Smith, Amanda Berry, 22
Smith, Hannah Whitall, 16, 42
Smith, Joseph, 18
Smith, Robert Pearsall, 16
Snyder, Alba, 130
Solano, Nueva Vizcaya, 113, 144
Soldier's Institute, 37–44, 47, 52, 64
South India Conference, 21, 25
Spanish colonial rule, 30, 48
Spanish-American War, 30, 51

INDEX

Spirit-filled, 8, 16, 83, 100, 113, 139, 144, 151. *See also* fullness of the Spirit; indwelling Spirit
spiritism, 111, 146, 168. *See also* folk religion/religiosity
Spottswood, Curran L., 166, 183
St. Peter MEC, Tondo, Manila. *See* Bancusay, Tondo, Manila
Sta. Maria, Ilocos Sur, 115, 115n85
Stagg Schism, 2n2, 9, 143, 151–56, 193. *See also* Stagg, Samuel W.
Stagg, Mary Boyd, 156, 159
Stagg, Samuel W., 2, 9, 34, 141–43, 141n8, 142n14, 149, 151–56, 152n50, 153n53, 154n56, 156n63, 159–60, 193
stereopticon projection, 55, 82, 103
Steward, Theopilus G., 37, 37n36, 39
Stixrud, Louise, 58, 68, 119–22
street preaching, 63, 72, 175. *See also* preaching, procession
Student Volunteer Movement (SVM), 17, 17n29, 19, 19n38, 23, 29, 99, 99n29, 142, 191
Stull, George C., 34–38, 34n23
Stuntz, Homer C., 21, 41, 49–50, 52–53, 67, 74–75
Sumrall, Lester F., 9, 167–77, 167n22, 168n26, 172n44, 181, 185–87
Sunday Schools, 40, 112, 115, 123, 170, 181. *See also* Ryan, Archie L.
Sunday School conventions, 81, 98, 100, 102–3. *See also* Sunday Schools
Supernaturalism, 111, 146, 192, 194. *See also* evil spirits, deliverance from

Talba, Bacolor, Pampanga, 118
Tamayo, Lorenzo T., 103, 114, 157
Tangog, Valentino, 73
Tapia, Elizabeth S., 196n6
Tarlac District, 144
Tarlac MEC, Tarlac, 98
Tarlac, Tarlac, 59
Taylor University, 99, 99n30
Taylor missionaries, 21, 21n45, 35–36, 41, 76–78

Taylor, William, xiii, 21–22, 21n43, 25, 41, 76, 78, 99
Taytay MEC/Methodist Church, 2, 114, 173–74, 177–78, 180–81, 188–89
Taytay Methodist Community Church (TMCC), 179–80, 179n66
Taytay, Rizal, xvii, 6, 114, 172, 178
Teatro Filipino (Filipino Theater), 31–33, 31n13, 36–37, 64
Teeter, Edna, 68–69
Teeter, Lilian, 69
Teeter, William, 67–69
testimonies, public, 13, 49, 85, 104–6, 120
Thoburn, James M., xiii, 8, 21–22, 24–26, 31–37, 32n14, 32n16, 32n17, 39–40, 42, 93
Thomas, J. Edna, 120–21
Tipton, Byron, 43, 43n59
tobacco use, 74–75, 110, 126, 144. *See also* betel leaf/betel nut chewing
Tolentino, Guillermo, 149
Tongue of Fire, 15, 75
tongues, speaking in, 170, 177–78
Torrey, Reuben A., 17
Tovera, Benito S., 130, 140, 157
Treaty of Paris of 1898, 30, 51
Tuason, Prudencio, 110
Tuesday Meetings, 13
Tuguegarao, Cagayan, 59, 140, 172

Umengan, Tita B., 122, 122n113
Union Theological Seminary, Manila (UTS), 116, 140, 143, 153, 174
University of the Philippines (UP), 147–50, 154
Upham, Thomas, 14

Valdez, Adolpho C., 167–68, 172
Valencia, José L., 172, 176, 178
Valenzuela, Pio, 128, 147
Van Cott, Maggie, 94, 94n1
Vaudeville shows, 110
Vennard, Iva D., 77, 77n26, 79
Victorian domesticity, 121
victorious life, 17. *See also* deeper life; higher life; Keswick movement
Vidal, Alejandro, 157

INDEX

Vigan, Ilocos Sur, 56, 83, 130, 138, 146
Villa, José Garcia, 149
Villanueva, Clarita, 167–69, 171–73, 175, 186
Vincent, John H., 40
Voice of Healing, 169, 173, 173n46. *See also* Lindsey, Gordon
Volstead Act, 149

Warne, Francis W., 8, 23–24, 27, 38n37, 39–40, 42–45, 61, 70, 75, 93
Washburn, Orilla F., 90
Watson, Richard, xii
Welch, Herbert, 154
Welsh Revival, 76
Wesley, John, xv, 11–14, 195
white man's burden, 30. *See also* benevolent assimilation; manifest destiny
Wilk, Helen, 156
Willard, Frances, 42n55
Williamsport Dickinson Seminary, 93
Wilson, Woodrow, 127
Wisner, Julia, 40, 61
witness of the Spirit, the, 115, 144. *See also* assurance, doctrine of

Woman's Foreign Missionary Society (WFMS), 8–9, 19, 20, 21n45, 39, 40, 42, 44, 57–58, 62, 90, 98, 114, 118–21, 137, 144–45, 151, 154, 156
Woman's Christian Temperance Union (WCTU), 40, 42–44, 42n55, 44n62, 47
Woman's Home Missionary Society, 77
Wood, John A., 14
World War II, 5, 87

Yangco, Luis, 34n22, 51–52
Young Men's Christian Association (YMCA), 17, 35, 37, 42–43, 80, 123, 142, 142n14, 148

Zamora family, 39
Zamora Schism, 2n2, 8, 81–84, 91, 193
Zamora, Jacinto, 51
Zamora, Nicolas V., 29, 37–40, 38n37, 47, 49, 52–54, 60–61, 67, 70–71, 73, 81–84, 116. *See also* Zamora Schism
Zamora, Paulino, 38, 51–52, 51n91, 71

www.ingramcontent.com/pod-product-compliance
Lightning Source LLC
Chambersburg PA
CBHW070248230426
43664CB00014B/2444